MONEY A TO Z

MONEY A TO Z
A Consumer's Guide to the Language of Personal Finance

Don German and Joan German

Facts On File Publications
New York, New York ● Bicester, England

The authors wish to thank their son, Bob German, for creating the computer program that appears in Section II, "Money Math."

MONEY A TO Z

Library of Congress Cataloging in Publication Data
German, Donald R.
  Money a to z.
  I. Finance, Personal—Dictionaries.
  I. German, Joan W.
II. Title.
HG179.G46   1984   332.024'003'21   82-15418
ISBN 0-87196-836-3

Printed and bound in the United States of America
10 9 8 7 6 5 4 3 2 1

With love to Merrill and Elizabeth Wolfe—
"Dad and Betty"

CONTENTS

Preface

Did you know that Fannie Mae will sometimes yield generously or that Ginnie Mae will yield to maturity and that neither is sexy at all? Did you know that the nice banker with whom you usually deal would like you to roll over and that your insurance agent says that you are now in an elimination period? And did you know that, as usual, the bulls and the bears are slugging it out on the Curb, while the gangs at the trading posts cheer?

If you're confused, try some alphabet soup. Everyone knows that CPA means certified public accountant, but how about defining CMA, CLU, CD, ACV, or DIDC? Or if you like tough ones, how about NASDAQ?

Money matters have become confusing, and money books often don't help. Take Individual Retirement Accounts, or IRAs, for example. References to IRAs may be found in a typical money book in chapters on retirement, savings, tax shelters, women and money, and banking and interest rates. But wouldn't it be nice to have a book in which all you need or want to know about IRAs is in alphabetical order, under "I"? *Money A to Z* is that book.

If you like getting the most from your money, you should learn the words used by those who deal in money. *Money A to Z* explains the language spoken by the bankers, brokers, and agents with whom you must deal. It will make it easier for you to deal with them and will make your money affairs more profitable. Thus, *Money A to Z* not only explains what the words mean, but what they mean to you.

MONEY A TO Z

SECTION I
DEFINITIONS
AND
CONSUMER TIPS

abatement See *tax abatement*.

absolute assignment See *assignment*.

abstract of title a history of the ownership of a piece of real estate as traced by an attorney who is preparing a title search.
   See also *title search*.

accelerated option a choice that allows a life insurance policyholder to use the policy's cash value and accumulated dividends to prepay the policy. It is available only on cash-value or permanent life insurance, commonly called "ordinary," "whole," or "straight" life. Typically, such a policy is paid up at age 99 or, with higher premiums, at an earlier age—often at 65, when a person retires. Using the cash value and dividends can cause the policy to be paid up even sooner than its normal maturity date.
   Consumer tip: In general, exercising

this option is not wise. It is usually better to keep the cash value as a reserve for low-cost loans and to use the dividends to buy one-year term additions or paid-up ordinary additional coverage—a very nice tax shelter, since both the dividends and the eventual death benefit are tax-free. There is seldom a viable reason to choose this option to prepay a policy, because it doesn't increase the death benefit, but only increases the cash flow and hence the profits to the insurance company.
   See also *dividend options; life insurance; paid-up additions*.

acceleration clause a provision that is fairly common in some loan agreements, especially those written to cover the purchase of household goods or appliances. Under the terms of an acceleration clause, the outstanding balance of a loan becomes immediately payable should even one payment be overdue. The lender is usually granted the right to repossess any property purchased with the borrowed funds, to sell that property and apply the proceeds against the loan, and then to collect any remaining balance due.

Consumer tip: Never sign a loan contract that contains an acceleration clause. If your credit is good enough to qualify for a loan with such a clause, it's good enough to qualify for a fair contract.

See also *conditional sales contract; confession of judgment;* Section II, "Borrowing," "Money Mistakes."

acceptance   a time draft on the face of which the drawee has written "accepted" and the date and place payable, then has signed the instrument. A bank acceptance is one that is accepted by a bank.

See also *draft.*

accidental death benefit   an extra payment, usually doubling the face of the policy, made under a life insurance policy in the event of accidental death.

See also *double indemnity;* Section II, "Life Insurance."

account   1) a record of financial transactions; 2) a business relationship maintained with a bank or brokerage house.

A *ledger account* is a listing of debits and credits of items relevant to each other; thus, cash would not be credited to the building account. The purpose of ledger accounts is to sort financial transactions relating to specific purposes into separate listings. Thus, with a minimum of effort, a person can see exactly how much has been accumulated or spent in such categories as

cash, office equipment, taxes, salaries, or raw materials.

Checking, savings, loan, and investment accounts are those most commonly established by consumers. Like ledger accounts, such consumer accounts are established for a specific purpose, such as issuing checks, saving money, or making investments.

See also *ledger.*

account executive   See *customer's representative.*

accounting   a system of setting up, maintaining, and proving financial records. *Bookkeeping* is concerned only with the maintenance phase of accounting; it involves the actual posting of transactions to financial records. Everyone should use a simplified bookkeeping system for financial records that conforms to generally accepted accounting practices. Most families use a simple cash method of accounting versus the more complicated accrual system used by many businesses.

It is important to understand the following terms:

income: money earned. *Accrued income* is money earned but not yet received.

expense: money spent. *Accrued expenses* are monies due but not yet paid.

asset: a thing of value owned, including cash, investments, cash due in (*receivables*), and real and personal property. Money in the bank is obviously an asset.

liability: money owed. This might include current debts, such as credit-card balances, and long-term debt, such as a home-mortgage loan. Traditionally, *current liabilities* are debts due within one year; *long-term liabilities* are those due in over a year. Incidentally, since a customer's savings or checking account balance is owed to him or her by the bank, from the bank's standpoint, that account is a liability, even though it is an asset to the customer.

capital: money invested in a business by its owners or stockholders. Capital is used to purchase goods or equipment that will, hopefully, result in a profit.

net worth: the total of assets less the total of liabilities. This is the most important figure in family accounting because it shows an exact financial standing as of a certain date. In other words, if a person owns assets worth $100,000 and has liabilities of $20,000, he or she has a net worth of $80,000. It is the amount in cash that would be left if all property were converted to cash and all debts were paid.

Consumer tip: Try to acquire a basic understanding of accounting principles. Especially realize the relationship between assets and liabilities and how proper spending and investing habits can contribute to net worth.

See also Section II, "Family Accounting."

accounts receivable money due or soon to come due. Receivables may be used as collateral for a bank loan if cash flow is a problem.

Consumer tip: Excessive receivables are one of the major reasons for small business failures. If you are in business, keep your receivables down; insist on cash or accept only bank credit cards.

accounts receivable loan a business loan in which a company's receivables are pledged as collateral.

See also *accounts receivable.*

accrual See *accrual basis budgeting.*

accrual basis budgeting a financial plan based on estimated income and expense for a future period. *Accrual* means to add income or assets as periodic gains, whether or not they are actually received, and to allow for accumulating expenses, even if they are not paid. Most people keep family financial records on a cash-in cash-out basis. Since the most complicated financial form they handle is their income tax, and since it is easy to complete with a cash system, this is fine. But for anyone not on a totally fixed income, there is a better way.

Accrual basis budgeting is a more realistic budgeting system than the simple cash-in cash-out method, since it includes anticipated income and expenses as well as cash received or spent.

Consumer tip: To make a periodic family or personal budget on an accrual basis is a very wise thing to do. It means knowing what income and expenses can be expected at a given time and should result in an approximate net-worth projection as well.

See also *accounting;* Section II, "Family Accounting."

accrued interest interest earned but not yet paid. For example, if $1,000 is borrowed with a finance charge of $100 for a term of one year, as the year goes by, the interest due but not yet paid adds up, or accrues. When the loan, with interest, is paid at the end of the year, the interest that has been accruing—or adding up—is paid. By the same token, if a person invests in a certificate of deposit for 18 months, all during that period interest will be adding up, or accruing, and he or she will receive it when the certificate matures.

accrued liability   See *liability.*

activity charge   a bank service charge applied to checking accounts when the earnings on the collected balance are not adequate to meet the costs of maintaining the account.

See also *service charge.*

actual cash value (ACV)   a term used in property insurance settlements that refers to the original cost of an item or items less depreciation. For example, if a table destroyed in a fire cost $100 20 years ago when it was new, an insurance adjuster may figure that it has depreciated by 75 percent and allow $25 for its actual cash value.

Consumer tip: People tend to think of their personal property in terms of its present cost, while insurance companies think in terms of present cost less depreciation. It's wise to pay a small extra premium to insure property for its current *replacement value.* The table in the above example might cost $500 to replace today. With replacement-value insurance coverage, this is exactly what you would collect. To offset the higher cost of this insurance, it is a good idea to take the maximum deductible that you can afford to pay in the event of a loss.

See also *replacement value*; Section II, "Property and Liability Insurance."

actuary   a person who computes insurance premiums. He or she determines just how profitable any insurance policy will be to the company by calculating the degree of risk the company undertakes on a particular policy and then assigns a premium that will cover that risk plus any operating and sales expenses resulting from the policy.

See also *standard mortality table.*

ACV   See *actual cash value.*

add-on rate method   one of the variables used in computing the finance charge on a consumer installment loan, using the following formula:

Finance Charge = Principal × Rate × Time

Suppose, for example, that a bank quotes an add-on rate of 6 percent for a loan of $2,000 for one year:

Finance Charge = $2,000 × .06 × 1 = $120. Thus, the total to be repaid is $2,120.

Note that lenders, by law, must now quote interest in terms of the *annual percentage rate (APR)* and must state actual finance charges in dollars and cents. Also note that the 6 percent add-on rate in the above example is actually an annual percentage rate of 10.9 percent.

Consumer tip: For comparison shopping, don't pay any attention to add-on, discount, or even simple interest rates. Instead, consider the annual percentage rate, which the Consumer Credit Protection Act requires must be quoted.

See also *annual percentage rate (APR); discount rate method; simple interest.*

adjustable-rate loan   See *variable-rate loan.*

adjustable-rate mortgage   See *variable-rate mortgage (VRM).*

4

adjusted gross income a figure used in the calculation of personal federal income taxes that represents the total income received minus adjustments to income. Adjusted gross income is reported on IRS Form 1040. *Taxable income* is adjusted gross income less deductions and exemptions.

Consumer tip: It is a good idea to reduce taxable income without reducing actual income. You can do this by itemizing deductions carefully and by investing in a tax-deferred Individual Retirement Account or a tax shelter.

advice a banking form sent to customers advising them that action has been taken on a bank account. This may be notification of the correction of an error or of the carrying out of instructions of a customer, such as to charge his account for checkbook printing or safe deposit rent.

Age Discrimination Act a law enacted in 1978 that raised the legal mandatory retirement age from 65 to 70 for everyone except tenured college professors and senior executives in business and that forbids job or employment discrimination against older workers.

Consumer tip: If a person elects to work past age 65, he or she continues to make payments to Social Security; in turn, when he or she retires, the Social Security payment will be higher than it would have been had the person retired at age 65.

See also *Civil Rights Act; Equal Credit Opportunity Act (ECOA); Social Security;* Section II, "Retirement Planning."

age-life depreciation the length of time a building can be expected to last, assuming normal maintenance. Determining this number of years is important for tax purposes for anyone who invests in real estate. Substantial tax savings can result from following IRS guidelines for estimating the depreciated value of a given building.

See also *depreciation.*

agency technically, the relationship existing between a principal and an agent, authorizing the agent to perform certain acts on behalf of the principal when dealing with other parties. A salesperson, for example, often has an agency relationship with the company he or she represents.

In common usage, an agency is a person or group of persons representing an insurance company to the public. A *direct agency* represents only one company; an *independent agency* represents more than one company.

See also *agent.*

agent a person authorized by another person or company to act on its behalf. The agents with whom most consumers deal sell insurance.

Consumer tip: When buying insurance, shop around. Letting an independent agent know that you are doing this will often result in extra efforts on his or her part to get you a better deal.

See also *agency; broker; life insurance; property insurance.*

agent's commission the fee paid by an insurance company to an agent or broker for selling a policy.

In property and casualty insurance, the agent's commission ranges from 15 to 40 percent of the annual premium, depending on the coverage and the company.

In life insurance, a typical commission for a term policy is 40 percent of the first year's premium. For an ordinary-life policy written by a company licensed to do business in New York, it is 55 percent of the premium for the first year and 5 percent for the next nine years; in the trade, this is called "55 and nine fives." However, it is not uncommon for commissions to range as high as 100 to even 200 percent of the first year's premium, so it pays to shop around.

Consumer tip: Choose companies that pay the lowest commissions, because these savings are passed on to you. In life insurance, the first choice is Savings Bank Life Insurance if you live or work in Massachusetts, New York, or Connecticut, because no commissions are paid. The second choice is a company licensed to sell in New York, because New York State limits the commission percentage.

alimony   a money allowance paid to a former spouse. Alimony was once paid strictly by former husbands to former wives, but now is sometimes paid by former wives to former husbands, and, in some cases, even to former lovers (*palimony*).

Usually, however, alimony is paid by the former husband to his former wife. Typically, the amount paid, counting child support, ranges from 30 to 50 percent of his income. In almost all cases, alimony payments stop when the spouse who is receiving payments remarries.

Alimony payments are supposed to cover household and personal ex-

penses. Even staunch feminists contend that women have a right to expect alimony because of possible inequities in a woman's earnings and because of the sacrifices a wife may have made to help her husband increase his earning power.

Normally, alimony payments are deductible from income for federal tax purposes, and alimony received is taxable income.

After a divorce, there are two alternatives to monthly alimony payments—the *lump-sum settlement* and the *alimony trust*. For the wife, a lump-sum settlement has one definite advantage if the former husband has the money to fund it: payments to the wife are guaranteed. The alimony trust is a fund set up by the husband and administered by a trustee, usually a bank.

See also *child support*.

alimony trust   See *alimony*.

allowances, children's   the money given to children on a periodic basis, usually once a week, for them to spend or save on their own. There are two purposes for a child to be given a money allowance—to give him or her some responsibility in handling finances; and to teach the child simple money management.

Consumer tips: How much should a child be given? It depends on his or her age, what expenses the allowance is expected to cover, your family circumstances, and how much his or her peers receive. Here are some basic guidelines:

• For the pre-schooler, the allowance should be sufficient to buy some small treats plus minor toys. Examples would be occasional ice cream or candy and crayons. A big doll or bike should be purchased by you.

- Elementary-school children should get a sufficient increase in allowance to cover gifts for others, contributions, movies, and some minor clothing purchases. Some experts suggest that children of this age pay for school lunches out of their allowances, but this often leads to skipped meals.
- High-school children need additional funds for grooming supplies, cosmetics, some jewelry, special clothing, and for dating expenses. In most cases, parents buy the child clothing as needed and with some degree of supervision.
- Young people in college are in a totally different situation. Many work part-time, so the allowance should be looked on as a supplement to earnings—after all, the main family contribution goes to pay for tuition, room and board, and books. The young person's total living budget, earnings plus allowance, must be sufficient to cover the costs of some clothing, transportation, meals, entertainment, travel, and so on. Again, parents typically contribute clothing, often as gifts or as part of an annual back-to-school stocking up.

For college students, an important question when it comes to money management is, "What kind of bank accounts do I need?" As a general rule, the student should have a checking account, into which the parents may regularly deposit an allowance. For older college students, especially those far from home who may have to face financial crises alone, a credit card is not a bad idea. In this case, however, the student must be extremely responsible and the credit limit should be severely restricted. The parents will have to co-sign the original application; and at the time application is made, they should instruct the bank to limit the young person's credit line to an amount the parents can afford to lose—$300 is a common limit. Keep in mind that banks typically increase the limit when accounts show a good payment record, so insist that this not be done until the student is on his or her own.

Here are three allowance rules that seem simple, but which are often ignored:

1. Make the allowance sufficient for the child's needs.

2. Don't make the allowance so generous as to make money-management principles useless.

3. Don't use the allowance as a wage for services rendered. Children should help around the home, but should not be paid for doing so.

See also Section II, "Family Accounting."

all-risk insurance property insurance that covers all risks except those specifically excluded. Wear and tear, rust, and termite damage are typical exclusions. All-risk insurance costs a bit more than specific coverages, but avoiding possible gaps in coverage is usually well worth the little extra. The most common all-risk insurance coverages are the popular homeowner's and tenant's policies.

See also Section II, "Property and Liability Insurance."

American Society of Chartered Life Underwriters insurance agents who have completed required courses of study in life insurance and estate planning. They may use the designation C.L.U. after their names. It is a 10-part course of study supervised by the American College, Bryn Mawr, Pa., and normally takes a minimum of two years to complete.

Consumer tip: A chartered life underwriter will know much more about life insurance coverages than a beginning agent; but he is also likely to be more of an expert in sales techniques. Despite the high turnover among life insurance agents, the agent with a C.L.U. is likely to survive and be there should you need him or her.

See also *life insurance.*

American Society of Chartered Property and Casualty Underwriters insurance agents who have completed required courses of study in property and casualty insurance. To receive the designation, a person must complete a 10-part course administered by the American Institute for Property and Liability Underwriters, Bryn Mawr, Pa. Some of the courses are interchangeable for credit with the American Society of Chartered Life Underwriters. Persons completing the course may use the letters C.P.C.U. after their names.

See also Section II, "Property and Liability Insurance."

American Stock Exchange (AMEX) See *Curb Exchange; stock exchange.*

AMEX the American Stock Exchange.

See also *Curb Exchange; stock exchange.*

amortization the liquidation of an obligation through regular payments, which include both interest and principal reductions. Amortization comes from the Latin words *ad* and *mors*, meaning "to death." Thus, an installment loan is amortized, or "killed," as it is paid off.

The most common current usage involves real estate mortgage loans. Until about 50 years ago, most mortgage loans were what are now called "balloon loans," i.e., the borrower paid interest in regular installments but made no principal reductions. As a result, when the loan matured, the entire principal came due and payable all at once. Therefore, even if every interest payment had been made on time, the lender could still foreclose. And this grim situation often did occur, especially during the Great Depression. So it was, in stage and movie melodramas, that the villain was often a hardhearted mortgage holder about to evict an upstanding family into the cold. At the last minute, the family was saved by the hero, who paid off the mortgage and married the beautiful daughter.

Most modern mortgage loans are paid in monthly installments that eventually wipe out the principal *and* pay the interest, so fewer beautiful daughters are now at risk.

At the time of the mortgage settlement, lenders usually give the borrower an "amortization schedule," which shows the portions of each payment that go toward principal and interest.

The following is an abbreviated amortization schedule for a $100 loan at 12 percent for a term of 25 years. To use this schedule, simply multiply the figures in the chart by the number of $100s in a proposed loan—i.e., for a $50,000 loan, multiply by 500. In this example, the monthly payment would be $526.50; and in the first year, the amounts paid on interest and principal would be $5,982 and $337.50, respectively. The year-end balance remaining would be $49,662.50.

TWELVE PERCENT, 25 YEARS
Monthly Payment 1.053 × number of
$100s borrowed.

Year	Annual Interest	Annual Principal	Year End Balance Due
1	11.964	0.675	99.325
2	11.878	0.761	98.564
3	11.782	0.857	97.707
4	11.673	0.966	96.741
5	11.550	1.088	95.653
6	11.412	1.226	94.427
7	11.257	1.382	93.045
8	11.082	1.557	91.488
9	10.884	1.755	89.733
10	10.662	1.977	87.756
11	10.411	2.228	85.529
12	10.128	2.510	83.018
13	9.810	2.829	80.189
14	9.451	3.187	77.002
15	9.047	3.592	73.410
16	8.591	4.047	69.363
17	8.078	4.561	64.802
18	7.500	5.139	59.664
19	6.848	5.791	53.873
20	6.114	6.525	47.348
21	5.286	7.353	39.995
22	4.354	8.285	31.710
23	3.303	9.336	22.374
24	2.119	10.520	11.854
25	.785	11.854	.000

See also *balloon payment;* Section II, "Home Financing."

ancillary benefits an insurance term referring to benefits for inciden- tal hospital charges such as lab fees, physical therapy, and drugs.

See also *health insurance.*

annualized average yield the average yearly earnings paid by an investment firm to its investors. The annualized average yield is affected by both earnings rates and administrative expenses.

annual percentage rate (APR) the amount, expressed as a percentage, of the yearly cost of credit. Under the provisions of the Truth-in-Lending Act, this figure is stipulated by all lenders so that borrowers can make comparisons. Before the passage of this regulation, borrowers were confused by the use of varying methods of calculating interest and the terminology used to describe them. In addition, some borrowers were bilked by unscrupulous lenders who quoted a low percentage rate and who were aware that the way the interest would be calculated would make the actual percentage—and the cost—much higher. The Truth-in-Lending Act, which became effective in 1969, ended the confusion and the efforts of some lenders to defraud by defining one standard way of stating interest and making it a matter of law that all lenders conform to it.

To help assure that all borrowers are quoted rates based on the same mathematical formulae, the Federal Reserve has made uniform rate charts available to lenders. The law also stipulates that every borrower must be given a *disclosure statement* by the lender that spells out the annual percentage rate charged, and this rate must be accurate to "at least the nearest quarter of one percent." The borrower must sign a copy of the disclosure statement certifying that he or she has received the information. Furthermore, under the law, the APR must also be used in advertising and in quoting interest rates.

Prior to 1969, there were three common ways to state interest: as add-on, as discount, or as a constant ratio. Here's the way they compare to the annual percentage rate:

Percent stated	Computation Method	Finance Charge Per $100	APR
4%	Add-on	$8.00	7.5%
4%	Discount	8.70	8.14%
4%	Constant ratio	8.01	7.51%
4%	APR	4.22	4%

The annual percentage rate can be calculated using this formula:

$$APR = \frac{2 \times \text{No. of Pmts./Year} \times \text{F. Charge}}{\text{Unpd. Bal.} \times (\text{No. of Pmts.} + 1)}$$

Here's an example. Assume a loan of $3,600 for three years with a finance charge of $864—that's 8 percent annual interest, using the old add-on method of calculation. To find the annual percentage rate:

$$APR = \frac{2 \times 12 \times \$864}{\$3,600 \times (36 + 1)}$$

$$APR = \frac{\$20,736}{\$133,200} = 0.1556756$$

So the APR in this case is 15.6 percent, not the 8 percent that lenders could once advertise without clarification. Most lenders do not make calculations in this manner, however, because they fear the penalties that would be imposed should they make an error.

Instead, they use the standard charts provided by government regulatory authorities, which were mentioned above.

See also *Consumer Credit Protection Act; finance charge.*

annual renewable term   a term life insurance policy that may be renewed each year at the option of the policyholder.

See also *life insurance.*

annuity   a series of equal payments made at fixed times. An annuity is usually sold by an insurance company. However, it is not insurance. It has been described as "insurance in reverse," because, with a typical annuity, the buyer (the annuitant) pays in a sum of money and then receives a lifetime of regular payments. But it is not that simple. The reason insurance companies issue annuities is because they are expert in playing the odds on life expectancies. And, basically, that's how an annuity works. To simplify, the company takes the amount invested by the annuitant, calculates probable earnings and the annuitant's life expectancy, then promises to pay him or her certain regular installments for life or a certain period of time. Naturally, the company shades the odds a bit in its favor and, if the annuitant outlives the odds, he or she beats the company—but if the person dies earlier than expected, the company wins.

The advantage of an annuity is that the earnings multiply tax-free until the contract matures and payout begins. Because most annuities are purchased for retirement, by the time payments are received, the annuitant is in a lower tax bracket and may have additional exemptions for age. Annuities also have great appeal for financial conservatives because they are usually very secure.

There are several types of annuities, including:

1. *Straight annuity,* which is, in essence, like the plan described above. The annuitant pays in a lump sum and receives an income for life.

2. *Guaranteed annuity.* This is the plan for the nongambler. Typically, if the annuitant lives, he or she receives payments for life; but, in any case, payments are guaranteed for a stated period—often 10 years—to either the annuitant or a beneficiary.

3. *Single-premium deferred annuity* allows an investment to be made years before the payout will begin, which lets earnings compound tax-free until the annuitant (the person who buys an annuity) is ready to collect, at which time he or she will be in a lower tax bracket and the then-taxable earnings will be less heavily taxed.

4. *Flexible-premium deferred annuity* is similar to the single-premium deferred annuity, except that, as the name implies, investments are made periodically out of present earnings. Usually, these plans are set up as Individual Retirement Accounts, which also gives the purchaser a current tax deduction.

5. *Tax-deferred annuity* is for employees of nonprofit agencies, and it can be a good investment. Authorized by federal law, this annuity has similar tax-deferment advantages to those offered by Individual Retirement Accounts and can be owned in addition to an IRA. This means that all premiums are tax-deductible, with no maximum as in the case of Individual Retirement Accounts, and the earnings grow tax-free

until the proceeds of the annuity are finally paid out. For teachers, hospital staff members, and other employees of eligible organizations, tax-deferred annuities can be worthwhile.

Consumer tip: Annuities are sold on both a *load* and a *no-load* basis, that is, with or without a sales commission. Obviously, if you want to buy an annuity, you are better off with the no-load variety.

An annuity lets the insurance company do your money managing for you; but, like all services, it will cost you—in this case, in terms of lower investment earnings. With an annuity, you can be sure that you will never outlive your savings, but you can usually get a much better return from a good mutual fund or even from bank certificates of deposit. One exception is the case in which a tax-deferred annuity will allow for extra tax savings, over and above an IRA. A typical example is that in which a husband and wife are both employed and both have maximum IRAs, but one spouse works for a nonprofit organization and can have a tax-deferred annuity as an additional tax-deferred investment.

See also *Individual Retirement Account (IRA);* Section II, "Retirement Planning."

ante-nuptial agreement See *pre-nuptial agreement.*

apartment house technically, a building with three or more self-contained dwelling units. An apartment house can be a good investment because the down payment is often low and the rents can not only meet the mortgage payments but can also net a profit.

Consumer tips: If you're a small investor, an apartment house can offer you a good return on your money if you follow certain rules:

1. Remember the three main factors of real estate investing: location, location, and location. Choose a spot where you are likely to get maximum occupancy, minimum vandalism, and can command respectable rents.

2. Stick to properties with fewer than five units; in this way, you can avoid some onerous federal housing laws.

3. Buy a building that will require a minimum amount of maintenance and do as much of it yourself as you can; also, act as your own rental agent.

4. Shop for the best mortgage rate that you can.

See also Section II, "Investments."

apartment, cooperative See *cooperative apartment.*

appreciation a growth in price or, more accurately, a growth in value. The word "appreciate" has the same Latin root, *pretium,* as the word "price." In investment terms, it means an increase in an owner's equity. Thus, if a stock appreciates by $5 a share, that means each share is worth $5 more to its owners.

See also *depreciation.*

APR See *annual percentage rate.*

APS See *attending physician's statement.*

arrears in modern financial usage, an amount of money due but unpaid. "Arrears" derives from the Middle English *arere,* which simply meant

"behind." The term is usually used in reference to past-due loan payments, mortgage loan payments, or taxes.

See also *delinquency.*

asked See *bid and asked price.*

assessed valuation the value of real estate, usually set by a governmental assessor, on which property taxes are based. In the past, assessed valuations were often set far below the fair market value of a property, but now more and more states are insisting on "100 percent" or "full and fair" valuation. To taxpayers, the important thing is that the assessed valuation be fair and equitable in relation to the market value.

Consumer tip: Because the property tax rate is fixed, the most common way to try for lowered taxes is to seek a lower assessed valuation.

Often, local tax authorities will increase valuations as property changes hands, which means that people who have bought a home recently may have higher assessed valuations than long-time homeowners in a community. To assess similar properties at different effective rates has been found, in some jurisdictions, to be illegal. If you're in this spot, ask an attorney if you can appeal your assessed valuation.

See also *property tax.*

asset a thing of value owned. "Asset" is derived from the Old French *asez,* which meant "enough." The word originally implied having enough to pay obligations, but now assets go far beyond that.

Some common variations include:

- *fixed asset:* a permanent asset, such as a building, land, or machinery, needed to conduct a business.
- *liquid asset:* cash or something that can be quickly converted to cash, such as stocks.
- *intangible asset:* something that has no physical existence but is still worth money. Typical examples are goodwill and patents or copyrights.

See also *accounting.*

asset-management account See *cash-management account.*

assigned risk the designation of an applicant for insurance coverage who is considered highly likely to have a loss claim. Usually used in connection with automobile insurance, this evaluation is based on the applicant's past loss record. State law may require that all insurance companies doing business within the state form a pool, and that people who are refused normal coverage be "assigned" for coverage to an insurer whose turn is next on the list. The applicant must pay higher rates than those paid by people who are not assigned risks.

Consumer tip: At all costs, try to avoid becoming an assigned risk; if you fall into this category, your premiums are going to be sky-high. Avoid filing every little claim possible; having the maximum deductible will keep you from doing so. A better way to avoid becoming an assigned risk is to drive safely and, above all, never to drive after drinking.

See also *automobile insurance.*

assignment a legal document that assigns the benefits of a life or property insurance policy to someone other than the owner or beneficiary.

There are two types of assignment—collateral and absolute. Under a *collateral assignment,* the person to whom the rights are assigned can collect only enough of the policy payout to cover any amounts due. The most common example is that of a mortgage lender having enough property insurance rights assigned to cover the outstanding loan balance.

Under an *absolute assignment,* the person to whom rights are assigned has the same rights as the original owner.

Consumer tip: When signing an assignment form, be sure you are giving up only collateral rights.

See also *automobile insurance; property insurance.*

assignment of lease a legal document whereby a tenant assigns his or her rights, under a lease, to another person or persons. This is not a sublease. With an assignment, the assignor gives up all rights; with a sublease, he or she retains them.

See also *lease; sublease.*

assumption of mortgage a financial plan under which a buyer of real estate, as part of the purchase agreement, agrees to pay any remaining mortgage installments when due. The down payment for the purchase of the property would equal the owner's equity, and the responsibility for the outstanding mortgage loan would simply be assumed by the buyer.

Here's an example: Suppose a piece of property sells for $100,000, with an outstanding mortgage of $20,000. The buyer makes a down payment of $80,000 and takes over payments on the $20,000 balance due on the loan. It is common for the owner equity to be higher than the mortgage balance under an assumption of mortgage. In such a case, the seller may give the buyer a *second mortgage* to finance a part of the down payment.

Consumer tip: Assumable mortgages are very seldom written nowadays, but if you can find a good property with an old, low-rate one, go to it. Just make sure that the payments on that mortgage plus any on a second mortgage from the seller don't add up to a budget breaker.

See also *second mortgage;* Section II, "Home Financing."

assurance the British term for "insurance," which is seldom seen except in the names of some insurance— or assurance—companies.

Consumer tip: Don't, for example, tell people you just spoke to your assurance agent or wrote an assurance policy, even if you deal with a British company, because they aren't likely to know what you're talking about.

ATM automatic teller machine.
See also *teller.*

attachment the taking of a debtor's property into legal custody by a court order. When attached, property cannot be sold without the permission of the court.

attending physician's statement (APS) a form filled in by a doctor so that a person can purchase life, health, or disability insurance.

attorney-in-fact a person who has the authority to make business transactions on behalf of another. Such authority is given by a written document, called a *power of attorney,* signed by the person who grants the power.

An attorney-in-fact may have full power, or, more commonly, the power may be limited to certain transactions, such as making withdrawals from or writing checks on a bank account.

A power of attorney must be executed before a notary public, and a certified copy must be filed with each person or firm with whom transactions will be made.

A person need not be a lawyer (an attorney-at-law) to act as an attorney-in-fact.

Consumer tip: Sign powers of attorney with great care—you may be setting yourself up to be ripped off! However, a safe deposit box, used by a husband and wife (or other relatives), is an excellent place to use one instead of having joint access. Then, should one party die, the other may have immediate access to the box, which may otherwise be denied pending estate settlement proceedings.

See also *power of attorney.*

attractive nuisance a potential hazard for small children that is maintained on a property. The property owner may or may not be aware of any danger involved. The most common attractive nuisance is a backyard swimming pool with no fence or an inadequate fence around it. The homeowner sees the pool as a family recreational facility; a small child sees it as an inviting place to play. If the child falls in and is injured or drowned, the pool owner may be sued for maintaining an attractive nuisance.

Not all attractive nuisances concern real estate. Another example is that of the automobile owner who leaves the keys in an unlocked car. A small child entering the car sees it as a toy to play with. If he or she is killed or injured, an attractive nuisance suit may be brought against the careless driver.

The courts have compared an attractive nuisance to baiting a trap to attract small children. The fact that a child may be trespassing is irrelevant.

Consumer tip: If you have a pool, secure it with a high, locked fence. Don't leave the keys in your car, or in a ride-on mower sitting unattended in your yard, or have any other hazard that may attract and then injure a small child. The child could lose his or her life, and you your property—all of it.

automatic overdraft account

See *overdraft checking account*.

automatic teller machine (ATM) See *teller*.

automobile insurance a combination protection program of risk coverage that provides liability insurance against injuring others or their property and, as an option, property insurance against damage caused by others. The sections of an automobile insurance policy are:

- *Bodily injury*, which covers the insured against loss if his or her car kills or injures other people. The usual way of stating coverage is as a fraction—$5,000/$10,000, which means that, in the event of an accident, the insurance covers loss to

any individual for $5,000 and for all injured parties up to a total of $10,000.

- *Property damage*, which covers claims made for damage to the other person's vehicle or other property.
- *Medical payments*, the section that covers costs of injuries to persons riding in the car of the insured.
- *Comprehensive*, which covers theft, fire, hail damage, vandalism, and other property losses to the insured's car.
- *Collision*, which covers losses to the insured's car should he or she have an accident and the insurance company not be able to recover from the other driver or his or her insurance company.
- *Uninsured motorist*, the section that covers medical expenses caused by an uninsured motorist.

Consumer tips: Most people have too much insurance at the low end of the possible losses and too little at the high end. Here's a way to have more insurance at less cost:

1. Drop collision insurance if your car is not financed (the lender will insist on coverage) and if it is old enough so that you can afford to replace it yourself.

2. Take the maximum deductible on collision that you must carry.

3. Take the maximum deductible on comprehensive coverage, but raise your bodily injury insurance limits to at least $100,000/$300,000 or, better still, to $250,000/$500,000. It would be even better to stick to $100,000/$300,000 and then write a personal liability rider to your homeowner's policy that increases all of your liability coverage to $1 million. Believe it or not, this will

usually save you money while it protects you against a catastrophic accident that could bankrupt you.

See also *homeowner's insurance*; Section II, "Property and Liability Insurance."

average maturity index a report, typically printed weekly in major newspapers, that shows the average term of investment for all money market mutual funds. Cash saved in money market mutual funds is invested in short-term loans or in short-term investments. Thus, for example, Fidelity Cash Reserves may, at a certain date, have an average maturity of 45 days. This means that, on the average, money saved in that fund has been invested for an average term of 45 days.

Because the average maturity index represents the average term of investment for all funds, it is an indicator of how the top money experts in the country feel the money market will go in the near future. The important thing to watch is the trend. If the index is shortening—that is, for example, going from 45 days last week to 40 days this week—that means the experts expect rates to rise and are trying to make funds available sooner for reinvestment at higher rates. If the index is lengthening, going, for example, from 45 to 55 days, then the experts expect rates to drop and are trying to lock in current higher rates for longer terms.

Consumer tip: If you're a small investor, checking the average maturity index is a good idea because it lets the experts do some of the guessing for you. When the index is lengthening consider investing in stocks or mutual funds; when it is shortening, consider locking some funds into current money market rates. In the latter instance, bank certificates of deposit may give guaranteed high rates for longer periods.

See also *money market mutual fund*.

averages statistical tools for stock market analyses, based on stock prices that include corrections for dividends and splits. Different experts have devised different statistical bases, of which they keep detailed records and from which they may plot trends and make predictions.

The best known average is the Dow Jones Industrial Average; others include the Dow Jones Transportation Average, the Dow Jones Utilities Average, Standard and Poor's Composite Stock Index (S&P 500), and the New York Stock Exchange Stock Index.

B

baby bond   See *bond*.

bait-and-switch   as defined by the Federal Trade Commission, "an alluring but insincere offer to sell a product or service which the advertiser in truth does not intend or want to sell. Its purpose is to switch customers from buying the advertised merchandise in order to sell something else, usually at a higher price or on a basis more advantageous to the advertiser. The primary aim of a bait advertisement is to obtain leads as to persons interested in buying merchandise of the type advertised."

Consumer tips: Although it is illegal, bait-and-switch advertising is a rather common fraud. How can you spot a bait-and-switch? Here are some typical indicators:

1. A salesperson refuses to show the product advertised.

2. A salesperson tries to put down the merchandise offered or the service on that product.

3. An insufficient number of the items are in stock to satisfy reasonable demand.

4. A refusal to give a customer a raincheck to purchase the product at a later and reasonable time.

5. A salesperson takes a deposit on the item advertised, then tries to switch the customer to a higher-priced item.

At times, even prestige stores indulge in bait-and-switch, if not as store policy, perhaps because of an overly eager local manager. If you spot a bait-and-switch, complain either to your state's consumer protection agency (it will be in your phone book under "Government-State") or to your Better Business Bureau.

See also Section II, "Consumer Frauds."

balance   settlement; the difference between the plusses on one side of an account and the minuses on the other; or the equality between the two sides.

17

The word is from the Latin *bilanc*, meaning "two-scale."

Thus, in a loan situation, if the total loan is for $1,000 and $400 has been paid, the balance is $600. On a financial sheet, if the assets (things owned) total $50,000 and the liabilities (amounts owed) total $10,000, the balance is $40,000. On the other hand, if the two sides are equal, the account is said to be *in balance*. In a checking account, if the deposits total $1,200 and the checks written total $1,500, there is a negative balance of $300 and the account will either be overdrawn or checks will be returned.

balance of trade the difference, expressed in dollars, of imports versus exports. If there is a favorable balance of trade, that is, if the United States exports more than it imports, it tends to strengthen the domestic economy. When we import more than we export, it weakens the economy and everyone suffers financially to some degree.

balance sheet the tally of the assets and liabilities of a person or company that shows that person's or company's net worth or lack of it at a particular time. The balance sheet is the end result of the accounting function. The accountant first enters transactions in a journal, then posts from the journal to ledgers, then from ledgers to income and expense statements, and from both ledgers and the I&E statements to the balance sheet.

Consumer tip: Work up your own balance sheet so that you'll know just where you stand financially.

See also *asset; financial statement; liability.*

balloon payment the common name for a loan in which the full amount due of both principal and interest must be paid in a lump sum at the end of the term of the loan.

When mortgage interest rates were at all-time highs in the early 1980s, some real estate agents spoke of "creative financing" as if they had discovered a new chapter of Holy Writ. Creative financing often involved a second mortgage with a "balloon payment."

Actually, there's nothing new about the idea. Balloon-payment mortgage loans were standard until the Great Depression kept hundreds of thousands of families from meeting the terms of their loans and caused hundreds of thousands of foreclosures. Business loans are almost always balloon-type loans.

Consumer tip: Balloon-payment loans are neither good nor bad; like many things, their advantages and disadvantages vary depending on your circumstances. If you are a salaried person, you are almost always better off with an installment-type loan, simply because the likelihood of making an orderly payoff is better. If you are a shopkeeper with a large seasonal income—Christmas sales, for instance—or if you know you will get a large sum that is guaranteed at a certain time, a balloon-payment loan is a good deal because the true rate of interest is lower than with an installment loan.

See also Section II, "Borrowing," "Home Financing."

bank a depository institution, operating under either a state- or federal-government charter, which accepts deposits and makes loans. American banks can be separated into three main categories:

1. *Commercial banks*, which traditionally offer all deposit and loan services and specialize in business and consumer loans.

2. *Savings institutions*, which may legally offer just about any service, but often specialize in consumer-level deposit accounts, home-mortgage and home-repair loans, and consumer loans.

3. *Credit unions*, which serve only their members. Once specializing in low-cost loans to members, they now offer a broader range of services. Their loan rates have now, in many cases, risen to equal those of other banking-type institutions.

These three categories of banking institutions can be further broken down as follows:

• *National banks.* These commercial banks operate under a federal charter and the supervision of the Comptroller of the Currency. National banks must belong to the Federal Reserve System and their deposits must be insured by the Federal Deposit Insurance Corporation (FDIC).

• *State commercial banks.* These banks, many of which are called *trust companies*, operate under charters issued by their states. Most, but not quite all, are insured by the FDIC, and they may or may not (most do not) belong to the Federal Reserve System. Those that do belong to the Fed are under the supervision of the Federal Reserve Bank Board, and those that do not, but are insured, are under the supervision of the FDIC. State banks are also su-

pervised by their own state banking departments.

• *Federal savings and loan associations (S&Ls)* are of two types, mutual and stock. The assets of a mutual association are owned by its depositors, those of a stock association by its stockholders. The deposits of all federal S&Ls are insured by the Federal Savings and Loan Insurance Corporation (FSLIC). Both are under the supervision of the Federal Home Loan Bank (FHLB).

• *State-chartered savings and loan (or building and loan) associations,* sometimes called *cooperative banks,* are also depositor- or stockholder-owned. Most are mutuals. The assets of most are insured by the FSLIC, though in some states, such as Maryland, Ohio, and Massachusetts, the insurance may be provided by a state agency. In a few cases, state-chartered associations are not insured at all. If federally insured, they are under the supervision of the FSLIC; if not, the supervision is provided by their state's banking department.

• *Federal mutual savings banks.* Chartered only since 1982, these institutions, like the federal S&Ls, are insured and supervised by the FSLIC and the FHLB, respectively, but have somewhat broader authority, especially in lending, than S&Ls.

• *State-chartered mutual savings banks* have the option of belonging to either the FDIC or, in some cases, to a state-sponsored insurance program. In the first case, they operate under the supervision of the FDIC and the FHLB, and in the

19

second, under the supervision of the state insurance department and the FHLB.

- *Federal credit unions* are the fastest-growing of all depository institutions. They are federally chartered and insured and supervised by the National Credit Union Administration (NCUA).
- *State-chartered credit unions* may be either insured or uninsured. Like the federal credit unions, these credit unions are insured by and under the supervision of the NCUA. Uninsured state CUs are under the supervision of the state banking department.

Under the Depository Institutions Deregulation and Monetary Control Act of 1980, the powers of all types of banking institutions have been broadened considerably. For example, until the time of the act, savings institutions could not offer checking accounts or make business-type loans. Now they can.

Here's some interesting banking history. The word "bank" comes from the Italian *banca*, or bench, and originally referred to the tables or benches of goldsmiths.

During the Middle Ages, as now, criminals abounded. People didn't like to carry money because they could so easily become victims of medieval muggers; and, if they kept money hidden at home, they could be robbed. The goldsmiths, however, had strong vaults and guards with swords and sturdy clubs. So, recognizing a good business idea, the goldsmiths began to rent space in their vaults in which

people could safeguard their money—which was made of gold and silver. When a person needed some of his money, he went to the goldsmith and got it from his supply in the vault. Still, the person could be robbed coming from the goldsmith, so the practice grew of paying bills, not with the actual gold or silver, but with notes that ordered the goldsmith who had the person's money on deposit to pay a certain amount to such-and-such a person or to the bearer of the note.

Thus, checks began—orders to pay money drawn on a depository. And since the goldsmiths knew and trusted each other, they soon began accepting such orders drawn on funds on deposit with each other. And thus banks were born.

Consumer tip: Shop carefully for a bank. Look for these things: the services you want or need, ease in getting a loan should you someday want one, a good return on your deposited funds, federal or state insurance of your account, convenience of location, and a friendly and helpful staff.

bank acceptance   See *acceptance.*

bank-at-home   See *home banking.*

bank card   See *credit card.*

bank holding company   See *holding company.*

bankruptcy   a legal declaration by a court that a person, corporation, or other business or organization is insolvent.

See also *bankruptcy, personal.*

bankruptcy, personal the conditions under which a person or persons are declared by a court to be financially insolvent. Personal bankruptcy is the last resort for people with too much debt to handle. Unfortunately, it is a common phenomenon in American financial life. Every week, 1,000 people seek relief in our courts. The average person who files for bankruptcy has assets of $10,000 to $15,000 and liabilities of $15,000 to $20,000.

Two sections of the Bankruptcy Reform Act of 1978 offer relief to the debt-ridden: Chapter 13 and Chapter 7.

Chapter 13 allows for debt reorganization—a much less drastic step than outright bankruptcy. A person files under this chapter through an attorney who is familiar with bankruptcy law. The person lists his or her debts and, with the attorney's help, prepares a repayment plan. This plan, which must give creditors at least as much as they would get under a regular bankruptcy, is filed with a federal judge, at which point, all creditors are immediately stopped from further collection proceedings. If the plan is approved, the judge appoints a federal trustee, and the person who has filed makes a monthly payment to him or her that is distributed to the creditors. All creditor interest charges and service fees also stop.

To qualify for a Chapter 13 reorganization, a debtor:

1. Must have a regular income.

2. Must not have more than $100,000 in unsecured debts and must have less than $350,000 in secured debts. Unsecured debts would include credit-card and personal-loan balances, and secured debts would include such things as an auto loan (secured by the car) or a home mortgage (secured by the house).

Chapter 7, personal bankruptcy, is the last resort. It is an emotionally painful procedure to go through, and has been compared to having root canal work done without anesthesia while the dentist uses a half-inch bit. But it is available.

To qualify for Chapter 7 a debtor:

1. Must have more liabilities than assets, even if some assets cannot be converted to cash for a long time.

2. Cannot have debts that are mostly secured by objects in which the debtor has substantial equity, such as boats, cars, and so on.

3. Must not have received a discharge in bankruptcy for at least six years or have had a Chapter 13 plan approved that paid less than 70 percent of his or her debts within the past six years.

4. Must not have a co-signer on some of his or her debts. Co-signers are protected under Chapter 13, but in a bankruptcy, creditors can go against them. In other words, debts that are co-signed are not included in the listing of liabilities, since creditors can collect directly from the co-signer outside of the bankruptcy settlement.

5. Must not have lied on a credit application.

If the debtor meets these standards, he or she may file for personal bankruptcy through an attorney. All of the debtor's assets that are not exempt are turned over to a court-appointed trustee who will convert them to cash and pay out proportionate amounts to creditors.

The list of exempt property that the bankrupt debtor may keep in spite of the bankruptcy is lengthy. It includes:

- All assets with no further payments due, except those against which creditors have liens;
- Equity in a home up to $7,500 ($15,000 if filing jointly);
- Exemption for any car, truck, or van up to $1,200;
- Up to $200 *per item* for clothing, books, or other personal or household property.
- Up to $500 on jewelry;
- Up to $750 for tools of a trade;
- Up to $4,000 worth of cash-surrender value in life insurance.

All assets as of the date of the filing plus all assets purchased for six months after filing are listed in the accounting. *Consumer tip:* If you get into financial trouble, try to work it out yourself or see a debt counselor (see listing). If that fails, see an attorney about Chapter 13. When all else fails, consider Chapter 7, but only as a last resort.

See also Section II, "Debt Management."

bank services   the various financial services offered by banks and savings institutions. By definition, banks accept deposits and make loans, but they also do much more. While services vary from bank to bank, the most common offered are:

DEPOSIT ACCOUNTS:
   checking accounts
   NOW accounts
   savings accounts
   certificates of deposit
   Individual Retirement Accounts
   Keogh Plan accounts

LOAN ACCOUNTS:
   credit cards
   overdraft checking
   unsecured consumer installment loans
   secured consumer installment loans
   home-mortgage loans
   business loans
OTHER SERVICES:
   safe deposit boxes
   traveler's checks
   debit cards

See also *bank*.

barter   *swap;* the direct transfer of goods made without the use of money as a medium of exchange. Originally, all trade was done via the barter system, but it proved unsatisfactory because it limited trading options and stunted economic growth. *Consumer tip:* Barter clubs are now springing up all over America in part because of the desire to avoid payment of income taxes. However, the tax laws do not exempt "income" that is received through an exchange of goods and services from taxation. If you join a barter club, expect to pay taxes on the fair value of the goods or services received—or expect a very upset IRS auditor to be checking up on you.

basis point   a banking term that refers to one hundredth of one percent. Thus, when rates rise 25 basis points, they rise one-quarter of one percent.

bear   a term applied to a person who expects business conditions to worsen, specifically one who expects stock prices to fall; the opposite of a "bull," who expects stock prices to rise. A bear will often sell stocks short, i.e., sell borrowed stocks in the hope of repurchasing them at a later time for a profit.

See also *bear market; bull; bull market; option; puts; sell short*.

bear market an extended period during which the prices of common stocks generally decline.

Consumer tip: Playing a bear market is highly speculative and not a game for amateurs. It involves either selling short or, even more risky, buying put options. When stock prices drop, interest rates in the money markets generally rise, so prudent investors usually withdraw from a bear market and invest in bank certificates of deposit or in money market mutual funds.

See also *bear; bull; bull market; option; puts; sell short*.

bearer bond See *bond*.

bearer instrument a check or other negotiable instrument payable to "cash" or to "bearer" or one that has been endorsed with just a signature. A bearer instrument may be cashed by anyone.

See also *endorsement*.

beneficiary one who profits or receives other advantages. This is usually a person who is designated to receive the proceeds from a life insurance policy, from the estate of a person who has died, or from the distribution of trust funds.

Primary beneficiary refers to the first person named to receive benefits.

Contingent beneficiary refers to the person named to receive benefits if the primary beneficiary is dead or otherwise cannot receive such benefits.

Irrevocable beneficiary refers to a person named to receive benefits whose name may not be changed by the person owning an insurance policy.

Change of beneficiary refers to an endorsement by the owner of a life insurance policy that names a new primary or contingent beneficiary.

Consumer tip: Choose beneficiaries with care. In general, parents should be named as beneficiaries for single young people and spouses as primary beneficiaries with children as contingent beneficiaries for married people.

See also *life insurance*; Section II, "Estate Planning."

benefit the money paid out under the terms of an insurance policy. A death benefit is the most common example.

See also *death benefit; life insurance*.

bequest a gift of personal property made under a will.

See also *inheritance*.

beta the measure of the volatility of the price of a stock compared to the market as a whole. A beta of 1.00 indicates that the stock price will likely fluctuate in proportion to the rise and fall of the market; a beta of less than 1.00 (.80, for example) indicates that the stock is proportionately less subject to market fluctuations than the average; a beta of more than 1.00 (1.40, for example) shows that the stock is proportionately more subject to market fluctuations than the average.

Consumer tip: If you are a cautious investor or if you think a market drop is likely, try for a portfolio of stocks with a beta of less than 1.00. If you like more risk or if you think the market is going up, choose a portfolio of stocks with a beta higher than 1.00. You can find the beta by checking *Value Line* through your broker.

bid and asked price   an *asked price* is the amount the investor must pay a broker or mutual fund to buy a share; a *bid* is the amount a broker or mutual fund pays an investor to buy back a share of over-the-counter stock or a share of a mutual fund at a specific time.

Consumer tip: If you want to buy shares in a mutual fund, for example, you will pay the current asked price; when you want to sell, you will receive the current bid price. The asked price may or may not include a load charge or sales commission.

See also *mutual fund; over-the-counter stock.*

Big Board   a slang term for the New York Stock Exchange, which refers to the large stock-quotation board once featured in the trading room at many brokerage offices.

See also *Little Board; stock exchange.*

big one   a slang term for $1,000. "It cost me five big ones," means that something cost $5,000. Interestingly, 10 years ago, "big one" meant $100, which shows how inflation can change our language, among other things.

billing errors   See *Fair Credit Billing Act.*

binder   a legal agreement issued by an insurance agent to provide temporary property or casualty coverage un-

til the company can issue an actual policy. A binder is written for a definite time, often a month, designates a specific company, and lists the risks covered. A charge is made for a binder similar to that for a policy issued for the same period of time; often, the policy is simply backdated to the date the binder was issued, which automatically takes care of the premium charge.

Also see *casualty insurance; property insurance.*

black market   the buying or selling of goods and services in violation of government regulations. A black market usually springs up during wartime or periods of crisis when rationing is imposed or shortages exist.

bland   See *cartwheel.*

blank check   a signed check on which either or both the amount or the name of the payee has not been filled in.

Consumer tip: Never, under any circumstances, sign a check unless every block is filled in, in ink or typewritten. An amazing number of people are victimized each year by issuing blank checks to criminals.

blank endorsement   See *endorsement.*

block   a large quantity of stock, usually 10,000 shares.

See also *lot.*

blowing off   a stock market condition characterized by a short-term trading peak following an extended market advance.

blue chip a company with good management, great financial stability, and a sound earnings history. A blue-chip stock is a share of common stock in such a company. It implies a very safe investment.

See also *stock, common*.

Blue Cross See *health insurance*.

Blue Shield See *health insurance*.

blue sky laws state laws designed to prevent fraud in securities transactions.

See also *Securities and Exchange Commission*.

boiler room a place that sells securities of dubious value through high-pressure sales techniques, often by telephone or through misleading literature.

bond a certificate of indebtedness on which interest is paid. Common types include:

baby bonds, which have a face value of $100 each or less.

bearer bonds, which are payable to the holder.

convertible bonds, which may be exchanged for other securities of the issuing company by the owner.

corporate bonds, which are issued by corporations.

coupon bonds, which are bearer bonds, the interest on which is paid by the owner, who cuts coupons from the bond and deposits them in a bank for collection.

debenture bonds, which are general obligation bonds for which no specific security is pledged.

government bonds, which are obliga-

tions of the U.S. government and are regarded as the safest investment available.

municipal bonds, which are issued by states, counties, cities, or towns, the income from which is exempt from federal income taxes.

registered bonds, which are the opposite of bearer bonds, in that the owner's name is designated and payment may be made to no one else.

Savings Bonds, which are issued by the U.S. government in face value denominations of $50 to $10,000. *Series EE bonds* earn varying interest rates and pay the face amount at maturity—which time varies as the rates change. *Series HH bonds* also have varying rates, but pay interest semiannually and mature in 10 years.

zero-coupon bonds, which are sold at much less than the face value (deep discount) and redeemed at face value at maturity. There are no interest payments to holders.

Consumer tip: It is common to think of bonds as very stable investments; but with the exception of U.S. government securities, this is not always so. Bond values can fluctuate widely, and unsophisticated investors can get hurt. If you wish to invest in tax-exempt bonds, one good way is through a mutual fund that specializes in these securities.

See also *Treasury securities; U.S. Savings Bonds*.

bookkeeping See *accounting*.

book value the net liquidation value of a corporation on a per-share basis, determined by adding up all of the assets of a corporation, deducting all liabilities and the value of any preferred stock, then dividing the balance by the number of shares of common stock outstanding. In other words, the book value is the worth of each share of common stock in the event of the dissolution of a company. As an example, the market price of a stock may be $50, and its book value $25. In most instances, book value will be less than market value, with one major exception; bank stocks usually have greater book values than market prices.

Consumer tip: Book value is used by some investors as a guide to the safety of an investment. If the selling price of a stock is at book value or below, it is considered relatively safe.

Boston Stock Exchange (BOX)
See *stock exchange.*

bottom dropped out, the   a slang term meaning that prices of common stock fell so rapidly as to cause a financial crisis.
See also *stock, common.*

bounce   a slang term referring to a check not honored by a bank because of no funds, insufficient funds, or no account with the bank. A check that bounces back to the person who first received it is said to do so because it is a *rubber check.*
See also *insufficient funds.*

BOX   the Boston Stock Exchange.
See also *stock exchange.*

bracket   See *marginal tax bracket.*

bracket creep   a status change that is created by a cost-of-living salary increase that forces a taxpayer into a higher marginal tax bracket. Thus, in

terms of purchasing power, the taxpayer is actually receiving less net income, despite the inflation-offsetting raise, because he or she is paying a higher percentage of his or her income in taxes.
See also *marginal tax bracket.*

broker   in investments, a person or firm that is a member of a stock or commodity exchange or who represents a member of an exchange and who can, therefore, handle orders to buy or sell securities.

In insurance, a broker is an agent who sells insurance. The term is usually used to describe an independent agent who may place insurance with any of a number of companies.

Consumer tip: There are a number of different kinds of stockbrokers. Full-service brokers offer investment advice based on extensive research by their own staff of experts. *Discount brokers* simply execute your orders to buy or sell. By dealing with a discount broker, you can save up to 70 percent of the commission charges made by a full-service broker, whose commissions vary widely because they are not regulated. Minimum commission, even at a discount brokerage, is usually about $30. You can save a lot by using a discount broker; however, you should do your own research in your local public library beforehand.
See also *agent; stock, common.*

bucket shop   an illegal operation in which customers bet on stock prices. No orders are actually taken or filled for these securities; bucket shops function strictly for gambling purposes and are banned by the Securities and Exchange Commission.

budget a financial plan based on current assets, current liabilities, estimated future earnings, and future expenses.
Consumer tip: Everyone should have at least a simple budget for basic financial planning.
See also *accrual basis budgeting;* Section II, "Family Accounting."

building and loan association
See *bank.*

bull a slang term for a person who expects stock prices, in general, to rise; the opposite of a bear, who expects stock prices to fall.
Consumer tip: If you're going to invest in common stocks or mutual funds based on common stocks, it is much safer to be a bull than a bear. Just be sure that you have good reason to expect prices to rise! This means more than just playing a hunch—it means doing some research and listening to experts with a proven track record.
See also *bear; bear market; bull market.*

bull market an extended period during which the prices of common stocks generally rise.
See also *bear; bear market; bull.*

buyer's market a situation under the law of supply and demand in which the supply of a product or service is greater than the demand. Thus, buyers have greater leverage to set the price and other conditions of sale.
See also *seller's market.*

call   in banking, a demand for immediate payment of a loan because the borrower has not lived up to the original terms of the loan agreement.

See also *demand loan*.

call options   See *calls*.

calls   also *call options*; a contract that allows an investor to purchase the right to buy a specified number of shares of stock on or before a certain date. Call option contracts are purchased in anticipation that a stock will go up in value. Each option represents 100 shares of stock. The advantage to buying call options is that they have a multiplier effect on any potential profits; the disadvantage is that the same multiplier effect increases potential losses.

Here's the way buying call options creates a multiplier effect: Assume that the price of PDQ stock is $50 a share, and assume that an investor has only $1,000 to invest, which would purchase 20 shares. However, that same investor can buy PDQ three-month call options at $5, which means that a $500 investment gives him the right to buy 100 shares of stock. Thus, if the investor buys the 20 shares and the price of the stock goes to $75 a share, he has a profit of $500; but if he buys two calls at $500 each, he would earn the profit on 200 shares, or $5,000. On the other hand, if the stock fell from $50 a share to $30, the investor who purchased the shares would have a loss of $400; if he had bought call options he would have lost the entire $1,000. The amount of the loss is limited to the total price of the options.

Consumer tip: Unless you really know the market, stay away from options. When you buy call options, you are not investing, you are gambling; what's more, you are betting against experts.

See also *leverage; option; puts*.

cancellation of insurance   the termination of an insurance policy before its expiration date. There are clauses in every insurance policy that allow for cancellation. The policy-holder may cancel at any time; more problematic, however, is company cancellation. Every policy allows the company to cancel for nonpayment of premium. Life policies allow a 30-day grace period after the premium due date before the company may cancel. Property policies may not be can-celled unless the company notifies the policyholder that it will do so if he or she has not paid within a certain time— usually 10 days.

Consumer tip: Beware of policies that allow the company to cancel for rea-sons other than nonpayment. Some property policies, for example, allow the company to cancel in the event of a certain number of loss claims. And some health insurance policies may be cancelled in the event of claims. The result is that when you might need in-surance most, you don't have it. The answer is to buy top-grade policies from reputable companies. As a rule, it pays to avoid companies that sell through the mail or through news-paper advertising inserts.

cancelled check   a check that has been paid by the bank on which it is drawn and that has been stamped "cancelled" or "paid" and is no longer negotiable.

Consumer tip: Your cancelled checks are legal receipts of bills paid for tax and other purposes. Keep them in a safe place for at least seven years.

capital   an investment term mean-ing the amount of money invested in a business.

See also *accounting.*

capital gains   the profits from the sale of investment assets. For ex-ample, if an investor buys stock for $1,000 and sells it for $1,500, there is a $500 capital gain. If he or she has owned that asset for one year or less, it is a *short-term capital gain;* if owner-ship was for longer than one year, it is a *long-term capital gain.*

There is an advantage to long-term capital gains. Federal income tax laws treat short-term gains as ordinary in-come, so they are taxed at the same rate as any other income. Long-term gains, however, are taxed on a differ-ent basis: Sixty percent of the gain is exempt from tax, so that only 40 per-cent is taxed at all; and on that 40 percent, the maximum tax rate is 50 percent, which means that, for some-one in the 50 percent marginal tax bracket, the maximum effective tax is 20 percent. So for a married couple fil-ing jointly with earnings of over $20,000 a year, or for a single person earning over $10,000 a year, long-term capital gains have distinct advantages.

Consumer tip: If you buy stocks or make other investments, try to hold onto them for at least a year and a day before selling them at a profit so as to have a long-term capital gain. Another way to avoid short-term capital gains taxes is to make your investments under an Individual Retirement Account or Keogh Plan account, because they are tax-deferred and thus exempt from short-term gains tax disadvantages.

See also *Individual Retirement Account (IRA), Keogh Plan; tax.*

capital intensive   the description of an investment that, in order to pro-duce profits, requires a substantial amount of new capital. War production tends to be capital intensive because new weaponry means expensive retooling. In general, capital-intensive investments tend to contribute to inflation.

See also *labor intensive.*

capitalism an economic system based on freedom of ownership of the means of production. The United States economic system is best described as "limited capitalism," because, while it has many industries that are capitalistic, there is also much governmental regulation of all industries as well as government-authorized monopolies (the phone companies, railroads), and government-operated industries (the Postal Service, the Tennessee Valley Authority).

See also *communism; socialism.*

captialist a person who invests in a business and/or espouses the concepts of free enterprise.

See also *communist; socialist.*

capital stock the permanent investments made in a corporation by its owners, either at the formation of the company or subsequently. Each equal portion of ownership is represented by a share, which in turn is represented by a stock certificate. There are two basic types of capital stock, common and preferred, with subtypes of each. Investors trade in stocks in two basic ways: either by putting venture capital into new issues, in which case the proceeds of the sale go into the corporation for its use; or, more commonly, by buying shares from another investor through a stock exchange.

See also *stock, common; stock, preferred.*

carrying charge See *finance charge.*

cartwheel a large-diameter U.S. silver or nickel-clad dollar coin, last issued in 1978 and last bearing the likeness of Dwight D. Eisenhower on one side (*Ikes*). Cartwheels were so named because they were said to be "big enough to be used as cartwheels." In the old days, they were called *blands*, after Richard Parks Bland, U.S. Representative from Missouri, who, in 1878, co-authored the Bland-Allison Act, which made silver legal tender in the United States.

See also *money.*

cash 1) money; 2) currency and coins.

See also *money.*

cash-back deposit See *split deposit*.

cash flow an often misused term for the difference between cash received and cash disbursed. Technically, cash received may not just be from income; it may also include borrowing or issuing stock. Cash disbursed may not just be for expenses; it may also include payment of dividends to stockholders. In general, a positive cash flow means there is more money coming in than going out, indicating a healthy business.

Consumer tip: In personal terms, a positive cash flow means spending less than you make. Having a positive cash flow is the surest way to financial stability.

See also Section II, "Cash Management."

cashier's check   See *official check.*

cash-management account (CMA)   a multi-service account offered by many brokerage houses and banks under which a customer can have a checking account, an investment account, a credit card, and a personal line of credit all in one service. Typically, the minimum balance required to open such an account ranges from $10,000 to $20,000. Some financial institutions charge an annual fee up to as much as $100 for these accounts; others offer the account free. Capitalized as "Cash Management Account," the term is a registered trademark of Merrill Lynch.

Consumer tip: With the multitude of new banking and brokerage services available, you can usually put together a cash-management account of your own and save the service fee.

See also Section II, "Cash Management."

cash-reserve insurance   See *limited-payment life; ordinary life.*

cash-surrender value   the amount a policyholder receives if he or she cashes in a permanent-type life insurance policy during the lifetime of the insured.

Consumer tip: Cash-surrender values are usually disappointingly small, so it may be wiser to convert an unwanted policy to paid-up insurance or, if the policy is old and loan rates are low, to borrow against the policy and invest the proceeds of the loan in high-yield investments.

See also *cash value; paid-up insurance; policy loan.*

cash value   the amount a policyholder may borrow against a permanent-type life insurance policy. This amount grows through the years, and may be increased significantly through policy dividends if they are allowed to accumulate.

Consumer tip: Many old life insurance policies have guaranteed loan rates as low as 5 percent, with 6 percent being very common. If you have such a policy, it makes sense to borrow the full cash value and invest it in high-yield bank certificates of deposit or other investments. And when you pay the interest on your policy loan, remember that it is tax deductible for extra savings.

cash-value insurance   See *ordinary life.*

casualty insurance   liability insurance that provides coverage against loss to another person. Automobile insurance is the most common example. See also *automobile insurance.*

caveat emptor   a Latin phrase meaning, "Let the buyer beware."

Consumer tip: Avoid "as-is" sales, especially for high-ticket items such as used cars. When the rule is "let the buyer beware," he or she usually has something to watch out for.

CBOE   the Chicago Board of Options Exchange. See also *stock exchange.*

CD   See *certificate of deposit.*

certificate of deposit (CD)   also *investment certificate*; a term or savings account with a bank, in which the depositor is given a certificate as a receipt of the amount on deposit, and that guarantees a payment of interest and a specified maturity of the account. In general, CDs are used for larger savings deposits and pay much higher rates of interest than *regular* or *passbook savings accounts*. As of October 1, 1983, all rate ceilings were eliminated by direction of the Depository Institutions Deregulation Committee (DIDC). This means that a bank or savings institution may:

- Issue a certificate of deposit for any time period it wishes;
- Set any interest rate it wishes as long as the certificate is for a period longer than 31 days.

In addition, the penalty for early withdrawal has been substantially reduced, so that it now amounts to:

- Loss of interest for 31 days for a certificate of one year or less; or
- Loss of interest for three months for a certificate of more than one year.

The elimination of rate ceilings means, in essence, that CDs now offer highly competitive savings opportunities.

Consumer tip: Bank or savings institution certificates of deposit are almost always insured by either a federal or state agency. Check to be sure before you invest. Then shop for the highest rate for the time period for which you want to invest. In general, the longer the term, the higher the rate should be. In a period of declining rates, invest for as long a period as possible;

this locks you into high earnings for a long term. When rates are rising, choose the shortest term possible; this allows your certificate to mature at a time when it can be rolled over into a higher rate.

See also Section II, "Bank Accounts."

certified check a personal or business check that has been certified by the bank on which it is drawn. Check certification works like this: Mary writes a check payable to Susan. Susan wants to be sure the check is good, so she takes it to Mary's bank. The banker makes sure there are adequate funds on deposit in Mary's account, then stamps the word "certified" across the face of the check and signs it. At that time, the funds for the check are taken from Mary's account and transferred to a bank general ledger account. The check, from that point on, is not payable by Mary, but by the bank from its funds.

A certified check is as good as an official check or cash. In some cases, sellers will insist on payment by certified check; when this happens, the person who writes the check simply takes it to his or her own bank and has it certified.

Consumer tip: Be sure to make a photocopy of any certified check you write. Because certified checks are paid out of bank funds, the bank will hold the cancelled check for its records.

Certified Financial Planner (CFP) a professional designation awarded to graduates of the College for Financial Planning, Denver, Colo. Graduates are certified in such subjects as retirement planning, risk management, tax planning, estate planning, asset management, investments, and other aspects of personal financial planning.

Consumer tip: If you choose to use the services of a financial planner, look for a CFP or other professionally trained person. Above all, expect to pay a reasonable fee for the service. Many life insurance agents or stockbrokers are now becoming financial planners, but their orientation suggests that they will emphasize life insurance or stock trading because that's what gives them a profit. Thus, you may end up paying much more in unnecessary premiums or trading commissions than you would have for a one-time fee to an independent planner. Also, you'll get a more balanced plan from a planner who has nothing to sell but advice.

See also *Chartered Financial Consultant (CFC).*

CFC See *Chartered Financial Consultant.*

CFP See *Certified Financial Planner.*

chain letter an illegal pyramid-type scheme used to defraud unsuspecting people. Here's the way it works: Someone receives a letter in the mail that relates that this person made a million dollars and that that person made a huge sum, and so on, just for continuing the chain by sending on the letter to others. In addition, the letter usually contains bad-luck horror stories about people who supposedly broke the chain by not sending on the letter. A list of names and addresses, usually 10, is also included in the letter. The recipient is instructed to send a sum of money to the first name on

that list. Then, eliminating the first name, the recipient adds his or her own name and address to the end of the list, and sends the new letter to 10 friends, who, in theory, will send it to 10 friends, and so on. The letter promises that when the recipient's name reaches the top of the list, he or she will be on the receiving end of a huge sum of money.

The fallacy is in the mathematics. If a person does add his or her name to the end of the list, before it would move to the top (and before that person would collect money), 1,111,111,111 names would have to be added to the list! That's almost $4\frac{1}{2}$ times the population of the United States!

So who makes out? The few who start the scheme in motion. A crook begins a scheme with a list of phony names at the top—all actually himself. Then he mails to names selected at random. If he's lucky, the scheme may go on for five or six levels, and he will net up to $100,000 or more at only a $1 ripoff from each sender—all for some stamps and envelopes.

Consumer tip: The postal authorities take a dim view of chain letters, so if you get one in the mail, don't throw it away; take or send it to the Postal Inspector at your nearest General Post Office. Your postmaster can give you the name and address. You'll be helping to stamp out a rotten scheme that often defrauds those who can least afford to lose money—desperate people who will try to get lucky or ignorant people who don't realize the odds against them. But crooks know about Postal Inspectors, too, and usually avoid the use of the mail. Thus, the scheme may be called a "pyramid club," with in-person payoffs, or a "bond club," which uses U.S. Savings Bonds, or whatever. The principle is the same. Some years ago, in New York and Philadelphia, there was even a "bottle club," using Scotch whiskey for pay-offs, that ran rampant through the banks and brokerage houses—which shows that even money experts can be fooled!

See also *pyramid scheme.*

change of beneficiary See *beneficiary.*

Chapter 7 See *bankruptcy, personal.*

Chapter 13 See *bankruptcy, personal.*

charge account a line of credit extended by a retail store to induce a customer to shop there. Normally, this is an account under which the customer can pay in full for goods purchased within 30 days after billing date. If the account has a budget-payment feature, as almost all do, the customer may elect to make a minimum payment each month instead of paying in full. If this option is chosen, there is a finance charge, usually at the rate of 1.5 percent per month on the over-30-day balance, or 18 percent per year.

Customer tip: Having charge accounts at local stores makes shopping really convenient and makes it possible to take advantage of bargains even if you don't have the cash in hand. It also reduces the potential loss should you be robbed. However, it does induce some people to overspend and to get into debt. So if you use a charge account, use it carefully.

See also *charge card; credit card; finance charge;* Section II, "Debt Management."

charge authorization a system that charge-account and credit-card issuers use to verify credit before allowing the charging of expensive purchases or the dispensing of large sums of cash. The authorization is given by either a credit department or a central file, and may be done by means of a phone-in system or, in some stores, by means of a computer hooked right into the cash registers. In local department stores, it is common for authorization to be required for all amounts over $25; for credit cards, $50 or $75 are more common limits.

charge card an identification card issued for credit purposes by a retail store or company for use in purchasing its products. A charge card differs from a credit card, which is issued by a bank, because a charge card is good only in the outlet of the company that issued it.

charge-off an amount owed that is written off by the lender as uncollectable.

See also *bankruptcy, personal;* Section II, "Debt Management."

Chartered Financial Consultant (CFC) a professional designation awarded to graduates of the Chartered Financial Consultant Program, American College, Bryn Mawr, Pa. This is the same college that awards the Chartered Life Underwriter and Chartered Property and Casualty Underwriter designations, so it tends to be insurance oriented. In fact, many of the students and graduates are life insurance agents.

See also *Certified Financial Planner (CFP)*.

Chartered Life Underwriter (C.L.U.) See *American Society of Chartered Life Underwriters*.

Chartered Property and Casualty Underwriter (C.P.C.U.) See *American Society of Chartered Property and Casualty Underwriters*.

chattel personal property as opposed to *real property*. Real property is permanent and unmovable; in other words, it is land and the buildings on land. An automobile, TV, and clothing, on the other hand, would all be chattel. The word "chattel" has an interesting derivation; it derives from the same Latin root as the words "cattle" and "capital," because wealth was originally measured in terms of cattle owned as personal property.

See also *chattel mortgage; real estate*.

chattel mortgage a legal document pledging personal property as security for a loan. An automobile loan is probably the most common example of a chattel mortgage loan.

check an order drawn on a bank for the payment of a designated amount of money to a person named on the check or to the bearer on demand. A check is a negotiable instrument, which means that it can be transferred from person to person.

Technically, a check must have five parts:

1. A date. If a check bears a future date, it is said to be *post-dated* and is not yet negotiable. A post-dated check is actually a promise to pay, not an order to pay. If a check bears a date that has long passed—usually more than 90 days—it is said to be *stale-dated*. The check is still good, but it's not a bad idea to get a new check to avoid hassle.

2. A payee. A check may be made out to a certain person or to the bearer. A check payable to cash is payable to the bearer.

3. The signature of the drawer of the check.

4. An amount spelled out in words. Every check has an amount in figures, but this is for efficiency; the amount in words is the legal amount. When the amount in figures and the amount in words don't agree, the check is said to be *informal*, and the bank may return it; but, technically, the amount in words is the legal amount.

5. A bank name and address upon which the check is drawn. Part of that address is a number that looks like this: $\frac{3-9}{310}$. The top number is the American Bankers Association (ABA) *transit number*; the bottom is the Federal Reserve *routing symbol*. Here's what the numbers mean: In the transit number, the figures 1 through 49 in the first portion designate major cities; numbers 50 through 100 designate states. The figure in the second portion designates a specific bank in that city or state. Thus, in the example, 3–9 means Philadelphia, Central Penn National Bank. The bottom of the fraction, the routing symbol, refers to the Federal Reserve Banks, which sort many of the nation's checks. In the example, the 3

means that the check should clear through the Federal Reserve Bank of Philadelphia, the 1 means that the bank is a member of the Philadelphia Clearing House Association, and the 0 means that credit for the check is immediately available.

Consumer tip: Never issue a check unless you have money in the bank and unless any checks you have deposited have had time to clear. Check with your bank if you're not sure; otherwise, you might be embarrassed by a bounced check.

Checks are probably the greatest financial convenience that you have, but be careful. Keep your checkbook safe. Most important, don't have your checkbook and your identification in the same place—women often carry both checkbook and driver's license in their purses and thus give crooks both checks and valid ID. Finally, use care in writing checks. Fill in every space, starting as far left as possible and drawing a line to complete the blank to the right of the amount written in words. This helps prevent forgers from altering your checks. And use non-erasable ink or a typewriter to fill them in.

See also *bank; draft; forgery; post-dated check; stale-dated check.*

checkless society   a description of our society as predicted by some experts who believe that credit cards and computer banking will make checks useless. Twenty years ago, these same experts predicted moving sidewalks in today's cities. People like checks, they like the receipts they provide, they don't trust computers completely, and they like to play the *float*. Checks will be around for quite awhile.

See also *electronic funds transfer system (EFTS); float.*

Chicago Board of Options Exchange (CBOE)   See *stock exchange.*

child support   payments made by a parent, under a separation or divorce agreement or a court order, for the maintenance of a child or children who are in the custody, at least part-time, of the other parent.

Christmas Club   a savings account, often with coupon deposits, designed to accumulate holiday funds for savers. The name "Christmas Club" is a registered trademark of Christmas Club, A Corporation, which bankers affectionately call "the corpse."

Consumer tip: Bankers love Christmas Club accounts because they pay little or even no interest. In many banks, the Christmas Club totals equal the deposits an additional branch would bring the bank. If you can't save small, regular amounts in any other way, try Christmas Club; it works. But if you have any discipline at all, you can do better in a passbook account.

See also *savings account;* Section II, "Savings."

churning   the illegal and unnecessarily frequent buying and selling of securities engaged in by a broker in order to earn extra commissions.

Consumer tip: Brokers get paid only when they buy or sell stocks or bonds; thus, even if you lose, they win, as long as buying and selling is going on. Although churning is against the law, it is common. Don't let a broker buy and sell for you just to keep the pot "churning" and his or her income rising.

See also *twisting*.

Civil Rights Act a federal law, passed in 1964, that forbids discrimination on the grounds of race, creed, color, national origin, or sex, in the use of public accommodations, membership in labor unions, in the use of employment agencies, and, most important from a financial standpoint, in employment itself. Specifically, it bans discrimination in pay scales, fringe benefits, and, as amended, specifies that pregnant women have the same rights to employment as other workers. If they become unable to work for medical reasons, they must have the same rights and benefits as other disabled workers. Abortion payments may be excluded from health insurance coverage, unless the abortion is necessary to save the life of the mother, but other benefits, such as sick leave and disability benefits, still apply.

Other major anti-discrimination laws are the Equal Pay Act and the Age Discrimination Act.

See also *Age Discrimination Act; Equal Pay Act.*

clear to have a check pass through the collection system and be paid by the bank on which it is drawn.

See also *check; collected funds.*

clearinghouse an association of banks in a local area at which checks

drawn on participating banks are exchanged to expedite their clearing.

See also *check.*

Clifford Trust a *reversionary trust* set up for at least 10 years. Under a Clifford Trust, a person may transfer title to income-producing property for a period of 10 years or more, at which time the property reverts to the original owner.

Consumer tip: This is a great way to put the kids through college tax-free or to help out aging parents. For example, if you have $25,000 in bank certificates of deposit paying 10 percent interest, and you are in the 30 percent marginal tax bracket, your earnings on those CDs are $2,500 per year, or, after taxes, $1,750. If you put the $25,000 into a Clifford Trust for your 13-year-old child, for example, that $2,500 will go to him untaxed, unless he has enough earnings from some other source to make him eligible to be taxed. The accumulated earnings should really help to put him through college. By the same token, you could set up a Clifford Trust for aging parents and augment their income, probably tax-free, by that same $2,500 per year. A lawyer should be consulted for details.

See also *Uniform Gifts to Minors Act (UGMA);* Section II, "College Costs," "Tax Savings."

closed-end fund an investment trust whose funds are pooled for common investment and whose shares are traded on a stock exchange or over-the-counter. By comparison, a mutual fund is an *open-end fund.* In a closed-end fund, there is a set number of shares, so when someone wishes to invest, he or she must buy shares from a present owner—just as with any stock. With a mutual fund, there is no set number of shares (hence the name "open end"); new funds are simply invested in additional securities.

Consumer tip: Closed-end funds are not nearly as popular as investments as are mutual funds. In the first place, there aren't as many of them. In the second place, since they are traded like common stocks, brokerage commissions are always involved. In general, most people are better off with mutual fund shares.

See also *mutual fund.*

closing a banking term for the signing of legal papers to transfer the ownership of property.

See also *closing costs.*

closing costs the charges imposed on the buyer at the time of a real estate settlement. Closing costs can be substantial and can easily amount to $1,000 to $2,000 or more. These charges may include fees for appraisal, credit-reporting, and a mortgage application, in addition to fractional interest for the year, the purchase of any oil remaining in a household tank, partial tax payments, partial insurance payments, a title search fee, title insurance costs, a document-preparation fee, attorney's fees, and a recording fee. The buyer may also have to pay *points,* a loan origination fee that is technically not included in closing costs but is an additional interest charge.

Consumer tip: The law requires that a buyer of real estate be told of any closing costs before the time of the actual closing or settlement. Unfortunately, this rule is sometimes ignored or, more commonly, the buyer is not told until it is too late to do anything about it. This often results in the buyer having to go into debt to meet the closing costs. So if you buy a home or other real estate, ask about closing costs early on and make allowances accordingly.

See also *mortgage loan; point;* Section II, "Home Financing."

C.L.U. Chartered Life Underwriter.

See also *American Society of Chartered Life Underwriters.*

club account a savings account in which funds are put aside for a specific purpose. These accounts do not always pay interest and usually mature one year after their opening. Christmas clubs, vacation clubs, tax clubs, and travel clubs are typical examples.

Consumer tip: If your club account does not pay interest, try to save in another manner.

See also *Christmas Club.*

CMA See *cash-management account.*

codicil a legal document that changes a will.

See also *will;* Section II, "Estate Planning."

coinsurance insurance in which risk is shared. Usually this term refers to the 80-percent coinsurance clause common in property insurance policies. Under this clause, if the property is not insured for at least 80 percent of its replacement value, the homeowner must share in any loss, proportionate to the degree of underinsurance. Thus, if the value of a home is $100,000 and the homeowner has only $50,000 in insurance and a $25,000 loss occurs, the insurance company will pay only $12,500, or 50 percent of the loss, since the homeowner has only 50 percent coverage. Coinsurance is also common in health insurance, whereby the insurance may cover 80 percent of medical costs with the policyholder paying the additional 20 percent.

Consumer tip: With health insurance, you may not have a choice. So if you are young and healthy, coinsurance is not an unacceptable risk. With property insurance, however, it is best to check your policy to be sure that you are covered within the limits required.

See also *property insurance.*

COLA   See *cost-of-living adjustment.*

collateral   security left with or pledged to a lender in order to assure payment of a debt. A mortgage is a legal document pledging property to a lender. A *hypothecation* is a legal document pledging securities.

Consumer tip: In general, you can get lower rates on loans if you put up collateral because that collateral decreases the lender's risks. Thus, it is usually cheaper to finance a car with an auto loan (chattel mortgage) than with an unsecured personal loan.

See also *installment loan; side collateral.*

collateral assignment   See *assignment.*

collected funds   checks that have been deposited in a bank account and have been paid by the bank on which

they were drawn and are now available to the depositor.

See also *uncollected funds.*

collection   1) the obtaining of payment of a debt through formal presentation of a claim; 2) the process used for payment of an item by a bank or company on which the item is drawn that must be accomplished before funds can be credited to the depositor's account. A bond coupon, for example, is a collection item, which means that the customer must deposit it, then wait until it has been honored by the bond issuer and funds have been transferred to the bank. Checks drawn on other banks are also credited to a customer's account subject to collection.

See also *collected funds.*

co-maker   See *co-signer.*

commercial bank   See *bank.*

commercial paper   usually, high-grade short-term certificates of indebtedness issued by corporations, to secure loans with maturities of 270 days or less.

See also *money market mutual fund.*

commission   the fee paid to an agent or broker.

See also *agent's commission; broker.*

commodities   products of trade, such as sugar, pork bellies, soybeans, coffee, and even gold and silver. People invest in commodities by buying commodity futures contracts or commodity options.

A *commodity futures contract* is simply a promise to buy or sell a certain amount of a specific product at a specified future date. Producers of these commodities offer their future products in order to raise immediate cash; buyers purchase these contracts with the hope that, by the time the date arrives, the value will have gone up and they can make a profit. Most commodity futures contracts are sold through brokers dealing on the Chicago Board of Trade—a kind of stock exchange of products.

Commodity options come in two varieties, call options, purchased by investors who expect prices to rise, and put options, purchased by investors who expect prices to drop. They give the buyer of the option the right to buy or sell a futures contract at a certain price during a specific time period.

Consumer tip: Investing in commodities futures is risky for the novice, and speculating in futures options is just plain gambling. These financial dealings are best left to specialists who can afford to take the risks. Most commodity trading is done with huge margins—i.e., with very little actual cash down—so that the trader can make relatively huge profits—or suffer huge losses.

See also *option*.

commodity cash market   See *spot market*.

commodity futures contract
See *commodities*.

commodity option   See *commodities; option*.

common disaster clause   See *Simultaneous Death Act*.

common stock   See *stock, common*.

communism   an extreme version of socialism in which all of the means of production and distribution of goods and services are owned by the state. It is quite possible for socialist countries to also be democratic, but communism, as promulgated by Karl Marx, teaches that it is necessary to have a period of "dictatorship of the proletariat," after which, theoretically, the state will simply wither away.

See also *capitalism; socialism*.

communist   a person who espouses the economic and political ideologies of communism.

See also *capitalist; socialist*.

community property   a legal definition recognizing the partnership that exists in a marriage and referring to property owned jointly by husband and wife. In community-property states, a husband and wife are considered to share equally in all property acquired during the marriage, in income received during that time, and in any increase in the value of assets owned. In some community-property states, if a spouse dies, the surviving spouse inherits all community property; in other states, if a spouse dies, the surviving spouse inherits one-half of the property and the remaining half goes into the estate of the deceased. Arizona, California, Idaho, Louisiana, Nevada, New Mexico, Texas, and Washington are community-property states.

Consumer tip: In these days of high divorce rates, it should never be assumed that any marriage is permanent. If either party owns any amount of property, it pays to have an attorney draw up an agreement defining the rights to such property in the event of a divorce or the death of either spouse. See also *joint property; prenuptial agreement*.

compound   interest interest earned on interest. Compounding applies primarily to savings interest, and may be calculated on a continuous, daily, weekly, monthly, quarterly, semi-annual, or annual basis. The more frequent the compounding, the higher the actual yield on the savings. For example, $100 that earns simple (uncompounded) interest of 10 percent per year will grow to $200 in 10 years; with 10 percent interest compounded daily, that same $100 will grow to $275.59.

Consumer tip: Always look for the deal for which interest is compounded as frequently as possible; however, note that daily and continuous compounding produce virtually the same results.

See also Section II, "Money Math," "Savings."

Comptroller of the Currency the federal officer responsible for chartering and supervising national banks. "Comptroller" is pronounced "controller."

computer   banking See *home banking*.

conditional receipt a receipt issued when an applicant pays for a life or health and accident insurance policy that has not yet been issued. The payment is accepted by the agent on behalf of the company on condition that the applicant meets the standards required for coverage.

conditional sales contract a legal document used when paying in in-stallments for a purchase, by the terms of which the buyer gets the use of the property but the ownership stays with the seller until the entire sum due has been paid. All payments must be made even if the product turns out to be substandard in quality.

Consumer tip: Never buy anything under a conditional sales contract. This device is normally used by merchants who specialize in victimizing poor or disadvantaged people in slum and ghetto areas.

See also *acceleration clause; confession of judgment*; Section II, "Borrowing," "Money Mistakes."

condo See *condominium*.

condominium also *condo;* a building, especially an apartment house, in which individual portions of space are privately owned. Common areas, such as elevators, are jointly owned by all of the private owners.

Consumer tip: In some areas, condos can be an excellent alternative to home ownership. All of the tax advantages of buying a home are there, and so are the benefits from any increases in value. Another advantage, in many areas, is the security offered residents from criminals, since condos are often well-protected. The disadvantages are their high cost and the danger of escalating maintenance fees over which the individual resident may have no control. Shop carefully before buying a condominium.

See also *cooperative apartment*.

confession of judgment a clause in a promissory note giving the lender the right to enter a judgment against the borrower with no further legal

41

proceedings if the loan should become delinquent.

Consumer tip: State laws vary and so do judgment notes, but the universal consumer rule is, never sign a note with a confession of judgment clause in it. You would be giving up a part of your legal rights. So if a lender insists, go elsewhere for the money.

See also *acceleration clause; conditional sales contract*; Section II, "Money Mistakes."

consolidation loan   a loan used to repay other outstanding loans. The theory is simple. If a borrower is having trouble meeting too many loan payments, he or she can take out one big loan, pay off the little ones, and have one payment instead of many.

Consumer tip: The theory can work, but only if the payments on the new loan are spread out over enough time so that the borrower can afford to make the payments. Otherwise, a consolidation loan is just a substitution of one big payment for a group of small payments for the same amount due. For many people sitting on huge home equities, a second mortgage can serve as a workable consolidation loan.

See also Section II, "Debt Management."

consumer   any person who purchases products or services.

consumer credit   a consumer loan made for the purpose of buying consumer goods.

Consumer Credit Protection Act   the official title of the truth-in-lending law passed in 1968. The main features of the Consumer Credit Protection Act are:

1. Lenders must disclose the true annual interest rate on almost all loans and credit sales. This interest is to be expressed as an *annual percentage rate*.

2. The actual finance charge must be disclosed.

3. The total cost of the product, including the finance charge, must be stated.

4. The borrower must be given a *disclosure statement* containing the relevant information.

5. A purchaser has the right to cancel a sales contract within three business days with a full refund of any deposit.

Consumer tip: Hooray for the Consumer Credit Protection Act! Be sure you not only get, but read any disclosure statement. Lenders often just say, "Here, this is for you—nothing important—just a formality," and hand you a folded disclosure statement. Read it and be sure you understand it; and if you don't, ask questions and be sure that you get honest answers.

See also *annual percentage rate (APR); finance charge.*

Consumer Price Index (CPI)   a statistical index compiled by the Bureau of Labor Statistics and based on an ongoing nationwide survey of prices. The CPI is designed to measure the cost of living and is a very useful tool. Despite recent corrections, however, it may tend to overstate the rate of inflation. Many salaries, wages, and pensions are geared to the CPI.

Consumer tip: Follow the CPI, but don't let it worry you. Remember that it is based on a fixed market basket and that your spending needn't be. In other words, the CPI may, for example, reflect a rising price of beef because it assumes that you will eat a certain quantity of beef—but you can beat an inflationary trend by switching to a less expensive protein source.

See also *cost-of-living adjustment (COLA)*.

contingent beneficiary   See *beneficiary*.

contingent liability   See *liability*.

contract   a legally enforceable agreement between two or more persons who mutually promise to do or not to do something. A contract may be written or oral, expressed or implied by the nature of the transaction, and unilateral or bilateral.

In general, a contract has five requirements to make it binding:

1. There must be mutual assent by the parties involved.

2. There must be consideration—in other words, not just a promise, but rather something tangible must be given up by the person to whom the promise is made. Usually, the consideration is payment for a good or service.

3. The object to be achieved by the contract must be lawful—a contract for murder, for example, would be unenforceable.

4. The contract must require performance within an agreed period of time.

5. The contract must be in the form required by the laws of the state in which it is made.

Consumer tip: People make routine contracts every time they do business. But making some contracts is serious business, so never do so without the advice of a lawyer. It is much cheaper to have a contract reviewed by a lawyer beforehand than to contest it in court later.

See also Section II, "Money Mistakes."

contributory negligence   a legal term describing a situation in which an injured party had not used proper care or had contributed to his or her own injuries. The most common usage is in automobile accident claims, in which contributory negligence is a defense or partial defense against the person bringing suit. In other words, the defense can try to prove that the accident was caused in part by the actions of the person bringing suit.

Consumer tip: In an auto accident, never volunteer anything except your name, address, auto registration number, and driver's license number. Saying, for example, "Oh, my God! I'm sorry!" and meaning that you're sorry the other guy hit you, may be construed by witnesses as an admission of contributory negligence on your part.

conventional mortgage   a mortgage loan, written for terms ranging from 20 to 30 years, with a fixed interest rate and monthly payments that reduce the principal as well as paying off the interest, so that, when the last payment is made, the loan is amortized, or paid in full.

See also *graduated-payment adjustable mortgage; rollover mortgage; variable-rate mortgage (VRM);* Section II, "Home Financing."

convertible   a security that can be exchanged for another. Most common is convertible preferred stock, which can be exchanged for common stock at the request of the stockholder.
   See also *stock, preferred.*

convertible bond   a corporate bond that may be exchanged for stock.
   See also *bond.*

convertible policy   a term life insurance policy that may be changed to an ordinary-life insurance policy at the request of the policyholder and upon the payment of an extra premium.
   Consumer tip: When buying term insurance, be sure that any policies are convertible and renewable. You may never want to convert, but if you should want to, you can. The best reason for converting is a situation in which health deterioration warrants extending your insurance beyond the period for which you had planned. Switching to permanent insurance will allow you to avoid future premium increases.
   See also *life insurance.*

convertible preferred stock   See *stock, preferred.*

co-op   See *cooperative apartment.*

cooperative apartment   also *co-op;* an apartment building that is owned by a corporation, with the shares of stock owned by those who live there. The first mortgage loan, if any, is owed by the corporation, and each "owner/renter" has a second mortgage. Financing is not easy to get.
   Most people buy into a co-op because the control of the directors of the corporation is almost absolute. And many people do so in order to prevent "undesirable" people from moving in as neighbors.
   The federal income tax advantages of a co-op are similar to those in owning a home, in that each shareholder can deduct his or her portion of the mortgage interest and property taxes on Schedule A.
   Consumer tip: There are few advantages to cooperative apartments for people with average incomes. They tend to have the most appeal for the very rich, who wish to restrict rentals.

cooperative bank   See *bank.*

corporate bond   See *bond.*

corporation   an organization formed under the law, with powers to make contracts, own property, and do business within the framework of its charter. In many ways, a corporation is an "artificial person" in the eyes of the law.
   See also *incorporation; stock.*

correspondent bank   a bank that functions as a depository for another bank. All banks have deposit accounts with other banks to expedite the clearing of checks and to establish relationships so that they can share the risks of large loans.

corridor deductible   the gap between health insurance benefits paid by a basic plan and those paid by a major medical plan. For example, a basic plan might pay the first $7,500 of expenses of an illness and the major medical provision might pay only the portion over $10,000, so the corridor deductible, which must be paid by the policyholder, is $2,500.

Consumer tip: Try to arrange your health insurance so that you don't have a huge corridor deductible.

See also *health insurance.*

co-signer   also *co-maker, guarantor;* a person who signs the note of another in order that that person can obtain a loan.

Consumer tip: Surveys have shown that, in over 50 percent of loans guaranteed by co-signers, the co-signers end up paying the debt. Before you co-sign a note for someone, ask yourself these two questions: Is this person reliable? And will I mind losing a friend? If you co-sign a note, the odds are that you'll lose both money and friendship.

cost of living   the amount of money it takes to maintain a reasonable standard of living. This is determined by comparing present prices for necessities against those for a base year—currently, 1967.

See also *Consumer Price Index (CPI).*

cost-of-living adjustment (COLA) a common clause in union wage contracts and some pension plans that provides for income to increase at a specified rate as the Consumer Price Index increases.

See also *Consumer Price Index (CPI).*

counterfeit   money   fraudulent money that is created by producing imitations of real bills. Savings bonds, checks, and other papers with value may also be counterfeited. People have even counterfeited certificates for free hamburgers.

Consumer tip: The law on counterfeit money requires that the bank or other place at which the money is presented confiscate the bill or bills as evidence. This means, if you get stuck with a counterfeit, that you lose the amount the bill represents. So be careful. Good money looks good. The paper is of good quality and has blue and red hair lines impregnated in it; the features of the portrait are crisp; the Federal Reserve seal is sharp-pointed; the green on the back is the distinctive money-green. Don't get stuck with a phony bill; but if you do, don't try to pass it on or you may be guilty of a federal crime.

See also *money.*

coupon   the detachable portion of a coupon bond redeemable for interest.

See also *bond.*

coupon bond   See *bond.*

coupon booth   a small courtesy room near a vault in which bank customers may have privacy while working with the contents of their safe deposit boxes. The name derives from banking history; during the 19th century, these rooms were places in which wealthy customers could clip their bond coupons. In fact, most banks still equip the rooms with scissors for this purpose.

covenant   a contract.

See also *contract.*

C.P.C.U.   Chartered Property and Casualty Underwriter.

See also *American Society of Chartered Property and Casualty Underwriters.*

crash a sudden and dangerous drop in stock prices or other business activity.

creative financing buying a home with multiple loans. Most typical is the purchase financed with a first mortgage at a bank or other prime lender and a seller-financed second mortgage.

Consumer tip: Creative financing was the common way to buy homes in the early 1980s when interest rates were high. The only reason that many borrowers didn't get hurt was because rates dropped, often making it possible to arrange refinancing at favorable rates through a bank or savings institution. Beware of creative financing unless you are absolutely sure you can meet any payments that come due.

See also Section II, "Home Financing."

credit 1) a loan; 2) a bookkeeping entry made on the right side of a ledger; 3) an increase in liabilities, income, or capital; 4) a decrease in assets or expenses.

See also *accounting; debit.*

credit bureau an organization that keeps central files on consumers who are located in a specific area. Credit bureaus keep records on people's paying habits and other personal-history items that might have a bearing on their ability and intent to repay a loan.

Consumer tip: Under the Fair Credit Reporting Act, if you are refused a loan, you have the right to know why. If the reason is a bad report from a credit bureau, you have the right to inspect your credit file and to have any erroneous data corrected. If the credit bureau does not cooperate, you should contact the nearest office of the Federal Trade Commission (FTC).

See also *Fair Credit Reporting Act.*

credit card a plastic card by means of which a person can get immediate credit for goods and services or even a loan in cash. Credit cards are of three basic types:

1. *Gasoline.* These cards are issued by oil companies and range from simple charge cards to those through which the cardholder can charge accommodations and meals and get cash advances.

2. *Travel and entertainment (T&E).* American Express, Diners Club, and Carte Blanche are the most common T&E cards. There is an annual fee, and installment payments are not encouraged. These cards are primarily used by business people, but are becoming increasingly popular with the general public.

3. *Bank cards.* The two main bank cards are VISA and MasterCard. There is usually an annual fee, and installment payments are welcomed. Interest is charged at rates that vary according to state law and range up to 23 percent per year, with 18 percent per year being the most common. Any good or service may be charged to a bank card and cash advances may be obtained at any participating bank. The minimum credit limit is often $300 per card, with maximums running as high as $5,000 or more.

Consumer tip: For most people, the bank card is the best deal. But beware! Half of all cardholders pay their bills when due and avoid interest charges; most of the other half pay in installments and effectively add 18 percent or more per year in finance charges to all of the goods and services paid for in this way. Credit cards have caused more debt problems than any other loan plan in history.

See also Section II, "Borrowing," "Debt Management."

credit disclosure   See *Consumer Credit Protection Act; disclosure statement.*

credit life insurance   term insurance sold through a lender to the borrower so that, should the borrower die, the loan will be paid off.

Consumer tip: Credit life insurance is expensive and usually unnecessary. However, most borrowers agree to take it so as not to offend the lender. Don't buy it. If you need extra insurance to cover your debts, buy an inexpensive term policy through an insurance company.

credit line   See *line of credit.*

creditor   1) a lender; 2) a person or company to which money is owed.

credit rating   1) the amount a lender or credit-rating organization believes that a specific borrower can safely repay; 2) a borrower's scoring based on his or her credit history, on which the granting of future loans might be based.

See also *Fair Credit Reporting Act;* Section II, "Borrowing."

credit union   See *bank.*

credit worthy   a person with a good credit rating is said to be credit worthy.

cumulative preferred stock   See *stock, preferred.*

Curb   See *Curb Exchange.*

Curb Exchange   also *Curb;* the American Stock Exchange. This exchange was originally and officially titled the Curb Exchange because it dealt in stocks not listed on the New York Stock Exchange, and the brokers literally traded on the curb of the sidewalk. In 1921, the Curb moved to 86 Trinity Place, New York, N.Y. In 1953, it became the American Stock Exchange.

See also *stock exchange.*

currency   in common usage, paper money; technically, both bills and coin.

See also *money.*

current asset   an asset that is expected to be converted to cash within a year.

current income   income expected to be received within a year.

current liability   See *liability.*

current yield   the annual income from an investment expressed as a percentage. For example, if a stock sells for $100 and pays $10 in dividends, the current yield is 10 percent.

See also *earnings yield.*

custodial account   a bank or brokerage account set up under the Uniform Gifts to Minors Act (UGMA).

See also *Uniform Gifts to Minors Act (UGMA).*

customer service representative See *teller.*

customer's representative also *account executive;* a registered representative of a brokerage house who has met the legal requirements to handle transactions for customers and who buys and sells securities on behalf of investors. Sometimes called a "customer's man," this person may also be a woman.

Consumer tip: If you plan to invest, choose your customer's representative with care. His or her advice and attention to your account can earn or cost you a lost of money. Pick someone you like, trust, and respect who will handle your account with your interests in mind.

See also Section II, "Investments."

cutting your loss selling a losing investment and taking a modest loss before the loss becomes serious.

See also Section II, "Money Mistakes."

damages money paid by a defendant at the direction of a court to the person who brought suit for a loss.

D&B See *Dun and Bradstreet*.

day order an order given to a broker to buy or sell stock that expires at the end of the business day if the transaction has not been made. All orders to brokers are automatically day orders unless the customer directs otherwise.

days of grace See *grace period*.

deadbeat a person who does not pay his lawful debts; usually a person who incurs the debts with no intention of repaying.

dead broke absolutely penniless.

dead hand the situation that occurs when the wishes of a dead person continue to be legally enforced even after they have become useless. The classic example is that of the kindly person who, in the 1800s, left a large sum to maintain watering troughs for city horses. If the will were inflexible enough, that money would still be there, growing at interest, and absolutely useless.

Consumer tip: When making a will, allow for change in the situations of your heirs and of society in general. Don't let your "dead hand" waste the money you leave. In some areas, there are discretionary accounts, administered by the courts, that allow people to direct their funds to be pooled for charitable purposes when the original intent of their wills is no longer relevant. In such a case, the money for the horse troughs, for example, could go to crippled children or for an animal shelter.

death benefit the amount payable on a life insurance policy on the death

of the insured. Death benefits are also payable under some accident policies.
See also *settlement option*.

debenture   an unsecured long-term debt; usually, a corporate bond for which no specific collateral is pledged.
See also *bond*.

debit   1) a bookkeeping entry made on the left side of a ledger; 2) an increase in assets or expenses; 3) a decrease in liabilities, income, or capital. Also, 4) a charge against a deposit account made by a bank.
See also *accounting; credit*.

debit book   See *industrial insurance*.

debit card   a plastic card with a magnetic stripe that allows a person to make financial transactions via automatic teller machines (ATMs) or point-of-sale (POS) terminals located in retail stores. Usually, a debit card is combined with a credit card by simply adding the magnetic stripe to a VISA or MasterCard.
See also *giro; on-line*.

debit man   See *industrial insurance*.

debt   money, services, or goods owed to another person.
See also *accounts receivable*.

debt collector   anyone other than a lender or the lender's attorney who collects debts on behalf of the lender.

debt counselor   a person who makes a living by advising people who are in debt. Member agencies of the National Foundation for Consumer Credit make no charge for this service, except for $5 to $10 a month for postage costs. They're paid by contributions made by banks and other lenders who are delighted to have a responsible agency helping to work things out.
Consumer tip: If you have excessive debts and need help, look in the Yellow Pages for the nearest affiliated agency, or write to the National Foundation for Consumer Credit, 8710 Georgia Avenue, Silver Spring, Md. 20910 for the address of the office nearest you.
See also Section II, "Debt Management."

decedent   a deceased person. This is usually used as a legal descriptive term, as in *decedent's estate*, meaning the money and property of a person who has died.
See also Section II, "Estate Planning."

decedent's estate   See *decedent*.

decree   a court order that must be put into effect.

deduction, tax   an allowed expense that may be legally subtracted from income in the computation of federal income taxes. These deductions are usually shown on Schedule A, Form 1040, but in special cases may be listed on other schedules.
Consumer tip: Every deduction reduces your taxable income, so don't miss any. For example, if you are in the 30 percent marginal tax bracket, a $100 deduction reduces your actual taxes by $30.
See also Section II, "Tax Savings."

deed   a formal, written document by which title to real estate is passed from one person to another. The deed contains the terms of the sale and a detailed description of the property. There are different types of deeds:

- A *general warranty deed* guarantees the title to the property against all claims.
- A *quitclaim deed* contains no warranty of title against any claims others may have to the property.
- A *special warranty deed* is one in which the seller defends the title against all claims but assumes no other liability.

Consumer tip: Don't ever buy property unless you receive a general warranty deed. If the seller won't guarantee his right to the title, you should not assume that risk for him. You might end up losing the property!

deed restrictions   provisions in a deed limiting the rights of the purchaser of the property. Restrictions made in violation of the law are not enforceable. A seller cannot, for example, prevent a new owner from transferring the property to anyone because of race, religion, or national origin.

defalcation   stealing or misappropriation of funds entrusted to one's care; embezzlement. Interesting fact: According to the semiannual FBI crime statistics report, about $10 is stolen each year from banks by officers and employees for every $1 taken by outsiders.

default   failure to live up to an obligation, such as failure to make a payment on time.

deferred annuity   an annuity that does not begin until after a certain period or until the annuitant reaches a certain age.
See also *annuity*.

deferred posting   also *delayed posting;* putting off making accounting entries until a future time.
Consumer tip: The most likely area in which deferred posting will affect you is in bank transactions made after hours. Many banks treat transactions made after a certain hour as being effective the next day. Thus, a deposit made on Friday evening may be credited on the following Monday, which means that plenty of time should be allowed before checks are written against such deposits, or the checks may be returned.
See also *uncollected funds*.

deficit   the amount by which spending exceeds income. Businesses and individuals cannot sustain a deficit for very long; lenders soon grow wary. Governments can and do live with deficits, however. *Deficit spending* is action by the government, usually federal, to deliberately approve a budget that calls for spending in excess of anticipated tax revenue.

deficit spending   See *deficit*.

deflation   a drop in the cost of living, which increases the purchasing power of the dollar; the opposite of inflation. In technical economic terms,

51

deflation is characterized by emergency liquidation of inventories, which results in an excess supply of goods on the market and thus to much lower prices.

Consumer tip: After suffering double-digit inflation, deflation sounds good to many people; but in reality it is as unhealthy an economic situation as excessive inflation. Deflation usually precedes a period of *depression*, at which time unemployment is high, industrial production is low, and the economy is sinking.

See also *depression; flation; inflation.*

delayed posting See *deferred posting.*

delinquency failing in an obligation. In personal finance, this usually refers to failure to make a payment on a debt when it is due.

Consumer tip: Most lenders extend a grace period before a loan payment is considered delinquent. This may be 30 days from the billing date for a credit-card payment, or 10 days or less for scheduled installment loan payments. Allowing payments to become delinquent can seriously hurt your credit rating.

See also *grace period.*

demand deposit funds on deposit that the owner may withdraw on demand, with no notification of any kind. Checking accounts are demand-deposit accounts. NOW accounts are technically savings accounts, but are in fact nothing more than interest-bearing checking accounts. In this sense, they too are demand deposits.

See also *time deposit.*

demand loan a loan for which the lender may demand partial or full payment at any time.

Consumer tip: Few individuals borrow with demand loans. However, in some cases, to do so may be advantageous. Demand loans are excellent in instances in which you know you will receive a large sum to repay the loan, but don't know exactly when you will get it.

See also *installment loan; loan;* Section II, "Borrowing."

deposit insurance insurance on bank deposits provided by various agencies. Most common is that provided by the Federal Deposit Insurance Corporation (FDIC), the Federal Savings and Loan Insurance Corporation (FSLIC), and the National Credit Union Administration (NCUA), all agencies of the United States government. Through these agencies, each depositor's account in participating institutions is insured for up to $100,000. Insurance is also available for savings institutions under state supervision in Massachusetts, Maryland, North Carolina, Ohio, and Pennsylvania. In addition, state-chartered credit unions are insured in 22 states, industrial banks in six, and commercial banks in Pennsylvania.

Consumer tip: Never keep funds in an uninsured bank or thrift institution. In 1983, over 90 banks and thrifts failed, and only depositors with funds over the insured limit, or those whose institution was not insured, lost money. It is possible for you to increase your insured funds in any bank by carefully designating separate accounts. For example, if you are a married man, you may have an account in your name, an account in your wife's name, a joint account with your wife, joint accounts between yourself and each child, and joint accounts between your wife and each child. Each will be insured up to the maximum of $100,000. But why bother? If you have that much money, use more than one bank.

See also *Federal Deposit Insurance Corporation (FDIC); Federal Savings and Loan Insurance Corporation (FSLIC); National Credit Union Adminstration (NCUA).*

deposit slip   an itemized list of cash and checks to be deposited to a bank account.

Depository Institutions Deregulation and Monetary Control Act   a bill passed by Congress in 1980 ordering the eventual deregulation of the banking system. The main provision established the *Depository Institutions Deregulation Committee (DIDC)*, composed of the Secretary of the Treasury and the chairmen of the Federal Reserve Board, the Federal Home Loan Bank Board, the Federal Deposit Insurance Corporation (FDIC), and the National Credit Union Administration (NCUA). The Comptroller of the Currency is a nonvoting member. The DIDC was charged to abolish all savings interest regulations by 1986; with the exception of passbook savings and NOW accounts, this has, in effect, already been accomplished.

In addition, the law overruled all state usury laws on home mortgages for over $25,000.

Depository Institutions Deregulation Committee (DIDC)   See *Depository Institutions Deregulation and Monetary Control Act.*

depreciation   the loss in value of property over a period of time. For tax purposes, it is the cost, less the final disposal sale value of an item, prorated over an allowable number of years.

Consumer tip: The depreciable item of greatest importance to most people is the automobile. Cars are expensive, and they depreciate at different rates for different makes and models. In general, however, here's how experts estimate depreciation for a car:

Year	Percentage of Depreciation
1	30–32%
2	24–26%
3	18–20%

A car costing $7,000 will depreciate as follows:

At the end of year	Depreciated value
1	$4,900
2	3,724
3	3,053

Inflation, of course, will tend to offset depreciation, at least in terms of inflated dollars.

See also *appreciation; straight-line depreciation.*

depression   a time period in the economic cycle during which production of goods and services is low, prices drop, purchasing power is greatly lessened and unemployment is high. There have been many depressions in American history, but the worst was the Great Depression of the 1930s, which began with the collapse of the stock market in 1929.

Consumer tip: Depressions don't happen without warning. The classic signs are decreasing productivity and increasing unemployment—signs also associated with recession. When a depression seems likely, that's the time to get rid of all investments that can fluctuate in value and to concentrate as much as possible in savings in insured bank accounts.

See also *recession.*

devaluation governmental action to reduce the relative value of its currency in terms of gold or other currencies. As an example of devaluation through gold content, in 1934, the gold content of the U.S. dollar was reduced from 25.8 to 15.2381 grains, .90 fine, as an anti-depression measure.

The gold standard is a thing of the past. As a result, the modern method of devaluation is simply to change the exchange rate of a nation's currency in terms of another currency (usually the U.S. dollar) or against a market basket of 16 major currencies as defined by the International Monetary Fund. Devaluation is an extreme step taken by a debtor nation to reduce its international debts and impede an outflow of funds to other nations.

Consumer tip: In recent years, Mexican banks were paying interest at rates much higher than American banks; also, some Americans thought they could evade federal taxes on the interest earned in Mexican bank CDs. Then, when oil prices dropped, Mexico devalued the peso, and many of those Americans lost half or more of their savings. It can be very risky to save in any country in which devaluation is a possibility.

DIDC the Depository Institutions Deregulation Committee.

See also *Depository Institutions Deregulation and Monetary Control Act.*

direct agency See *agency.*

direct deposit a system whereby income due a person is deposited directly into his or her bank account. Many companies meet their payrolls by making deposits directly to employees' accounts in banks; but the most common use is made by the federal government, whereby Social Security payments are sent directly to recipients' banks. The advantage to the company or government is that much of the cost of issuing and mailing individual checks is eliminated.

Consumer tip: If you are eligible for direct deposit of funds due you, be sure to give your approval. For one thing, you usually get your money faster. For another, you are protected against muggers and mailbox theft. In the case of Social Security, some banks guarantee your deposit, which means that, even if the bank doesn't receive it on time from the government, it still credits your account. Ask if your bank offers this service.

disclosure statement a statement issued to borrowers by lenders that spells out the terms of the loan. Disclosure statements are now required by federal law.

See also *annual percentage rate (APR); Consumer Credit Protection Act.*

discount a deduction of some sort.
Consumer tip: If you're buying, a discount means a reduction in price, and

that's good. If you're selling, it's not so good, although discounts are often offered to encourage prompt payment. You should try to avoid *discounted loans*, which means that you pay the interest in advance.

See also Section II, "Borrowing."

discount broker   See *broker*.

discounted loan   See *discount; discount rate method; rediscount*.

discount rate   the interest, expressed as a percentage, charged by the Federal Reserve Bank for loans made to its member banks.

discount rate method   a technique for computing interest on a consumer installment loan in which the interest is prepaid when the loan is made. Using the discount rate method favors the lender, in that the interest as stated seems lower than it actually is. For example, for a loan of $2,000 at a discount rate of 6 percent for one year, the computation would be:

$2,000 × .06 × 1 = $120

The finance charge of $120 would then be subtracted from $2,000, and the borrower would receive only $1,880, while the lender would receive the interest payment in advance. Thus, the borrower, repaying $2,000 but receiving only $1,880, would actually be paying $120 interest for a $1,880 loan, for a true interest rate of 6.383 percent. In addition, in the above example, the annual percentage rate (APR)–the rate that is the legal standard–would actually be 11.58 percent, because the borrower would not have the use of the entire amount for

the full term but would be charged as if he or she did.

Consumer tip: Although few lenders still make them, you should avoid discounted loans. Rely on the annual percentage rate, which all lenders must state under the Consumer Credit Protection Act.

See also *add-on rate; annual percentage rate (APR); simple interest*.

discretionary trust   a trust that gives the administrator the right to decide when and how much of the income and/or principal to disburse to the beneficiary. Discretionary trusts are common in cases in which the person setting up the trust questions the judgment of his or her heirs.

dishonored check   See *notice of dishonor*.

disintermediation   the taking of money from bank savings accounts for investment in higher-yield accounts, especially money market funds and bonds, thus bypassing the banks as intermediaries in the investment process. The effect of disintermediation is that banks have fewer dollars to lend and that loan interest rates then tend to rise.

disposable income   personal income less all taxes. In other words, what a person has left to spend on his or her own needs.

Consumer tip: Disposable income is more important than gross income. There are two ways to increase disposable income; one is to increase gross income, the second is to reduce taxes.

See also *spendable earnings;* Section II, "Tax Savings."

distribution of risk   See *diversification.*

diversification   also, *distribution of risk*; an investment strategy that calls for having several varied holdings so that, if one drops in value, losses will be minimized.

Consumer tip: The average person can use the principle of distribution of risk simply by investing in mutual funds rather than specific stocks.

See also Section II, "Investments."

dividend options   a choice in the use of dividends under the terms of an ordinary or cash-reserve participating life insurance policy. The owner has the following options regarding dividends. He or she may (1) receive them in cash; (2) use them to reduce premiums; (3) leave them with the company to accumulate at interest; (4) use them to buy paid-up additional insurance; (5) use them to purchase one-year term additions.

Consumer tip: If you are young and need extra coverage, go for the fifth option—the one-year term additions. If you don't especially need the extra coverage, choose option four and buy paid-up additions of ordinary life. There are no agent's commissions or underwriting fees, so you get a good price, and you gradually add to your permanent insurance so that eventually, when the term insurance becomes prohibitively expensive, you can reduce some of it. Also, you pay no income tax on the dividends nor will your heirs pay them on the death ben-efits, so you have a perfectly legal tax shelter here.

See also *settlement options.*

dividends   earnings as a portion of net profits. Banks pay *interest* on savings; companies pay dividends to stockholders.

Savings and loans that are mutually owned by depositors also pay dividends. For tax purposes, however, these dividends are classified as savings interest. In addition, earnings from money market mutual funds are called dividends, but are also classified as savings interest for tax purposes.

Consumer tip: The first $100 of dividend income from stock holdings ($200 for a married couple filing jointly) is excluded from taxable dividends income; but the Economic Recovery Tax Act of 1981 rescinded the tax exclusion that was previously allowed on savings interest. The rescinding of this tax exclusion is patently unfair to people of modest means who are more likely to have savings than stock holdings. It's a good idea to keep enough in dividend-paying investments to qualify for the tax exclusion and thus maximize your earnings.

See also *interest.*

dollar   the basic monetary unit of the United States. A dollar is equal to 100 cents. Money is called "dollars" in other foreign cities and countries, including, among others, Australia, Canada, Guyana, Hong Kong, Jamaica, New Zealand, Singapore, Taiwan, Trinidad and Tobago, and Zimbabwe. These, of course, are not U.S. dollars.

The word "dollar" is an Anglicization of the Low German word *daler*, which is adapted from the German *thaler*. The first large, silver "thalers" were minted in Joachimstal (Joachim's Dale) in Bohemia in 1518 and were called "Joachimsthalers," or "thalers," for short. Later, the Spanish made a large silver coin that, in the American colonies, was dubbed the "Spanish dollar," which became the basis for our first national coinage. Because of a shortage of smaller coins, it became customary to cut these Spanish "dollars" into eight smaller pieces of equal size for change, hence our slang terms of "two bits" for 25 cents, "four bits" for 50 cents, and "six bits" for 75 cents.

dollar cost averaging an investment technique of buying a security at fixed intervals with a fixed dollar amount. This means that when prices are high the investor gets fewer shares, and when they are low he or she gets more shares. This automatically gives the investor a median price and can help assure a favorable investment in the long term.
See also Section II, "Investments."

domicile a legal residence. In these days of fluid populations, establishing domicile is very important. Retired people, for example, may have homes in New York and Florida. When they die, which state gets the inheritance tax? Too often, the answer is both.
Consumer tip: If you have residences in two or more states, take steps to establish a domicile right away. Be sure to register to vote in one state; have a notarized statement of intent as to your choice of domicile; have your driver's license and auto registration from that

same state. In short, do everything to show that you live in the desired state and visit the other as a tourist. It's a good idea to ask an attorney in the state you do not wish as your domicile for advice on how to circumvent his or her state laws.
See also Section II, "Estate Planning."

double indemnity a clause in a life insurance policy providing for double death benefits in the event of an accidental death. Naturally, there are specific exclusions limiting the claim.
Consumer tip: A double indemnity clause is a sales gimmick used by many companies to induce younger people to buy insurance—the rationale being that most deaths of younger people are accidental. However, you should never count the doubled value as the amount of insurance you actually have. Buy any insurance you actually need and look on an accidental death benefit for what it is—a gamble.

Dow Jones Averages the indexes most commonly used to judge the performance of the stock market, based on prices of shares traded on the New York Stock Exchange. Actually, there are four Dow Jones Averages: Industrials, based on the stock prices of 30 carefully chosen companies; Utilities, based on 15 public utility stocks; Transportation, based on 20 stocks; and a composite based on all 65 of these stocks. When people refer to the Dow Jones Average (or Dow, for short) they almost always mean the industrial average, as most of the stocks people buy are industrials.
See also *averages; Standard and Poor's*

Composite Stock Index (S&P 500); Section II, "Investments."

down payment   a partial payment for goods or services made in advance to induce a lender to finance the balance. Amounts of down payments vary, but 20 percent of the total sale price is most typical.

See also Section II, "Borrowing."

down tick   a stock transaction at a lower price than the transaction immediately preceding.

See also *up tick.*

draft   an instrument similar to a check that may be payable at a future date and need not be payable at a bank. The difference between a check and a draft is that a check must be payable at a bank; a draft may be payable by anyone. Drafts are usually used for commercial transactions, with the seller submitting a draft, with shipping documents attached, through his or her bank for collection from the buyer.

A *sight draft* is payable on presentation to the drawee. A *time draft* is payable at some time after the draft is presented. A *trade acceptance* is a draft used in a transaction involving the sale of goods. NOW accounts were originally begun by savings banks that could not pay checks, so the negotiable order of withdrawal was technically a sight draft.

See also *check.*

drawee   a person or, more commonly, a bank on which a check or draft is drawn; the paying bank.

See also *check.*

drawer   a person who issues a check or draft.

See also *check; draft.*

due and unpaid   See *past due.*

Dun and Bradstreet (D&B)   the leading firm in the business of credit analysis and reporting. To "D&B So-and-So" is to order a credit investigation of that person or firm.

earnest money money given to bind an agreement; a nonrefundable down payment.

See also *down payment*.

earning power a person's potential ability to earn money over a period of time. This figure is important in making future projections for determining needed life insurance or for the settlement of injury or death claims by the courts.

Usually, earning power is estimated by multiplying the person's annual income, adjusted for inflationary and merit increases, times the number of years he or she would normally continue working. For example, assume that a man, aged 55, is totally disabled. At the time of his disability, he is earning $20,000 a year. At retirement, senior people in his position earn $40,000 a year. Assuming an annual inflation rate of 6 percent, that means his total inflation-adjusted earnings for the 10 years he cannot work would amount to about $420,000.

Consumer tip: Knowing your own earning power is important because it helps you to put your future finances in perspective.

See also Section II, "Money Math."

earnings yield the reciprocal of the price-earnings (P/E) ratio of a common stock, which is calculated by dividing the P/E into 100. Thus, a stock with a P/E of 6 has a per-share earnings yield of 16.67 (6 into 100).

Consumer tip: Always try to buy stocks with a high earnings yield. Even though you may not receive these earnings as dividends, they will at least be used to expand the company and the value of the stock may rise accordingly. However, don't go by the earnings yield alone; be sure also that the stocks you choose are those of financially sound companies with growth potential.

See also *price-earnings ratio (P/E)*; Section II, "Investments."

easement rights held by one person in the real estate of another. The right to cross a person's property to gain access to one's own property is a good example.

ECOA See *Equal Credit Opportunity Act*.

economics the study of the production and distribution of goods and services offered to satisfy human needs.

Economic Recovery Tax Act of 1981 a legislative attempt to provide tax relief by reducing taxes overall, by reducing the effect of *bracket creep*, by raising the *zero bracket* amount, and by raising personal exemptions. Other important provisions were:

- The maximum tax on long-term capital gains was reduced to 20 percent. (Sixty percent of long-term gains are exempt from taxes, and the maximum rate on the balance is 50 percent.)
- If both a husband and wife work, they may deduct a portion of the salary of the lower-paid partner. In 1983, this was 10 percent, up to a maximum of $1,500.
- All working persons may deduct up to $2,000 for contributions to an Individual Retirement Account or to a qualified voluntary thrift plan.
- Estate and gift taxes were reduced. Estate taxes for a surviving spouse were eliminated.

See also *bracket creep*; *zero bracket*; Section II, "Estate Planning," "Tax Savings."

education loan a loan, usually made or secured by the U.S. Department of Education, to finance college or vocational training. Education loans can be made by the student for repayment beginning after graduation or by the parents with repayment beginning immediately. Application should be made through a local bank unless the family is especially needy, in which case direct loans may be made through the college the student will attend.

See also Section II, "College Costs."

EEOC See *Equal Employment Opportunity Commission; Civil Rights Act*.

EFTS See *electronic funds transfer system*.

Electronic Fund Transfer Act Title IX of the Consumer Credit Protection Act, implemented by Federal Reserve Regulation E, under which banks must disclose certain information to consumers using such services as direct deposit of Social Security or payroll checks, automatic teller machines (ATMs), telephone bill paying, and automatic transfer from savings to checking accounts or vice versa.

Consumer tip: Ask your bank for a brochure on Regulation E. The law required banks to send these out, which they did in 1980. Becuse they were lengthy and involved, a new record in consumer boredom probably was set when they were received, but they are important, so read your brochure if you use any of these services.

electronic funds transfer system (EFTS) a computerized system through which a bank may conduct routine business.

elimination period the time gap between signing up for a health insurance policy and when it takes full effect. Health insurers are nervous about people with terminal or lingering illnesses signing up, so there is a period during which "preexisting conditions" are not covered.
See also Section II, "Health Costs."

embezzlement See *defalcation*.

eminent domain the power of some government bodies or agencies to take title and possession of property, usually real property, by paying the owner a fair price. The classic example is that of a state highway department taking homes and land that are in the path of a proposed highway.
Consumer tip: If your property is ever to be taken by eminent domain, it is most important that you get the fair price to which you are entitled. You should be represented by an attorney who is qualified to deal with such cases.

Employee Retirement Income Security Act (ERISA) a law, signed on Labor Day 1974 by President Ford, that attempts to protect the interests of workers and their beneficiaries who are covered by private pension plans. Its main purpose is to assure that employees are not required to meet unreasonable age or service requirements before becoming eligible for a pension. Specifically, employees are entitled to:

- Receive literature explaining any pension plan in "easy-to-understand" language.
- Know how much they may expect to get, and when.
- Get statements when they retire that tell them how much they will get.
- Annual notification of where their pension money is invested, how well it is earning, and who is managing it.
- The right to sue if they feel they have been fired or discriminated against to avoid paying them a pension.
- Be told why they do not qualify for a pension.

Consumer tip: Even with ERISA, many employees do not receive the pension they expect. Pension plan managers must tell you how to qualify for a pension, but they often fail to spell out clearly how you may become disqualified. It's a wise precaution to save for retirement on your own behalf—and Individual Retirement Accounts (which were originally authorized under ERISA) make it possible to do so.
See also Section II, "Retirement Planning."

encumbrance a legal claim on real estate. An encumbrance may be in the form of a lien, an easement right, or even a pending lawsuit. It doesn't prevent the sale of the property if the buyer is willing to accept the encumbrance, but it does lower its value. An encumbrance will show up during a title search.
See also *lien; title search.*

endorsement a signature written on the back of a negotiable instrument, such as a check, that passes title to the rights of the instrument to another person, company, or bank. When handling checks, there are four kinds of endorsements:

1. The *blank endorsement*. This consists solely of a signature. Legally, it converts a check into a *bearer instrument*—which means that anyone can cash or deposit it. A check endorsed in blank is the same as a check payable to "bearer" or to "cash."

2. The *restrictive endorsement*, as its name suggests, restricts the transfer of the check. Most common is the endorsement that reads, "For Deposit Only," followed by the name of the payee. A check so endorsed can only be deposited to the account of the payee and, if lost or stolen, is worthless to anyone who finds or steals it.

3. A *special endorsement* names a new payee. For example, a check made out to Peter Smith and so endorsed might read on the back, "Pay to the order of John Doe, (signed) Peter Smith." No one can use this check except John Doe, and he may endorse and use it as he wishes.

4. A *qualified endorsement* limits the liability of the endorser. As an example, a check might be endorsed, "Without recourse, (signed) John Smith." This means that if the check bounces, no one can collect from John Smith. Banks do not cash or accept checks for deposit that have qualified endorsements.

Consumer tip: Never use a blank endorsement unless you are signing and cashing the check right in the bank so there is no chance of loss. Do endorse all checks you are depositing as soon as you get them with the words, "For Deposit Only." Then, if one is lost or stolen, you needn't worry about it. If you wish to pass on a check made out to you to someone else, use a special endorsement, again, as soon as you get the check. And, like your bank, don't accept a check with a qualified endorsement. If someone offers you a check so endorsed, assume that he or she knows something about the maker that you don't—so beware.

With robbery and mail theft so common, using the proper endorsements can save a lot of grief.

endowment insurance policy a life insurance plan under which premiums are paid for a set period, usually 10 or 20 years, at the end of which time the person covered collects the face value of the policy. If the insured person dies before the policy matures, a named beneficiary collects the face amount.

Consumer tip: Endowment policies used to be very popular ways to save, especially for educational purposes. Bought for a child at birth, they covered the child's burial expenses should he or she die and, at maturity, helped pay for the child's education. When savings interest rates were at 1 and 2 percent, this wasn't a bad idea. But with today's higher interest rates, endowment insurance is almost always a very poor investment.

See also Section II, "Life Insurance."

entrepreneur a person who assumes the financial risks of starting a new company or business venture.

Equal Credit Opportunity Act (ECOA) a law, passed in March 1977, that prevents lenders from discriminating against anyone on the basis of sex, marital status, color, religion, national origin, or, with a few exceptions, age. The Federal Trade Commission (FTC) is charged with enforcing this law. The main impact of the ECOA has been to reduce sexual discrimination. Under this act, a woman loan applicant:

- May not be refused credit because she uses her maiden name, a combined or hyphenated last name, or her own first name with her husband's last name. In other words, she does not have to apply as Mrs. John Doe.
- May not be made to reapply for credit if her marital status changes.
- May not be asked about her plans for having children or about her birth control methods.
- May not be asked her marital status, except in community-property states (Arizona, California, Idaho, Louisiana, Nevada, New Mexico, Texas, and Washington).

Also, creditors:

- May not refuse to consider alimony or child support payments as income if the payments are regular and reliable. However, the woman does not have to list such income unless she chooses.
- May not refuse to consider a woman's income because it comes from part-time work, if that work is regular. This is especially important on mortgage applications for which a wife's part-time income can make a lot of difference.
- May not require her husband to co-sign her loans.

Consumer tip: If you are a married woman, you should establish credit in your own name by having your own bank account, by having your own credit and charge account cards, and by requesting that creditors report information on joint accounts with your husband in both spouses' names. If you feel you are being discriminated against on a loan application, contact the Women's Bureau, U.S. Department of Labor, 200 Constitution Avenue, N.W., Washington, D.C. 20210.
See also *Equal Pay Act;* Section II, "Borrowing."

Equal Employment Opportunity Commission (EEOC) an independent government agency established to monitor and correct cases of discrimination in employment.

Equal Pay Act a federal law, passed in 1963, that requires men and women to be paid equal wages for the same work. The act prohibits lowering men's wages to achieve equality.
Consumer tip: Some employers get around this law by using different job titles for the same work. One small publisher, for example, used the job title "circulation manager" for men and "circulation supervisor" for women doing the same job, but paid the women about half of what the men made. You can report such violations to the Women's Bureau, U.S. Department of Labor, 200 Constitution Avenue, N.W., Washington, D.C., 20210.
See also *Equal Credit Opportunity Act (ECOA).*

equities common stocks.

equity the difference between the value of a property and any outstanding loans for which the property is pledged as collateral. For example, if a home is valued at $100,000 and the outstanding mortgage is $20,000, the equity is $80,000.

Consumer tip: Using home equity as collateral is an excellent way to borrow large sums for long periods at low rates.

See also *reverse annuity mortgage (RAM); second mortgage;* Section II, "College Costs."

equity fund   1) a mutual fund that invests in common stocks; 2) a combination of life insurance and mutual fund investment in which the fund shares are pledged as collateral for a loan that pays the insurance premium.

See also *growth fund; income fund; universal life insurance.*

equity investment   the purchase of a portion of the ownership of a corporation through buying common stocks, as opposed to the lending of money, or debt investment, such as that used to buy bonds, savings accounts, or Treasury securities.

Consumer tip: As a rule, equity investments are a bit riskier than debt investments, hence they should pay a higher rate of return. However, this doesn't always work out, so investing in common stocks, or "equities," should be done carefully.

See also Section II, "Investments."

ERISA   See *Employee Retirement Income Security Act.*

escalator clause   provision in a contract for automatic increases in payment scaled to the inflation rate or some other index.

Consumer tip: Check to see that your homeowner's or tenant's property insurance has a clause that raises its face value as property values increase. It's a good way to avoid the penalties of becoming a coinsurer.

See also *coinsurance.*

escheat   the taking of unclaimed property by the state. In all states, there is a set time period, typically ranging from three to seven years, during which bank-account transactions must take place; if a depositor makes no deposits or withdrawals or fails to have interest posted before the end of this time, and if the bank cannot locate the depositor, the account reverts to the state treasury. Also, people who die without a will and with no next of kin have their property escheated to the state.

Consumer tip: Know where your bank accounts are and keep them reasonably active; at the least, have interest posted once a year on savings accounts and write an occasional check on checking accounts. In addition, have your attorney prepare a will to avoid escheat.

See also Section II, "Estate Planning."

escrow   a written agreement setting aside funds to be held by a second party to eventually benefit a third party. Most common is an escrow account in which property taxes or homeowner's insurance premiums are prepaid and accumulated until due.

Consumer tip: Bankers love escrow accounts; they often pay little or no interest on them. If your mortgage lender requires you to make escrow payments to guarantee the bank's interests—so that taxes and insurance premiums will be paid on time—you may have to do so for a while. But after a year or so, after you have established your reliability, ask that the escrow account be closed and that you be allowed to save your own funds—and earn your own interest.

estate the real estate and personal property owned by a person at the time of his or her death. This includes homes, cars, money, securities, interests in businesses, and so on. In fact, it includes about everything except life insurance proceeds that go to a named beneficiary.

See also Section II, "Estate Planning."

estate planning a plan established during a person's lifetime providing for the distribution of his or her property after death and the minimizing of federal and state estate and inheritance taxes.

See also Section II, "Estate Planning."

estate tax a federal or state tax on assets left by a deceased person that must be paid before distribution can be made to the heirs.

See also *inheritance tax;* Section II, "Estate Planning."

Eurodollars U.S. dollars on deposit in European banks. Since 1957, and in response to the decline in the use of the pound sterling as an international standard, Eurodollars have become that standard. The importance of Eurodollars is that their value relative to that of other currencies is completely outside governmental jurisdiction. This means that, in times of tight money, Eurodollars may be more available than money from domestic banks. During such times, some money market mutual funds often invest heavily in commercial paper involving Eurodollars.

even lot See *lot.*

eviction in popular usage, a dispossession from use of property by court order. A landlord has the right to evict any tenant for violation of a substantial part of the lease, such as failure to pay rent, use of the property for illegal purposes, damaging the property, or even keeping a pet when "no pets" are stipulated in the lease.

Consumer tip: Tenants' rights vary in interpretation from state to state, so if you are ever threatened with eviction, see a lawyer at once.

excess coverage clause a clause in property insurance policies that excludes paying more than the property is worth no matter how much it is insured for.

Consumer tip: Since you can't profit from a property loss because of this clause, be sure to avoid letting the insurance company profit by your being overinsured.

excise tax a tax on the manufacture, sale, or use of certain goods; a tax on the privilege to do something, such as engage in a certain business. Excise taxes on jewelry, automobiles, and sporting events are common.

See also *sin tax; tax.*

ex-coupon (X-C) a bond sold with the coupon for the interest currently due removed. This does not affect the net price of the bond because the value of the coupon is deducted.

ex-dividend (X-D) the period during which the amount of a dividend payment is excluded from the quoted price of a stock because that sum goes to the seller. This happens because dividends are paid to those who hold the stock as of a certain date, so sales of the stock made between that date and the actual disbursement are made ex-dividend.

executor a person named in a will to administer the estate after the maker of the will has died.

Consumer tip: Always have a will, even if you own little and it is in joint name. Other property can turn up, and if you have no will and name no executor, the state will appoint an administrator. This will cost more because executors who are family members or friends usually work without a fee. Of course, if a bank or attorney is appointed, a standard fee will be charged. Also, a will helps guarantee that your wishes will be carried out.

expense See *accounting.*

extended term insurance life coverage provided by an insurance company for a specific time period after an ordinary policy has lapsed. When a cash-value life insurance policy is allowed to lapse because of nonpayment of premiums, it is customary for the company to use any accrued values to buy extended term insurance in the name of the insured person. That way, the company gets to keep the money and the insured person has a little coverage until he or she can make other arrangements.

Consumer tip: If you can't afford a policy or if you want to get rid of one for any reason, avoid lapsing into extended term. Unless you die during the extended term period, you lose everything. Ask an agent of that company to switch you to more suitable or affordable coverage or apply for your cash-surrender value.

extra dividend also *special dividend;* a cash dividend over and above the regular dividend paid by a corporation to its shareholders. When earnings are unexpectedly high, rather than increase the regular dividend, corporations declare an extra dividend to indicate that the increase may not continue in the future.

face amount in life insurance, the amount to be paid in the event of the death of the insured. The face amount may be decreased by loans or increased by additional benefits due.

face value See *par value*.

Fair Credit Billing Act an amendment to the Consumer Credit Protection Act that allows credit-card users to have the same legal rights against banks or other credit-card lenders that they previously had against merchants. Customers have always had the right to refuse full payment to a merchant who sold them unsatisfactory merchandise. But prior to 1975, if that merchant "sold" his accounts receivable to a bank, the customers who then owed the bank for the merchant's goods had to pay the bank even if the goods were shoddy; their recourse was against the merchant, but without the right to withhold payment, these rights

were almost useless. The new law changed that. It also provided relief from billing errors.

Consumer tip: Here's the way to take action if you have charged defective goods or poor service on a credit card and the amount in question exceeds $50:

1. You must have made the purchase within your home state or within 100 miles of your current address.

2. You must request the merchant or supplier of the services to make amends or accept a return of the goods.

3. You must notify the credit-card company of the dispute.

4. If this doesn't work, you may withhold payment of the portion of the credit-card bill that covers the disputed goods or services.

If you discover an erroneous charge on your bill, you should:

1. Notify the credit-card company within 60 days of the date the bill was mailed to you, pointing out the error.

Send this notice by certified mail, return receipt requested.

2. Do not send original documents to back up your claim; keep these to protect yourself, but do send photocopies.

3. Once the creditor has your letter, he cannot close your account, send you collection notices, threaten your credit rating, sue you, report the disputed amount as delinquent to a credit bureau—though he can report that you are in a dispute—or turn the matter over to a collection agency or an attorney.

4. The creditor must acknowledge receipt of your notification within 30 days.

5. Once you have sent your letter, you do not have to pay the amount in dispute, although you still must pay any undisputed amount when due.

6. If the creditor is wrong, you cannot be charged interest on the amount in dispute.

It is a good idea to pay bills for potentially disputable goods or services with a credit card. Auto repairs, for example, are often disputed. If they are on your credit card, and if you properly refuse payment, the bank or credit-card company will join you in putting pressure on the mechanic to make things right.

See also *holder in due course;* Section II, "Borrowing."

Fair Credit Reporting Act a
federal law establishing the rights of borrowers to see and correct the files kept on them by credit reporting agencies. Under this act, if credit or employment are denied because of a poor credit rating, the person has the right to:

1. Be told which credit bureau issued the negative report.

2. Be told what information that credit bureau has on file about him or her.

3. Know the sources of this information.

4. Be told who has received copies of reports based on this information within the past six months, or, if used for employment references, within the past two years.

5. Have incomplete or incorrect information corrected and added to the file, and to have anyone the person names apprised of the corrections.

6. Have his or her side of the story added to the file on any items in dispute.

In addition, credit bureaus may not report negative information that is more than seven years old, except for bankruptcies, which they may report for 14 years.

Consumer tip: If you fail to get a loan or a job because of a negative credit report, check out the report yourself and, if a mistake was made, demand that it be corrected.

See also Section II, "Borrowing."

Fair Debt Collection Practices Act the law, signed by President Carter in 1978, that made it illegal for bill collectors to harass debtors by use of threatening words, late-night phone calls, or by damaging reputations. For example, it is illegal for collectors even to use a name in the return-address portion of their envelopes that might indicate the nature of the letters inside.

See also Section II, "Debt Management."

Fannie Mae See *Federal National Mortgage Association.*

FDIC See *Federal Deposit Insurance Corporation.*

federal credit union See *bank.*

Federal Crime Insurance coverage against burglary, larceny, and robbery losses offered through the Federal Insurance Administration, Department of Housing and Urban Development, in areas where commercial insurance is unavailable. This insurance is sold to both homeowners and to tenants.

Consumer tip: If you live in a high-crime area where coverage is not sold by regular insurers, apply for federal coverage through your insurance agent. The premiums are relatively low.

Federal Deposit Insurance Corporation (FDIC) a government-sponsored agency that insures deposits up to a legally set amount for all national banks, all state banks that are members of the Federal Reserve, and all other banks that request the coverage. Almost all banks in the United States are covered. In addition, the FDIC acts as the regulatory agency for all insured commercial banks that are not members of the Federal Reserve system.

Consumer tip: Never choose a bank where deposits are not insured by the FDIC, the Federal Savings and Loan Insurance Corporation (FSLIC), or a reputable state agency.

federal funds usually, excess reserves of banks that are members of the Federal Reserve. These funds are available for loans to banks whose reserves may be temporarily short.

Consumer tip: Federal funds have no great interest for the average person, but the interest rate charged to banks that borrow them is very important as an early-warning indicator of major changes coming in the economy. The federal funds rate is reported daily in *The Wall Street Journal;* if the rate is rising, it might indicate an inflationary trend.

Federal Home Loan Bank (FHLB) the federal agency that charters and supervises federal savings and loan associations and federal mutual savings banks. In addition to its supervisory functions, the FHLB acts as a mortgage credit reserve for member institutions. Thus, members may borrow from the FHLB under certain conditions and may get advances on home mortgages that they own when they are pledged as collateral to the FHLB.

Federal Home Loan Mortgage Corporation (Freddie Mac) a government agency affiliated with the Federal Home Loan Bank Board, designed to aid in raising funds for residential mortgages through the sale of bonds issued specifically for that purpose. Freddie Mac works by purchasing home mortgages already made by savings institutions that are members of the Federal Home Loan Bank. Once a bank has sold a mortgage to Freddie Mac, it then has additional money to lend to another would-be homeowner.

Freddie Mac bonds are of two types: *pass-through participation certificates,* which means that monthly earnings are passed on to bondholders as income is received; and *guaranteed mortgage certificates,* which operate like bonds with semiannual interest payments.

Consumer tip: Freddie Mac bonds can be an excellent investment; the yield is often higher than that on corporate bonds or Treasury securities. And, while they are not technically guaranteed by the government, they are considered almost as safe as Treasury bonds. They are also highly liquid because they are bought and sold through brokers. The income is taxed as ordinary income. Unfortunately, the certificates are sold in minimums of $100,000, which puts them out of reach to most investors.

See also *Federal National Mortgage Association (Fannie Mae); Government National Mortgage Association (Ginnie Mae).*

Federal Housing Administration (FHA)

a government agency whose function it is to promote home ownership and home improvement by guaranteeing loans made by commercial lenders to home buyers and owners.

Consumer tip: You can often save money through an FHA mortgage and buy a home with a relatively low down payment. The problem is the interminable red tape and the waiting. A money-saver that many people overlook is a Title I FHA home improvement loan. The rates are low and the repayment periods are long. Money cannot be used for luxury improvements such as swimming pools, however. Ask your bank for complete details.

See also Section II, "Home Financing."

Federal Insurance Contributions Act (FICA)

the federal law that establishes Social Security taxes and benefits. The portion of your income on which Social Security taxes must be paid is called FICA wages or FICA income.

See also *Social Security.*

Federal National Mortgage Association (Fannie Mae)

a private corporation, chartered by the federal government and designed to help mortgage lenders obtain additional funds for home purchasers by purchasing mortgages from those lenders. Fannie Maes are *debentures,* which means that they are similar to bonds. They are sold for a minimum of $10,000, with additions available in multiples of $1,000.

Consumer tip: Like Freddie Mac securities, Fannie Mae securities can be excellent investments. They are similar in earnings, risk, and tax status to Freddie Macs.

See also *debenture; Federal Home Loan Mortgage Corporation (Freddie Mac); Government National Mortgage Association (Ginnie Mae).*

Federal Reserve Banks (FRBs)

the operating arms of the Federal Reserve Board whose main function is to control the nation's money supply. They do this by issuing currency, or *Federal Reserve Notes,* which constitute the main portion of the legal tender of the United States. They also do this by controlling the *discount rate,* or the interest rate that banks must pay to borrow from the Federal Reserve. As the discount rate is raised, so are bank interest rates, since banks must charge more interest than they pay for money in order to show a profit. The Federal Reserve Banks and their branches also play a key role in clearing the billions and billions of checks written each year.

There are 12 FRBs with 25 branches and 11 check-processing centers serving the U.S. banking industry. Banks are located in Boston, New York, Philadelphia, Cleveland, Richmond, Atlanta, Chicago, St. Louis, Minneapolis, Kansas City, Dallas, and San Francisco. Branches are located in Buffalo, Cincinnati, Pittsburgh, Baltimore, Charlotte, Birmingham, Nashville, Jacksonville, Miami, New Orleans, Detroit, Louisville, Memphis, Little Rock, Helena, Oklahoma City, Omaha, Houston, El Paso, San Antonio, Denver, Seattle, Portland, Salt Lake City, and Los Angeles.

See also *money; money supply.*

Federal Reserve Note   See *money.*

federal savings and loan association   See *bank.*

Federal Savings and Loan Insurance Corporation (FSLIC)
an agency of the Federal Home Loan Bank (FHLB) that insures all accounts maintained in insured savings institutions up to the limit mandated by federal law. All federal S&Ls and most state-chartered S&Ls are insured by the FSLIC.

Consumer tip: Before you open an account in any savings institution, be sure that it is insured either by the FSLIC, the Federal Deposit Insurance Corporation (FDIC), the National Credit Union Administration (NCUA), or a state-supervised insurance program.

See also *Federal Deposit Insurance Corporation (FDIC); National Credit Union Association (NCUA).*

FHA   See *Federal Housing Administration.*

fiat money   money that has no gold or silver backing, i.e., it is issued and has exchange value solely by government authority. U.S. money has been fiat money since 1975, when Federal Reserve Notes replaced silver certificates.

See also *gold standard; silver certificate.*

FICA   See *Federal Insurance Contributions Act.*

finance charge   the cost of a loan in dollars and cents. Under the Consumer Credit Protection Act, all lenders must disclose this amount to borrowers before the loan is made.

Consumer tip: When borrowing, shop around. Rate is important, but so are the total finance charges. Time is the important factor here. If you borrow $1,000, for example, for three years at an annual percentage rate of 10 percent, your monthly payments will be $32.27 and your finance charge, or total interest paid, will be $161.62; if you borrow $1,000 for four years at the same rate, your monthly payments will be $25.37, but your finance charge will be $217.40. Borrowing for the shortest term possible at the lowest rate available is the best way to reduce the finance charge.

See also Section II, "Borrowing," "Money Mistakes."

finance company   technically, any lender that is not a bank; in common usage, a firm that makes consumer loans. Many people feel that it is easier to get credit at a finance company than at a bank; this is sometimes true, but not usually. Like banks, finance companies expect to be repaid.

Consumer tip: Finance companies were

once ideal for short-term unsecured loans. Now most consumers can get this service through cash advances on their bank credit cards or through an overdraft feature of their checking accounts. Before you borrow from a finance company, try a bank or two. You can almost always save money—and if the bank does turn you down, it probably won't hurt your chances with a finance company.

See also Section II, "Borrowing."

financial statement an accounting form that reflects the financial strength of a person or company as of a certain date. A financial statement is simply a balance sheet that contains more specific detail than an ordinary balance sheet. For example, whereas a balance sheet might show a total for securities, a financial statement would require a detailed listing of each security, including the number of shares and the market value. Financial statements are usually rendered for purposes of obtaining credit.

See also Section II, "Family Accounting."

first mortgage a real estate loan backed by a claim that takes precedence over any other claims against a piece of real property. Almost all homes and investment properties are financed by first mortgages.

Consumer tip: First mortgages come in many types, including conventional mortgages, graduated-payment adjustable mortgages, rollover mortgages, and variable-rate mortgages. Before you finance a property, check to see which type is best for your needs.

See also *second mortgage;* Section II, "Home Financing."

fiscal pertaining to financial matters.

fiscal agent a bank appointed by a company to act on its behalf in certain situations. Typically, a fiscal agent issues dividend checks, redeems bond coupons, and performs other such functions.

fiscal year a company's accounting year, as opposed to the calendar year. The fiscal year of most business firms corresponds to the calendar year. The federal government, however, operates on a fiscal year that begins October 1 and ends September 30.

fixed asset See *asset.*

fixed income income that does not change with the cost of living. People on fixed incomes are usually retired or disabled and are thus the least able to cope with inflation.

See also *inflation.*

fixed income tax See *tax.*

fixed liability See *liability.*

flation a period of economic stability. The prefix "in" makes the word mean instability through rising prices; the prefix "de" makes the word mean instability through falling prices and production.

See also *deflation; inflation.*

fleece slang, meaning to cheat or defraud. The word comes from "shearing the sheep."

See also Section II, "Consumer Frauds."

flexible-payment mortgage an alternative mortgage loan in which, typically, only interest is paid during the first five years, then payments of principal and interest begin.

Consumer tip: This is a good type of mortgage to avoid. Interest accounts for about 90 to 98 percent of the payments on a conventional mortgage during the first five years, so the monthly cost differential is negligible. All a mortgage of this type accomplishes is to put the borrower five years behind in building equity, while it costs much more in total interest paid.

See also Section II, "Home Financing."

flexible-premium   deferred annuity   See *annuity*.

float   money in the process of collection between one bank and another. Here's the way it works: If a person deposits a check in his or her account, and that check is drawn on a bank other than the person's own, a period of time is required for the check to go from the person's bank to the other bank and for credit for the amount of the check to be sent back. That period is called the float. This means that, when a person pays a bill with a check, he or she has the use of the money in his or her account for a few days while the check clears.

Consumer tip: Play the float. Always use an interest-paying or NOW account; it gives you the benefits of float automatically. You could even open an account in an out-of-town bank to add time to the check clearing and add to the float, although this would be impractical for most people.

See also Section II, "Cash Management."

forced sale   the sale of property against the wishes of the owner, usually as a result of a bankruptcy.

foreclosure   a legal action against a mortgagor who is in default on a loan. Since a mortgage is a legal agreement pledging property as security for a loan, if payments on the loan are not made within a reasonable time as defined in the agreement, the lender will start a foreclosure action, and if that proves successful, take title to the property.

Consumer tip: If for any reason you can't make mortgage payments, sit down and talk to the lender. Few banks or other lenders want to go into the real estate business, so they will go to great lengths to avoid foreclosure, as long as you are cooperative. If your back is to the wall and foreclosure is imminent, see an attorney at once; legal delays are available.

See also Section II, "Debt Management."

foreign check   a check drawn on any out-of-town bank.

foreign exchange rate   the value of a national currency in terms of the value of another nation's currency. Since August 1971, the rate is no longer expressed in terms of gold; rather, rates have been allowed to "float free" in relation to each other. Rates are determined much as prices on the stock market are determined, that is, by bidding; and relative rates are established daily on major currency exchanges. The computations are made on the basis of the relative purchasing power of each currency against its counterparts.

forgery   a false writing or alteration of any legal instrument with the intent to injure or defraud another. For example, if someone signs an endorsement on a check that is payable to someone else, then cashes it and keeps the money, that's forgery. However, if someone writes another person's name on the back of a check, then deposits it in that person's account, it would not be forgery because there was no intent to injure or defraud. The most common forgeries are endorsements on stolen checks; also common are signatures on stolen checks or savings bonds.
Consumer tip: Protect yourself from forgery loss by endorsing checks as soon as you get them with a special endorsement—"For Deposit Only." Keep your checkbook and identification in different places so that you aren't giving prospective forgers both your checks and your ID. Write the amount on checks as far to the left as possible, then fill in the rest of the line to prevent the alteration of the amount.
See also *check;* Section II, "Consumer Frauds."

franchise   a distribution privilege sold to a dealer by the manufacturer or the holder of rights in a good or service.
Consumer tip: Buying a franchise can be a good way to go into business for yourself, or it can be a financial disaster. Before you invest, investigate. Ask your banker, your lawyer, and your Better Business Bureau for information about any company before you buy a franchise.

fraud, consumer   illegal actions undertaken by a seller to misrepresent a product or service to a consumer.
See also Section II, "Consumer Frauds."

Freddie Mac   See *Federal Home Loan Mortgage Corporation.*

freeze   the seizing or impounding of property by a government.

front-end load   See *load.*

frozen account   See *sequestered account.*

frozen asset   something owned by a person or company that cannot be used until legal action determines rights of ownership.

FSLIC   See *Federal Savings and Loan Insurance Corporation.*

fudge factor   adding to estimated figures an amount that is based on an educated guess because the figures developed by other means seem, by common sense, to be inaccurate.

full faith and credit   a pledge by the government to back something financially. The best example is the Congressional pledge to cover all insured savings accounts, above and beyond any coverage by the Federal Deposit Insurance Corporation (FDIC), the Federal Savings and Loan Insurance Corporation (FSLIC), or the National Credit Union Administration (NCUA), with the "full faith and credit" of the United States. This

74

to run out of money when paying losses, the Treasury would cover deposit losses.

See also *Federal Deposit Insurance Corporation (FDIC); Federal Savings and Loan Insurance Corporation (FSLIC); National Credit Union Administration (NCUA).*

full-service bank   a bank that offers a range of services designed to meet every community, business, or individual need.

See also *bank.*

futures   See *commodities.*

futures exchange   a place where commodity futures are traded. The New York Commodity Exchange deals in gold, silver, platinum, and copper; the Chicago Board of Trade deals in agricultural commodities. Exchanges are also located in Kansas City and Minneapolis.

future value   the amount that a certain sum of money today will be worth on a definite future date, assuming a fixed rate of interest and method of compounding. As an example, a one-time deposit of $1 invested today at 10 percent annual interest, compounded daily, will grow to $2.75 in 10 years. Or, as another example, $1 deposited each week at 10 percent annual interest, compounded daily, will grow to $901.69 in 10 years.

Consumer tip: Future value shows how your savings can be expected to grow over a period of time. Learn to use future value formulas; they're explained in Section II, in "Money Math." They'll help you to make better savings and investment choices.

See also *present value;* Section II, "Money Math, " "Money Mistakes."

garnish   to attach, through legal action, monies due a person. Creditors use this technique to recover seriously overdue debts. The most common method is that in which a creditor obtains a writ from a court directing the debtor's employer to pay a portion of the debtor's wages directly to the creditor. Garnishment is a harsh way to collect a debt. It has been completely outlawed in some states, including Connecticut and Texas, and its use is restricted to some degree in every state.

See also Section II, "Debt Management."

general-obligation debentures
bonds that are not secured by specific property but only by the overall financial condition of the issuer.

See also *Federal National Mortgage Association (Fannie Mae.)*

general warranty deed   See *deed*.

gentlemen's agreement   an unwritten, unsigned contract based only on the good faith of the parties involved.

Consumer tip: Any unwritten contract is as good as the paper it's written on. Even if the deal is with your best friend, put it in writing. Why? Because things can go wrong, even among friends. Suppose you lend your best friend money. Of course, you trust him to repay it, but suppose he gets killed in an auto accident and his heir is his second cousin? Do you trust his second cousin? Get it in writing!

gift tax   a tax on gifts, imposed by the federal government and some state governments, that is paid by the giver. Under federal law, a person may make any number of gifts of up to $10,000 to each recipient each year without using up any exemption. Gifts made jointly with a spouse may be for as much as $20,000. A tax attorney or accountant should be consulted for full details.

Consumer tip: Making annual gifts to your children into a custodial account set up under the Uniform Gifts to Minors Act (UGMA) is an excellent way to fund a future college education. The gifts are tax-free, and, in most cases, so is the interest in the minors' trust accounts.

See also Section II, "College Costs," "Tax Savings."

Ginnie Mae   See *Government National Mortgage Association.*

giro   an automatic payment plan, relatively new to American banking, but in use in Europe for some time. With a giro account, a depositor instructs the bank to automatically transfer payments he or she owes directly from his or her account to the accounts of creditors and to advise the creditors when this is done.

Consumer tip: The giro account may never catch on in the United States because the point-of-sale (POS) debit card may supersede it.

See also *debit card.*

glamour stock   any popular common stock in which many people invest that tends to rise in price over a period of time.

GNP   See *gross national product.*

going public   having a stock newly listed on a major exchange.

gold   a precious metal long regarded by many as the ideal basis for value. Gold is highly durable and has little industrial value, hence it has been estimated that over 98 percent of all gold ever mined is still in use. However, most modern economists reject gold as the ultimate standard of value, preferring instead the raw materials and industrial capacity of a nation.

Consumer tip: If you want to buy gold as an investment, forget those newspaper ads. The best deal is to buy directly from the U.S. government and save on commissions. Simply pick up an application form at your post office, phone the toll-free number on the form for a price, send in your payment and application, and you'll get the gold in return. The government charges a standard $14-per-ounce surcharge; most dealers charge 6 or 7 percent. Thus, if gold is $400 an ounce, you'll pay $414 for an ounce from the government and $424 to $428 from a dealer.

gold standard   having all of a nation's currency backed by gold. The United States was on the gold standard until 1933. At that time, it became illegal for Americans to own gold except as coin collectors. However, the gold standard applied in foreign trade until 1971. Then, with rising oil prices, it became risky to continue to back dollars with gold, the value of which was set by law at $35 an ounce. What would happen, for example, if an oil sheikdom suddenly presented the U.S. with hundreds of billions of dollars and demanded Fort Knox? So the U.S. went off the gold standard completely, and citizens were again allowed to own gold. Gold is now traded on the commodity markets, so its price fluctuates from day to day.

See also *gold*.

good-till-cancelled order an order to buy or sell stock that is good until the transaction is made. Most stock orders are day orders and expire at the end of the business day upon which they are made.

goodwill an intangible asset; the positive public image of a company that enables it to sell more on a per-capita basis than most companies in a similar business would sell.

See also *asset*.

government bond See *bond*.

Government National Mortgage Association (Ginnie Mae) an agency under the U.S. Department of Housing and Urban Development that buys mortgages insured by the Federal Housing Administration (FHA) and the Veterans Administration (VA) from banks and other lenders in order to stimulate the flow of mortgage money into the economy. Ginnie Mae is the largest of the federally sponsored mortgage buy-back agencies. Also, unlike the Federal National Mortgage Association (Fannie Mae) and the Federal Home Loan Mortgage Corporation (Freddie Mac), Ginnie Mae securities are fully insured by the federal government. The bonds sold by Ginnie Mae are *pass-through certificates,* which means that interest is paid to the bondholders monthly as income is received.

See also *Federal National Mortgage Association (Fannie Mae); Federal Home Loan Mortgage Corporation (Freddie Mac).*

governments slang for Treasury securities.

See also *Treasury securities.*

grace period a courtesy period extending the time during which payment without penalty may be legally made. Lenders commonly add a few days of grace before a loan is considered past due; life insurance companies usually allow 30 days of grace before a policy lapses; and property insurance companies usually extend 10 days of grace after a cancellation-for-nonpayment notice is sent to the policyholder.

Consumer tip: To keep your money working for you, use your grace periods, but do so carefully. Don't let your loans go past due or your insurance policies lapse.

See also Section II, "Cash Management."

graduated income tax a tax in which the percentage paid rises as the income rises. The federal income tax is graduated. Some state taxes are, while others consist of a flat tax rate regardless of income.

graduated-payment adjustable mortgage a mortgage loan with payments set below the amortization rate for the first 10 years and with the interest rate varying with the cost of living.

Consumer tip: These mortgage loans are not very popular, and for good reason. Delaying the full amortization means a higher cost impact on the home buyer in the long run, and the variable rate is not as desirable as a conventional loan.

See also *amortization; conventional mortgage; rollover mortgage; variable-rate mortgage (VRM)* Section II, "Home Financing."

grandfather clause a clause in new laws or regulations that protects people currently doing something from having to make drastic changes. The name dates back to Reconstruction days when it was common in some areas to restrict the rights of blacks to vote by making it a law that no one could vote whose grandfather hadn't voted—and, of course, slaves couldn't vote. This was ruled illegal, but the phrase "grandfather clause" stayed in the language. Now it usually means that a company doing business in a certain way need not change to meet the requirements of a new rule.

greenback See *money.*

greenlining an action against supposed redlining that is taken by citizens who withdraw their accounts from the offending institution as a protest.
See also *redlining.*

Gresham's Law the economic premise that money of less real value tends to drive money of more real value from circulation. For example, people now get very few pre-1965 silver dimes, quarters, or half-dollars in change because these coins are so often hoarded for their silver content. Clad coins of little intrinsic value have replaced them.

gross national product (GNP) the total retail value of all the goods and services produced in a given country in any given year.

gross profit all income for a specified period, less only the cost of goods sold, which includes production and sales costs.
See also *net profit.*

gross sales the income from total sales over a specified period, even before customer returns.

group insurance an insurance plan under which a number of people are covered by a single policy.
Consumer tip: If possible, buy all health insurance under a group policy, and, if you are in poor health, try for group life insurance as well. Companies give lower rates for group policies because they tend to spread the risk over a broader base. For example, on an individual basis, more sick people will buy health insurance than well people; but under a group policy, everyone is covered. Therefore, the per-capita risk is lowered substantially.
See also Section II, "Health Costs."

growth fund a mutual fund that tends to invest in the more speculative stocks with an eye to future growth rather than current income.
Consumer tip: If you are young and have adequate savings, consider a good growth fund with a solid track record in investments.
See also *equity fund, income fund;* Section II, "Investments."

growth stock a common stock deemed likely to grow in value over a period of time, but not likely to pay high current earnings.
Consumer tip: If you want to buy growth stocks, buy several or invest in

a growth fund. In that way, you spread your risk. Remember, growth stocks are more speculative than income stocks.

See also *growth fund; income stock;* Section II, "Investments."

guaranteed annual wage a plan under which employers guarantee to pay workers a minimum wage each year. The theory is that this will add economic stability to the individual and to the community.

guaranteed annuity See *annuity.*

guaranteed interest a rate of interest that is assured for a specified time period. All interest paid by banks, except for variable-rate certificates of deposit, must be guaranteed.

guarantor See *co-signer.*

guaranteed student loans loans made by banks for which repayment is guaranteed by the federal government. This encourages lenders to make the loans and thus aids students in obtaining college educations. During the time the student is in college, the government pays the interest. Six months after graduation, the student begins to repay the loan.

Consumer tip: There are limits on family income to qualify for these loans, so ask your bank or school guidance counselor for current details.

See also Section II, "College Costs."

guardian a person appointed by a court to oversee the financial and/or personal affairs of someone who is incapable of handling his or her own affairs. Guardians are appointed for minors, people who are insane or retarded, or others who are incompetent.

hard money originally, coins as opposed to bills. Now, the term generally refers to *stable currency*, which does not fluctuate wildly in terms of purchasing power and other national currency values. Occasionally, the term is used to mean so-called "tight" money. See also *tight money*.

health insurance insurance coverage against the risks presented by the high cost of health care. Common plans include those offered by:

- Blue Cross, a nonprofit corporation that insures against hospital and ancillary costs.
- Blue Shield, a nonprofit corporation that insures against physicians' bills.
- Medicare, government-sponsored health insurance for those 65 years of age and above.
- Health maintenance organization (HMO) plans, which are sponsored by hospitals or physicians'

clinics and offer coverage to those who pay membership fees.
- Private insurers, which offer health insurance plans ranging from excellent to awful.

Consumer tip: If you can belong to Blue Cross and Blue Shield on a group basis, this is the best deal available. If not, shop for an HMO. Next, if you are eligible, opt for Medicare, but have additional coverage for your protection. As a last resort, buy Blue Cross and Blue Shield on an individual basis. Don't buy health insurance by mail. See also *Medicaid;* Section II, "Health Costs."

health maintenance organization (HMO) See *health insurance.*

hedge to offset an investment with another investment. Thus, someone may buy a stock that will go up in price should another stock that he owns go down. It is becoming more common to use options as a hedge against a changing market by buying call and put options on the same stock at the same time; the potential loss is limited, and yet the potential gain is not.

See also *calls; option; puts; spread.*

heirs   those who inherit property on the death of another.

See also Section II, "Estate Planning."

hidden assets   things of value owned by a company that are not listed openly on its balance sheet.

See also *asset.*

hidden tax   a tax, usually hidden in the cost of an item, that the buyer cannot identify.

high flyers   1) speculative stocks that can move up or down several points in a day or so; also, 2) the people who speculate in such stocks.

See also Section II, "Investments."

HMO   health maintenance organization.

See also *health insurance.*

hold   a banking term that refers to the setting aside of a portion of a customer's balance until a specific check has passed through the collection process or a specific deposit has been credited.

holder in due course   a person, company, or bank that accepts an instrument (such as a check, a draft, or certain notes) under these four conditions: (1) the instrument must be complete and regular on its face; (2) it must not be overdue or dishonored; (3) it

must be taken in good faith and for value; and (4) at the time it is taken, no notice may be given of any defect in the instrument.

Consumer tip: If you accept a check payable to another and endorsed on the back to you, you become a holder in due course. This means that you have the right to the money the check represents. It also means that, if you pass on the check to another person or deposit it and it is returned, you become liable for the amount of the check in your turn. Of course, you can pass it back to the previous holder, if you can find him. This is the basis of the cardinal rule banks have for check-cashing: "Know your endorser!"

Years ago, the holder-in-due course status also applied to a person who bought goods on time and whose loan was sold to another person. This meant that, even if the goods were defective, the loan agreement was a separate transaction and the debtor remained liable for the amount due—at that point, payable to a bank or finance company. This doctrine was largely wiped out by various state and federal laws, including the Fair Credit Billing Act.

See also *Fair Credit Billing Act; returned check.*

holder of record   the person who owns specific shares of stock as of the date dividends are declared. The dividend is paid to the holder of record, even if he or she has since sold the stock.

See also *ex-dividend (X-D).*

holding company   a company that owns the stock of another company and thus controls its management; also, a *bank holding company,* or corporation that holds the stock of and controls the management of one or more banks. This is often used as a device to circumvent state restrictions against establishing branches.

A *one-bank holding company* is a corporation that owns just one bank. Its purpose is to allow the corporation to conduct related business that is not provided for in the bank's legal charter, but that is in conjunction with the bank. Typical of such business would be running a title insurance company to insure the titles of property pledged to the bank.

See also *subsidiary.*

holographic will   See *will.*

home banking   also *computer banking, bank-at-home;* the ability to conduct almost all banking business, except the making of deposits and cash withdrawals, directly from a person's residence through a telephone hookup between a home computer and the bank. This concept, in conjunction with home computer shopping, is spreading across the country as personal computers become more common. The advantage of home banking is that people can conduct banking business at any hour on any day.

home financing   See *real estate mortgage.*

home improvement loan   a loan made for the specific purpose of modernizing, expanding, or repairing a home. Home improvement loans are of three types: Title I FHA insured, short-term unsecured, and secured.

Consumer tip: Which type of loan to use depends on the purpose and amount of money you need. If the amount is really large and the loan is not for a luxury improvement, such as a swimming pool, the best choice is a low-rate FHA Title I loan (the Federal Housing Administration won't allow loans for luxury improvements), because the borrower can take a long time to repay. If the loan is for a small amount, the best deal is probably an unsecured loan for the shortest term possible, because the finance charges will be lowest this way. Finally, for an in-between loan amount or for a large luxury improvement loan, the best deal is usually a longer-term loan secured with a second mortgage on the property.

See also *Title I FHA loan;* Section II, "Borrowing."

homeowner's insurance   a type of property insurance that covers a broad range of risks. Typically, such insurance covers loss to the homeowner's house and other structures from fire and all other hazards except those intentionally caused by the insured person, those arising from the business pursuits of the insured, losses caused by freezing pipes unless the insured attempted to heat the building or drain the pipes, vandalism against property left vacant for more than 30 days, continuous leakage of water or steam from a pipe for an extended period, rust or mildew, environmental pollution, shrinking or settling of the house, or damage from animals or bugs. It also covers loss by fire and theft and most other hazards to the personal property of the residents of the household, and the personal liability, including medical payments for injuries caused to

83

others, of the members of the household. A variant of homeowner's insurance is available to people who rent as tenant's insurance.

Consumer tip: Homeowner's insurance is obviously a necessity for every family. You can save money by shopping for rates, by taking the maximum deductible, and by installing a burglar alarm and smoke detectors. In addition, you can save money and increase your protection by limiting your personal liability coverage to $100,000, by doing the same with your auto insurance, and then by writing a blanket $1 million personal liability rider to continue the coverages on both home and car.

See also *automobile insurance;* Section II, "Property and Liability Insurance."

home service life insurance   See *industrial insurance.*

honor   to pay a check or draft when presented.

HR 10 Plan   See *Keogh Plan.*

hypothecation   See *collateral.*

I

I&E statement   See *income and expense statement*.

identification   documents that prove to a banker or other check-casher that a person is who he or she purports to be. The best identifier is a current driver's license bearing the person's name, photograph, and signature. Such things as Social Security cards, library cards, and voter registration cards are useless for this purpose.

Consumer tip: Always carry your identification in a place separate from your checkbook.

See also *endorsement*.

Ike   See *cartwheel*.

illiquid asset   a fixed asset. Illiquid assets are financial holdings that cannot be converted into cash easily or quickly, including real estate holdings, collections, and other things difficult to sell fast.

See also *asset; liquid asset*.

IMF   See *International Monetary Fund*.

implied easement   unauthorized use of property that has gone unchallenged for so long that its eventual authorization is implied. An example is the continual and long-term crossing of a portion of one person's property to gain access to another's. If unchallenged, this could eventually become a right.

See also *easement*.

implied warranty   See *warranty*.

impound   to hold property by a court order. The police, for example, may impound a car for nonpayment of traffic tickets, or financial records may be impounded during an audit.

inactive account a bank account that has no activity over a period of time, usually a year or more. If an account is inactive for a long enough period (state laws vary widely on the time required), the account may revert to the state treasury if the owner cannot be located.

Consumer tip: Keep your accounts active, even if you only have interest posted or write a check once a year. Better yet, put inactive dollars to work in profitable investments.

See also *escheat.*

income money earned by selling goods or services, including such common types of income as salaries, wages, commissions, royalties, rents, dividends, and interest.

See also *accounting.*

income and expense statement also *I&E statement, profit and loss (P&L) statement;* an accounting form that shows all of the income and its sources less all of the expenses and their sources. If income exceeds expense, the person or firm is operating at a profit, or in the black; if expenses exceed income, the person or firm is operating at a loss, or in the red.

Consumer tip: Some people may complete a personal financial statement, but few ever do an I&E. However, even if you're on a fixed salary, it's a good idea to know where your money goes. The personal income and expense chart in Section II, "Family Accounting," will help.

See also Section II, "Family Accounting."

income fund a mutual fund whose investments are selected to provide as much current income as possible. Income funds tend to be quite conservative in their investment approach and to stick mainly to high-yield blue-chip stocks and preferred stocks.

Consumer tip: Income funds are ideal for older people who cannot risk holding an investment for long enough to allow for a market recovery.

See also *equity fund; growth fund;* Section II, "Investments."

income stock a stock that pays regular and relatively high dividends.

See also *stock, common; stock, preferred.*

income tax See *tax.*

income tax lien See *lien.*

incorporation the act of forming a corporation. The letters "Inc." or "Corp." after a company's name indicates that the firm is incorporated.

See also *corporation.*

incumbrance See *encumbrance.*

indebtedness See *debt.*

indemnify to pay for an actual loss. When an insurance policy guarantees to indemnify a policyholder, that means it will pay the actual amount of a loss that has occurred, but no more.

See also Section II, "Property and Liability Insurance."

indemnity a guarantee against loss.

independent agency See *agency.*

index a financial measurement of data as compared to identical data in another specified year. The Consumer

Price Index (CPI), for example, compares the price of a fixed market basket of goods and services against the price of those same goods in 1967.

individual account a personal bank account in the name of one person as opposed to a joint account or a business account.

See also *joint account;* Section II, "Bank Accounts."

Individual Retirement Account (IRA)

a tax-deferred self-created retirement plan authorized by Congress to allow working people to systematically accumulate funds to augment Social Security and company pension-plan income.

Under the Economic Recovery Tax Act of 1981, all employed persons may deposit (the technical term is "contribute") up to $2,000 a year in an IRA in any approved investment plan of their choice. In addition, if a worker has a nonemployed spouse, a spousal IRA may be opened in his or her name, but the total deposits made by the couple may not exceed $2,250, at least $250 of which must be in the account of one of the spouses, but which otherwise may be divided in any way they choose. This means that a single, working taxpayer may deposit up to $2,000 a year; a married working couple may deposit up to $4,000 a year, with $2,000 in each name; and a couple with one spouse working may deposit up to $2,250 a year. (As of early 1984, legislation was pending that would increase the limit for nonearning spouses from $250 per year to $2,000 per year. Legislation was also pending to allow each contributor to deposit an additional non-tax-deductible $1,750 per year, which could still grow in the IRA, with interest tax-deferred.)

IRAs may be opened at almost any bank, with any mutual fund or brokerage office, or may even be invested in government savings bonds.

The money may not be withdrawn without penalty until the saver reaches age 59½, and withdrawals must begin by age 70½. Withdrawals may be made in a lump sum or staggered over a period of time or even over the anticipated lifetime of the person. Money withdrawn is taxed as ordinary income; but, because the taxpayer is retired, it is likely that his or her tax rate will be significantly lower. Also, as the money grows, the tax-free compounding of interest has a multiplier effect that not only allows it to grow at an extremely rapid rate, but even totally offsets early withdrawal and tax penalties after about five to seven years, depending on the earnings rate.

In addition, IRA deposits are deducted from income on IRS Form 1040, which means that a substantial portion of the taxes on that income is deferred. Thus, a taxpayer in the 50 percent bracket who deposits $2,000 actually has an immediate tax saving of $1,000 because his or her taxes are reduced by $1,000; a taxpayer in the 40 percent bracket who deposits $2,000 has a tax saving of $800; a taxpayer in the 30 percent bracket would save $600; and a taxpayer in the 20 percent bracket would save $400 in taxes.

Consumer tip: Every employed taxpayer should have an IRA—it is the best tax savings device available to most people, with the possible exception of home ownership. Don't be misled by advertising—you needn't deposit the entire $2,000 a year; that's a maximum. For example, if you are 30 years old and deposit only $100 a year, at 10 percent interest, compounded daily, by age 65, that will grow to a little over $32,000. If that amount is left to earn at 10 percent while withdrawals are being made, you can withdraw $320 a month for the next 17 years!

See also Section II, "Retirement Planning."

indorsement   See *endorsement.*

industrial insurance   also *home service life insurance;* life insurance sold door-to-door, often in amounts of $1,000 or less, and with weekly or monthly premiums collected by an agent. This agent is called a *debit man* because he carries a large register, or *debit book*, in which he records the payments. Industrial insurance is still fairly common in city slum areas, where people buy it to cover burial expenses. Industrial insurance is extremely costly because it is expensive to write such small amounts of insurance and because the premiums must pay the costs of door-to-door collections. In 1980, there were still 62 million industrial policies in force in the United States.

Consumer tip: Never buy industrial life insurance. It is far too costly.

See also Section II, "Life Insurance."

inelastic demand   an economic term used to describe a situation that occurs when a rise in price does not result in a drop in sales.

Consumer tip: Buying stock in a company that produces goods and services for which demand tends to be inelastic makes sense. As the prices rise, so do the profits, since the price rise doesn't mean a loss in sales revenue.

See also *inelastic supply; supply and demand.*

inelastic supply   an economic term used to describe a situation that occurs when a price change does not cause the supply of the goods or service to change.

See also *inelastic demand; supply and demand, law of.*

inflation   a time period in the economic cycle during which the cost of living increases as the purchasing power of the dollar decreases. Over the long term, the U.S. economy has tended to be somewhat inflationary.

The main problem with inflation is that it does not impact equally on everyone. If, for example, the cost of living rose at a rate of 10 percent per year, and if everyone's income rose at that rate, and if all interest, dividends, income, and expenses were indexed to increase at that rate, inflation would have no impact at all—it would just be annoying. But it doesn't work that way. Retired people on fixed incomes have a loss in real purchasing power every time the cost of living rises. Young couples buying homes pay many times the real worth of a home relative to the prices paid in former years, which means that couples living side by side in identical homes may have similar incomes but vastly different mortgage payments.

Consumer tip: Protect yourself against inflation by making investments that tend to be anti-inflationary. An Individual Retirement Account (IRA) is a good example; the taxes deferred now are paid at a later lower rate and then in inflated dollars. Do shop for high interest rates on your investments and, unless you are ready to retire, consider having some money in growth stocks or mutual funds.

See also *deflation, flation.*

informal check See *check.*

inheritance originally, 1) the passing of real property by descent; in modern usage, 2) the passing of real or personal property to heirs, either through a will or by court action.

See also *will;* Section II, "Estate Planning."

inheritance tax a tax imposed by a state on property left by a person who dies.

See also *estate tax;* Section II, "Estate Planning."

installment credit See *installment loan.*

installment loan also *installment credit;* a loan on which interest and principal are repayable in regular, equal installments so that, when the last payment is made, the loan is paid in full. Most personal and mortgage loans are payable in installments.

See also Section II, "Borrowing."

instrument a formal, legal document.

See also *check; negotiable instrument.*

insufficient funds also, *not sufficient funds (NSF);* the situation existing when the balance in a depositor's checking account is insufficient to pay a check when it is presented at the bank. When this happens, the bank has two recourses. One is to overdraw the account and let the check be paid. In this case, the bank is making an unauthorized, interest-free loan to the depositor, so it will usually impose a service charge. More often, the bank will simply return the check to the last holder in due course, who will return it to the person from whom he or she received it, and so on until it gets back to the original payee. This is known as *bouncing* a check. At this point, the payee may attempt to redeposit the check or may seek redress from the issuer of the check. In every state, issuing a check for insufficient funds and then failing to make it good promptly is a criminal offense.

Consumer tip: Writing checks in anticipation of income is dangerous. If you are often short before payday, open a checking account with automatic overdraft privileges. In this way, should a check clear before your paycheck is credited, your bank will simply create a loan for you. On the other hand, if you receive a check that bounces back to you, in most cases, the best thing to do is redeposit it and see if it clears the second time. If it does not, ask the person who issued the check for payment in cash. If he fails to make that payment, tell him that you plan to turn the returned check over to your attorney for collection and possible criminal action. Chances are, you'll get your money quickly.

See also *bounce; uncollected funds.*

insurable interest a condition that must be met before an insurance policy is issued, under which, in the case of life insurance, the person buying the policy must have a valid relationship with the person whose life is insured.

89

Otherwise, anyone could insure a stranger, then kill him or her for the insurance. Thus, an insurable interest is held by anyone who would suffer financially if the insured person were to die. This would include close relatives and even some business associates.

In the case of property or liability insurance, an insurable interest is held only by those who would suffer financially if a property were destroyed or if action were successfully brought against the owners. These restrictions prevent people from insuring buildings in which they have no interest and then burning them down or otherwise trying to fraudulently abuse the insurance.

See also Section II, "Life Insurance," "Property and Liability Insurance."

insurance   a sharing of risk by the contribution of many people into a common fund from which claims are paid. Contributions to the common fund are called *premiums*, the amounts of which are based on the statistical probability of risk. In life insurance, this statistical base is called the *standard mortality table*. It shows statistically how long anyone of a given age can expect to live. Eventually, everyone dies. But out of 1,000 people aged 30, 1.7 are expected to die. Therefore, ideally, the cost of $100 in life insurance for a person aged 30 should be 17 cents, which, from 1,000 people, would create a pool of $170 to pay the 1.7 people who die at a rate of $100 per claim. Obviously, insurance companies stack the odds a bit more in their favor. For one thing, they add in sales and administrative costs and projected profits. For another, mortality tables

are not updated as quickly as they should be. Insurance companies benefit because of this and because people are living longer.

Property insurance has a different statistical base than life insurance. A life can be insured for any amount; property can be insured only for its actual cost of repair or replacement. In property insurance, the theory is also that of spreading risk; but calculations are based on the likelihood of a total or partial loss of the property, and factors ranging from the character of the person applying for insurance to the neighborhood in which the property is located are considered.

In addition to life and property insurance, it is common for people to insure against loss from illness, income impairment because of disability, and from legal claims based on personal liability. Americans, it is estimated, spend about one month's income per year on all types of insurance, making it a major consumer expense.

Consumer tip: Shop around for whatever kind of insurance you buy. You can save a lot of money by carefully choosing your coverage and your insurance companies.

See also Section II, "Life Insurance," "Property and Liability Insurance."

insurance policy   a legal contract between the insurance company and the insured, specifying the amount of insurance, the risks covered, and the premiums to be paid.

insured account   a bank account in which deposits are guaranteed up to a certain amount by the Federal Deposit Insurance Corporation (FDIC), the Federal Savings and Loan Insurance Corporation (FSLIC), the National Credit Union Administration (NCUA), or a state agency.

See also *Federal Deposit Insurance Corporation (FDIC); Federal Savings and Loan Insurance Corporation (FSLIC); National Credit Union Administration (NCUA).*

intangible asset   See *asset.*

interest   the amount a bank pays or charges for the use of money, which is expressed as a percentage or as a flat fee. The inventory of a bank is the money it receives in deposits. It lends this money for a fee, which is called interest. It also pays a fee for what it "borrows" from savings customers. This is also called interest. Naturally, a bank pays out less in savings interest than it charges in loan interest. This spread—less operating costs—accounts for a bank's profits. Interest is also paid by issuers of bonds to the owners of those securities.

Consumer tip: Obviously, it pays to shop for the highest savings rates and the lowest loan rates, yet many people fail to do so. Rates can differ, and widely, from bank to bank.

See also *dividends;* Section II, "Borrowing," "Savings."

intermediation   the use of funds deposited in banks and savings institutions to make loans and other investments.

See also *disintermediation.*

Internal Revenue Service (IRS) the subdivision of the U.S. Treasury Department charged with the collection of federal taxes.

International Bank for Reconstruction and Development   the World Bank; an organization formed as a result of the 1944 conference held at Bretton Woods, N.H., to help provide funds for reconstruction after World War II. Now, the main purpose of the Bank is to make loans for development to Third World and other underdeveloped countries.

International Monetary Fund (IMF)   an international banking organization formed in 1947 to help stabilize international exchange. Member nations may borrow foreign currencies under specified requirements. Also, membership in the IMF is necessary in order to belong to the International Bank for Reconstruction and Development, better known as the World Bank, which makes loans to developing nations.

See also *International Bank for Reconstruction and Development.*

in terrorem   a clause added to a will that threatens a possible beneficiary. Usually, this is used as a threat of disinheritance to discourage anyone who might contest a will.

See also Section II, "Estate Planning."

inter vivos trust   literally, a trust between the living; therefore, a living trust.

See also *living trust;* Section II, "Estate Planning."

intestate   without a valid will. When a person dies intestate, the court appoints an administrator who attempts to distribute the assets of the estate according to a formula set up by state law, usually awarding a certain percentage to a surviving spouse and the remainder to any children. Lacking those relatives, distribution may be made in varying orders to other relatives.

Consumer tip: Have a will drawn up by an attorney in the state in which your principal residence is located. This can avoid much family bitterness and save a substantial amount in inheritance or estate taxes and in administrative costs.

See also Section II, "Estate Planning."

in the black operating at a profit.
See also *in the red.*

in the money a term relating to stock options in which the *striking price,* the price at which the option takes effect, is below the current stock price for a call option or above the current stock price for a put option. When an option is in the money, there is no point in buying it because the goal for which the option would have been purchased has already been reached.

See also *calls; option; out of the money; puts.*

in the red operating at a loss.
See also *in the black.*

investment certificate See *certificate of deposit (CD).*

investment club a group of people who pool their money for investment, usually in common stock.

Consumer tip: If you have limited funds or if you are a real stock market novice, an investment club is an excellent way to diversify your risks and to learn by sharing information. Ten people contributing $25 a week each have a pool of over $1,080 a month or $13,000 a year to invest. This lowers brokerage commissions because they can buy in larger lots. The normal procedure is to assign different people to investigate possible stock investments and to hold a monthly meeting to make an investment decision. When a person wants to leave the club, a new member may buy his or her share or he or she may be paid off by the existing members.

investor a person who buys securities, hoping for a generous and regular income as opposed to a quick profit.

See also *speculator;* Section II, "Investments."

IOU short for "I owe you"; a promise to pay, usually informal.

IRA See *Individual Retirement Account.*

iron law of wages the economic theory postulated by English economist Thomas Malthus (1766–1834) holding that wages tend to equal what employees need for subsistence and no more. Parson Malthus, incidentally, was not a cheerful economist; his theories led some people to call economics "the dismal science."

irrevocable beneficiary See *beneficiary.*

irrevocable trust a trust that cannot be changed or cancelled by the person setting it up.

See also Section II, "Estate Planning."

IRS See *Internal Revenue Service.*

itemized deductions a listing of deductions from taxable income as authorized by law, usually made on Schedule A, IRS Form 1040.

J

joint account a bank or invest-ment account owned by more than one person. Usually, funds may be with-drawn on the signature of any of the people named, although countersign-ing may be required as a condition of the account as described in the docu-ments executed when it is opened. Most joint accounts are in the names of husbands and wives or parents and children. The title of the account is often something like, "John and Mary Doe as tenants in common."

Consumer tip: Do not have a joint ac-count with anyone you do not com-pletely trust. Relationships do end, and when they do, either party can clean out the account. Or if two signatures are required to withdraw funds, an angry party can refuse to co-sign and thus tie up the property or money of the other party indefinitely.

See also *joint property.*

joint and last survivor a type of annuity in which payments are made jointly to two annuitants until one dies, at which time payments continue to be made to the other person until his or her death.

Consumer tip: This is probably the best all-around type of annuity for a hus-band and wife to have because the in-come continues for as long as either party lives.

See also *annuity.*

jointly and severally together and individually; a term common in loan agreements, meaning that each person is individually responsible for the entire loan and the group as a whole is also responsible.

joint property property owned in common by more than one person. There are three types of joint owner-ship, and their differences are impor-tant:

1. *Tenancy in common.* In this type of joint ownership, there is no *right of survivorship.* This means that, on the

94

death of one person, all of the property in this case does *not* pass to the other person. Also, either person may sell or transfer his or her interest without the approval of the other.

2. *Joint tenancy.* In this type, there is the right of survivorship; but, while both parties are alive, either may sell or transfer his or her share and thus force a partition.

3. *Tenancy by the entirety.* In this type, there is the right of survivorship, and neither party may sell or transfer his or her share without the approval of the other party, so neither party may force a partition. This type of joint ownership is available only to married couples.

Consumer tip: Joint ownership has been called the "poor man's will" since some people think it avoids probate and estate settlement costs. It does not. Under joint ownership, a person's share is often taxed at death. Even though the unlimited marital exclusion has eliminated federal estate taxes between husbands and wives, it is sometimes wiser to have property owned by one spouse or another in order to avoid onerous state inheritance taxes. But where husbands and wives do have joint bank accounts, they should be held as joint tenants. Bank accounts between children and parents are usually as tenants in common. Except for close relatives, it is usually a bad idea to own any joint property.

See also *joint account.*

joint tenancy   See *joint property.*

judgment   a court ruling that establishes that a person owes a specific debt. When a person is sued for an amount owed, or when a money amount is assessed against a person, the court issues a judgment against him or her. If he or she fails to pay this judgment to the person to whom the money is due, that person then has a legal claim to collect it.

Consumer tip: As they say on the TV show, "People's Court," if you have a claim, take it to court. It costs little to bring a case into small claims court; and if you're in the right, you can get a judgment without too much effort.

judgment note   a promissory note that authorizes the lender to enter an automatic judgment against the borrower in the event of nonpayment, with no need for court action.

Consumer tip: Judgment notes are common among shady lenders, especially those who sell overpriced goods to poor slum dwellers. *Never* sign a judgment note. It is always a mistake to give up any of your legal rights.

See also *confession of judgment;* Section II, "Borrowing."

jumbo CDs   bank certificates of deposit in amounts of $100,000 or more.

Consumer tip: Because $100,000 is the legal limit on deposit insurance, it is always unwise (as the bankrupt Penn Square Bank CD holders learned the hard way) to buy CDs of over $100,000. Diversify your holdings!

Keogh Plan   also *HR 10 Plan;* a tax-deferred retirement plan, based on legislation sponsored in 1962 by Congressman Eugene J. Keogh, Democratic Representative from Brooklyn, N.Y. "HR 10" refers to the bill number. Keogh plans are for the self-employed and are somewhat similar to Individual Retirement Accounts (IRAs) except that the limits are broader. Under such a plan, a self-employed person may:

1. Invest up to 20 percent of his or her annual self-employment income, up to a maximum of $30,000, in an approved Keogh Plan.

2. That investment is deductible from income right on the face of IRS Form 1040.

3. Although it is easier to use a trustee with an approved plan, the person may act as his or her own trustee and may borrow from Keogh Plan funds.

4. The original plan must be set up prior to December 31 of the taxable year, but additional contributions may be made up until the person's tax is filed—usually April 15. Contributions may be made in later years up to the time that the tax is filed for that year.

5. The self-employed person must contribute to the retirement funds of all full-time employees who have worked for him or her for three or more years at the same rate as the self-employed person contributes to his or her own.

6. The self-employed person may have an Individual Retirement Account in addition to a Keogh Plan if he or she chooses.

7. A person whose annual income from all sources does not exceed $15,000 may put 100 percent of self-employment income or $750, whichever is less, into a Keogh Plan. This is popularly called a *Mini-Keogh Plan.*

Consumer tip: For many self-employed persons, the Keogh Plan is just as good a tax shelter as a personal corporation. The clinker is the requirement that some employees be included; but for the one-person business or husband-and-wife business, Keogh is ideal. The tax deferral can save thousands of dollars a year in tax payments; the multiplier effects of compound interest and investment growth further decrease the eventual impact of taxes. And with the new regulations, Keogh funds can be self-administered and even borrowed against for personal use.

Any bank or brokerage house can set up a Keogh Plan; in fact, it's a good idea to have two, one at a bank with insured CDs for safety and income, and one at a brokerage house with mutual fund or stock investments for growth.

See also *Individual Retirement Account (IRA)*; Section II, "Retirement Planning."

Keynesian economics   the economic theories of John Maynard Keynes, a British economist who died in 1946. Keynes taught that national income and employment levels are dependent on real investments and consumer spending. The Roosevelt "New Deal" policies were the first practical application of his ideas; they tried to stimulate the economy by creating employment and thus stimulating consumer spending. Modified Keynesian theory is the basis of many governmental policies today.

kickback   an illegal rebate given to obtain favors.

killing   a very profitable transaction, as in, "He made a killing in the stock market."

kite   an illegal system of building the balances in accounts at two different banks by floating bad checks between them until the paper balances seem enormous, at which time the kiter usually draws checks for cash and skips town. Also, a person will sometimes kite checks so as to establish a falsely favorable credit report, then simply let the balances return to normal without stealing any money. Kiting requires a detailed knowledge of check-clearing procedures and schedules.

A variation on kiting is the filing of a phony income tax return showing an inflated income. The kiter files an amended return with the IRS, but uses a copy of the original to show a prospective lender.

Consumer tip: Kiting is dangerous and illegal.

L

L See *money supply.*

labor intensive production requiring an additional use of labor to increase earnings.

Consumer tip: As a rule, labor intensive production leads to high employment rates, consumer spending, and economic stability. It includes housing and other building trades, the automotive industry, major appliances, and other consumer-oriented production.

See also *capital intensive.*

laissez-faire French, meaning "allow to act." In economics, the term describes an economy having little or no government regulation.

lamb an unsophisticated investor, who, like a lamb, is ready to be fleeced, or defrauded.

See also Section II, "Consumer Frauds."

landlord's warrant a court-issued order allowing a landlord to seize a tenant's personal property as security against past-due rental payments.

See also *eviction.*

lapse automatic cancellation of an insurance policy because of nonpayment of premium.

See also *grace period;* Section II, "Life Insurance," "Property and Liability Insurance."

last will the final will executed by a person.

See also Section II, "Estate Planning."

late charge See *late-payment penalty.*

late-payment penalty also *late charge;* an extra fee imposed by a lender because a loan payment is made after the due date and after the grace period, if there is one.

Consumer tip: There are two things to remember about late-payment penalties: Avoid them because enough of them can hurt your credit rating; and if you do incur one, be sure to take it as an income tax deduction under the Interest Expense section of Schedule A, Form 1040.

See also *grace period; penalty clause;* Section II, "Debt Management."

lawful money See *legal tender.*

leading indicators 12 economic factors, chosen by the Bureau of Economic Analysis, that supposedly reflect future trends in the U.S. economy. The leading indicators for the previous month are reported monthly. They are:

1. The national average work week.
2. Average weekly initial unemployment claims.
3. New orders for materials and manufactured and consumer goods.
4. Vendor performance in filling orders.
5. Net business formation.
6. Contracts and orders for plants and equipment.
7. Building permits.
8. Change in inventories on hand and on order.
9. Changes in sensitive material prices.
10. Common stock prices.
11. The money supply.
12. Changes in credit—business and consumer borrowing.

lease a contract between a renter and a property owner or his agent for the right to use property for a certain period of time for a specified amount of money.

Consumer tips: Before you sign a lease, read it carefully, keeping in mind the old adage, "The large print giveth, but the fine print taketh away." Ask yourself, "What do I need from this lease?" And beware of the following traps that many landlords slip into leases:

1. A provision for a security deposit to be held until the premises are vacated. You may not get it back, so try instead to have it apply to the rent after a reasonable period of time.
2. A provision making you responsible for all repairs, including normal maintenance.
3. A restriction against subletting.
4. A requirement that you give 30 to 60 days' notice for nonrenewal of your lease.
5. A clause that allows the landlord to have the right to show the house or apartment to prospective renters at any time.
6. A waiver-of-notice clause that allows the landlord to evict you if you violate even one of the fine-print provisions in the lease.
7. A waiver-of-liability clause that absolves the landlord if you are injured through his negligence.
8. A confession-of-judgment clause whereby you waive your rights to a defense in court.
9. A lease-cancellation clause should the owner sell the building.
10. A clause that requires you to pay property taxes.

lease-purchase a lease that provides that all or some of rents paid will be applied toward the purchase price of a property.

ledger 1) a book or other place of record where financial accounts are recorded; in accounting, 2) a book of final entry as opposed to a journal or book of original entry.

legacy a bequest; a gift made through a will.
See also *inheritance;* Section II, "Estate Planning."

legal custody 1) guardianship; 2) placement in strict safekeeping by order of a court.

legal entity a person, government body, company, corporation, or other organization that has the legal ability to make a contract and to be sued if the contract is not honored.

legal interest the maximum rate of loan interest allowed by state law.

legal obligation a debt that can be collected through court action, if necessary.

legal rate See *legal interest.*

legal residence See *domicile.*

legal tender also *lawful money;* coin or currency that, by law, must be accepted in payment of a debt unless the original contract specifies another form of payment. In the United States, all coins and currency, except for pennies, are legal tender.
Consumer tip: Don't try to pay $1,000 in taxes or a disputed bill with 100,000 pennies. The tax collector or creditor can refuse them, and you'll have to lug back about 695 pounds of pennies. Try nickels instead—they're legal tender!

lend to allow another to use property without giving up title to that property.

lending institution any organization that lends money and charges interest for its use, including a bank, a finance company, a mortgage company, an insurance company, or even a pawnbroker.

letter of administration a document issued by a court showing that a named person had been legally appointed as administrator of the estate of a person who died intestate, or without a valid will.
See also *intestate; letters testamentary.*

letter of credit a document issued by a bank showing that a person's or company's credit is backed by the bank's guarantee to honor its trade acceptances up to a certain limit.

letters testamentary a certificate issued by a probate court to the executor of an estate appointed under a will. This certificate is used as authority to dispose of property, open and close bank accounts, and otherwise perform the duties of liquidating the estate.
See also *short certificate.*

level-payment loan an installment loan or mortgage that is amortized with regular monthly payments of the same amount. The last payment may vary slightly to cover fractional interest due.
See also Section II, "Borrowing."

level-premium insurance See *ordinary life.*

leverage the use of credit to increase potential profits. For example, assume that a stock is selling for $50 a share and that a person has $500 to invest. He or she can buy 10 shares. Or the investor can buy on *margin*, that is, by making down payment and buying additional shares on credit. Thus, if the margin is 10 percent, the investor in this case could use his or her $500 as a down payment and obtain credit for $4,500, thus buying 100 shares. If the price of the stock rises to $60 a share and the investor merely has the 10 shares, the profit is $100. On the other hand, if leverage is used and the investor buys the 100 shares, the profit is $1,000. Of course, if the stock goes down, the investor stands to lose proportionately. There is also great leverage possible in real estate investments.

Consumer tip: Don't use leverage in your investments unless you are as prepared to lose a large amount as you are to make one. Buying on margin is a dangerous game for amateurs.

See also *margin;* Section II, "Investments."

liability money owed. Liabilities include unpaid taxes, loans, unpaid bills, rent due, interest due, and all other financial obligations. Liabilities are of many types, including:

- *Accrued liabilities,* which are debts that are accumulating but not actually due, such as interest on a one-payment loan.
- *Contingent liabilities,* which are obligations that might come into being

because of the action of another person; the most common example involves the co-signer of a note who might become responsible for the debt.
- *Current liabilities,* which are bills due at this time.
- *Fixed liabilities,* which are debts that will not come due within the current period, usually considered to be one year.

To a bank, a depositor's account is a liability because the bank has an obligation to repay that money.

See also *accounting;* Section II, "Family Accounting."

lien a claim on property against an outstanding debt. Liens may be either voluntary or involuntary, but in common usage, the term implies a lack of consent on the part of the debtor. The three most common liens are:

- The *income tax lien,* which is a claim against bank accounts and real and personal property until overdue taxes are paid.
- The *property tax lien,* which is a claim against real estate until overdue taxes are paid.
- The *mechanic's lien,* which is a claim against personal or real property until a debt is paid, such as payment owed to a contractor for improvement made to a home.

See also Section II, "Debt Management."

life annuity an annuity that provides an income for life and then ceases.

See also *annuity;* Section II, "Retirement Planning."

life beneficiary   also *life tenant;* a person who receives income from an estate or trust for as long as he or she lives, but who may not bequeath the property in turn to a person of his or her choosing.

life estate   a trust established to benefit a person for as long as he or she lives. Upon that person's death, the property remaining goes to whomever the originator of the estate has directed.

life income   See *settlement options.*

life-income-with-installments-certain   See *settlement options.*

life insurance   a pooling of funds from many people to provide money benefits to the beneficiaries of each at the times of the deaths of the insured. There are two aspects to life insurance: the protection of beneficiaries from loss caused by the death of the insured, and a savings feature that is built into many policies.

The cost of pure protection is based on the statistical probability of death of each insured person during the current year. Thus, if there are 1,000 insured persons in the pool and the odds are 1 in 100 that any one of them may die, each will contribute $10 to assure a payout of $1,000 to each of the 10 who will probably die. A savings feature is added to many policies through an additional premium charge and the investment of these funds by the insurance company. A portion of the earnings from this investment are passed on to the policyholder in the form of growing cash values and, with participating policies, as dividends. If the savings feature is added, the costs rise dramatically.

The common types of life insurance include:

- *Term,* which is pure protection, with no savings feature.
- *Ordinary life;* also called *whole life, straight life, cash-reserve, cash-value, level-premium, and permanent insurance.* There are many variations, including executive life, life paid up at 65, 10-payment life, 20-payment life, and so on.
- *Endowment,* which is primarily a savings plan with an insurance feature tacked on.
- *Industrial,* which is the most costly of all insurance, since premiums are collected door-to-door by a debit man.
- *Credit life,* which is insurance sold through a lender to secure the loan.
- *Group life,* which provides coverage of an entire group under a single policy, usually a "free" fringe benefit of employment.

Consumer tip: Life insurance allows anyone to create an "instant estate" to care for loved ones, but life insurance costs account for a large part of the average family's budget, so shop carefully. In general, avoid credit and industrial insurance because they are very expensive, and concentrate needed protection in low-cost term insurance. Never use life insurance as an investment or as a savings plan; it is very uneconomical for either use.

See also *endowment insurance policy; industrial insurance; limited-payment life; ordinary life; standard mortality table; term life insurance;* Section II, "Life Insurance."

life insurance trust an estate-planning technique of creating a trust with the proceeds of life insurance. Other assets may or may not be included in the trust. These trusts are most often established by people of limited means to create assets and to guarantee care for a person or persons who cannot handle their own financial affairs competently.

Consumer tip: If you have a minor child or a retarded or otherwise handicapped person in your care, or even a spouse who cannot really handle money, and if you don't have many assets, a life insurance trust is ideal. Ask your bank's estate planning officer for advice. He or she will help you plan an insurance program, and then your attorney can create a trust to administer the money that will become payable at your death.

See also Section II, "Estate Planning."

life tenant See *life beneficiary.*

limited-installment payments See *settlement options.*

limited order an order to buy or sell stock within set price limits.

limited-payment life a cash-reserve life insurance policy with premiums payable only for a limited period of time, usually 10 or 20 years or until age 65. These policies are frequently called "10-payment life," "20-payment life," "executive life," or "life paid up at 65." The idea is to concentrate all payments into peak earnings years. For example, a 10-payment or a 20-payment life policy might have appeal to a baseball or football player who

is earning millions until age 40, and whose income will then drop sharply.

Consumer tip: Limited-payment life plans are expensive. It is almost always a better deal to buy term insurance for needed protection and to invest the difference. Chances are, the earnings on the investments will more than offset the cost of future insurance needs.

See also *life insurance; ordinary life; term life insurance;* Section II, "Life Insurance."

limited warranty See *warranty.*

line of credit an agreement by a bank to guarantee a set credit limit for a customer, subject to the customer's continued good credit rating. Lines of credit were once only for business firms, but now they are commonly extended to consumers. A bank credit card, for example, extends a line of credit; so does an automatic overdraft checking account.

Consumer tip: Having a line of credit via a bank credit card and/or an overdraft account is a good idea if you don't abuse it. You should be aware at all times of your credit limit.

See also Section II, "Borrowing," "Money Mistakes."

liquid asset property that can be converted into cash quickly. Liquid assets include bank deposits, money market fund accounts, mutual fund shares, government bonds, and common stocks.

Also see *asset; illiquid asset.*

listed security a stock or bond listed on a stock exchange.

Little Board the American Stock Exchange.

See also *Big Board; stock exchange.*

living trust a trust set up from the assets of a living person.

See also Section II, "Estate Planning."

load a charge made at the time a securities transaction is made to cover the sales commission. Most charges are *front-end loads,* that is, they are incurred when a security is bought and no charge is made when it is sold. The charge is usually from 6 to 8 percent of the cost of the securities.

Consumer tip: When buying mutual funds, consider the no-load variety. They have just about as good a record as the load variety, and they save you money. For example, if you invest $1,000 in an 8 percent front-end load fund, you actually make an investment of $920 and pay a charge of $80— which works out to a true rate of 8.696 percent. Your investment must earn 8.696 percent before you are even. Check *The Wall Street Journal* or *Money* magazine for information on excellent no-load funds.

See also *low-load; mutual fund; no-load;* Section II, "Investments."

loan to allow the temporary use of property. A fee may or may not be charged for this service. In financial terms, a loan means granting the use of money for a fee, referred to as *interest.* Loans are of several kinds, including the following (note that different lenders may use other descriptive titles for advertising purposes):

1. *Personal-type loans* almost always feature installment repayment plans. These include:

- *Mortgage loans,* made to finance the buying of real property and secured with that property as collateral.
- *Chattel mortgage loans,* made to finance the purchase of personal property, such as automobiles, and secured with that personal property.
- *Personal unsecured loans,* made on a person's signature alone, relying on his or her good credit history as the basis for the loan. Unsecured personal loans tend to have slightly higher rates than secured loans.
- *Revolving credit loans,* which include credit cards and automatic overdraft checking accounts. With this type of loan, a credit limit is established and, as repayments are made, the borrower may again borrow up to the set limit.

2. *Business-type loans* may have installment repayments or, more commonly, may require a single payment when the loan matures. They include:

- *Unsecured time loans,* made for relatively short terms, usually 30, 60, 90, or 120 days, with possible agreements for review and renewal, usually after a partial payment has been made. These loans are often made for seasonal production needs or inventory replenishment.
- *Secured time loans,* which are similar to the unsecured, except that they are collateralized, often with the goods they are used to finance.

- *Accounts receivable loans*, which are secured with the accounts receivable of a business. As credit cards take more and more business away from the direct extension of credit by merchants, these loans are becoming less widely used, although they remain important.
- *Demand loans*, which are payable, as the name implies, on demand by the lender. They may or may not be secured by collateral of some type.

Consumer tip: Borrowing is an important part of modern life. The trick is to find the lowest finance charge for the specific purpose at hand. This usually means looking beyond the obvious ease of using a credit card for long-term borrowing. Often, good customers can borrow on a business basis at their local bank and save substantial amounts.

See also *accounts receivable loan; demand loan; interest; mortgage loan; open-end credit;* Section II, "Borrowing."

loan fee   a charge, in addition to the finance charge, made by a lender to a borrower as a condition of the loan.

Consumer tip: Pay any loan fee at the time the loan is made and with a separate check; this fee is tax deductible on Schedule A, Form 1040, if paid in a lump sum and not amortized with the loan. As always, you should have proof of payment, hence the separate check.

Also see *point;* Section II, "Borrowing."

loan shark   a person who makes loans for instant cash and charges such exorbitant interest that the borrower

can often never get caught up. If the victim quits paying, he or she is often physically abused by the loan shark or someone he hires.

Consumer tip: If you heed only one tip in this book, make it this one. Never, never borrow from a loan shark! They are vicious predators who can destroy innocent people.

See also Section II, "Borrowing," "Debt Management."

Lombard Street   the English equivalent of Wall Street; the financial district in London.

long   owning a large number of stocks in a company. For example, "She is long on Ford," means that she owns a lot of stock in Ford Motor Company. "She is long 1,000 Ford," means that she owns 1,000 shares of this stock.

long position   the description of an owner of a number of shares of a common stock who is holding the shares in the expectation that they will be profitable.

long-term capital gains   See *capital gains.*

loophole certificate   a device used in the late 1970s by banks to get around the requirement that minimum deposits in six-month certificates of deposit be at least $10,000. With a loophole CD, the depositor put up the amount of money he or she could, then the bank lent the customer the difference so that he or she could buy a $10,000 CD. The rate charged by the bank was for the interest that would be earned on the loan portion, plus a little, so that the depositor came out ahead. Eventually, though, the IRS ruled that the income on the entire $10,000 was taxable, even though the depositor didn't receive it; and, of course, the loan interest was deductible. Because it didn't work, the loophole certificate went the way of the dinosaur.

Consumer tip: The important message of the loophole certificate is that, before you jump into something new, you should think twice. Many savers got hurt with loophole CDs because they owed back taxes on them. Remember, if a deal looks too good to be true, it probably is.

lot   a quantity of stock. A *round lot* or *even lot* is usually 100 shares of stock, although, in some very inactive stocks, a round lot is 10 shares. An *odd lot* is any quantity of shares less than a round lot. The brokerage commission rate is lower on a per-share basis on round-lot transactions than on odd-lot transactions. However, if an investor buys a number of shares exceeding the basic round-lot number, i.e., 112 shares, he or she pays the round-lot rate for the entire transaction.

Consumer tip: Brokers charge less per share to buy or sell stocks in even lots.

So if you have $2,000 to invest and are torn between buying 20 shares of a stock at $100 each or 200 shares at $10 each, all other things being equal, take the latter because you'll pay less in commissions.

See also Section II, "Investments."

low-load   a mutual fund sales fee that is between the regular fee and no fee. Typically, a normal load is from 6 to 8 percent, so a low-load fee will average about 3 to 4 percent. These fees were unknown before 1980, but are becoming increasingly common.

See also *load; mutual fund; no-load;* Section II, "Investments."

lump sum   payment in full made all at one time.

lump-sum payment   See *settlement options.*

lump-sum settlement   See *alimony.*

luxury tax   a state or federal excise tax on goods or services not considered essential for daily living; taxes on jewelry are a good example.

See also *sin tax.*

macroeconomics the study of the whole economy as opposed to *micro-economics*, which is the study of individual economic units or firms.

See also *microeconomics*.

make a market making specific over-the-counter stocks always available for buying and selling by a broker.

See also *National Association of Securities Dealers Automated Quotations (NAS-DAQ); over-the-counter stock;* Section II, "Investments."

maker see *payer.*

manipulation making securities transactions so as to create an appearance of market activity, thus raising or lowering the price and inducing others to buy or sell. Manipulation is a form of securities fraud forbidden by Securities and Exchange Commission regulations.

See also *Securities and Exchange Commission (SEC).*

margin the down payment made by an investor when making a securities purchase on credit. Obviously, the investor's equity will change as the price of the securities changes, but Federal Reserve Regulation T sets the initial margin required at a varying percentage of the purchase price.

Buying on margin gives an investor considerable leverage; that is, for a much lower investment, potential profit can multiply dramatically. Thus, if the margin required is 50 percent, and the stock the investor wishes to purchase is selling for $25 a share, and if he has $10,000 to invest, by buying on margin, he can buy 800 shares instead of 400—that is, he can borrow another $10,000 from the broker to buy the additional stock. If the stock goes up in price, everything is fine; but if the price of the stock drops, the investor must put up additional money to maintain his margin at the legal limit. If he doesn't have the extra money on hand, the broker must sell all or part of the stock, even at a loss, to make up the difference.

Consumer tip: Buying on margin is a risky business for all but the most sophisticated investor. If you really are confident that a stock will rise in price and you wish to multiply the earnings effect, buy call options instead, or, if you believe a stock will drop, buy put options. The multiplier effect is greater and the risk is usually less. However, such options are available on relatively few stocks. Remember the old investment adage: "Bulls make money, bears make money, but pigs never make money."

See also *leverage; option;* Section II, "Investments."

margin account   a special account with a brokerage house enabling the holder of the account to buy stocks on credit.

See also *margin.*

margin call   a demand by a broker for an investor who has purchased securities on margin to put up additional equity.

See also *margin.*

marginal tax bracket   also *tax bracket;* the federal income tax rate imposed on the last dollar earned. The marginal tax bracket is extremely important because any deduction from income is also deducted from the last dollars earned. Here's an example: In 1982, John and Mary earned $32,000. They paid $6,275 in federal income tax, which is 19.61 percent of their in-

come. But they were not in the 20 percent marginal tax bracket—they were in the 33 percent marginal tax bracket, because they would have to pay $33 in taxes on every additional $100 they earned; also, they would have saved $33 in taxes for every $100 in additional deductions they could have taken.

Consumer tip: Know your marginal tax bracket. You can easily find it by looking up the Tax Rate Schedules in the information booklet that comes with your tax form. Just find your category (single, married filing jointly, or whatever), then your taxable income level under that category. Your marginal tax bracket is the percentage rate shown to the right of that amount.

See also Section II, "Tax Savings."

marital deduction   previously, the amount allowed to be excluded from federal estate taxes on the portion of an estate left to a spouse. The Economic Recovery Tax Act of 1981 established an unlimited marital deduction. This means that no part of an estate left to a surviving spouse is federally taxable.

See also Section II, "Estate Planning."

market   a place where people who desire to buy and those who desire to sell can come to an agreement.

market value   1) the price of a security on the latest quotation: 2) the price that can be obtained when selling a piece of real estate or other property.

markup   the increase between the cost and the selling price, expressed in dollars or as a percentage.

marriage penalty the relatively higher federal income taxes paid by married couples as compared to single people. It is mathematically impossible to have an income tax that has income-related progressively rising rates, that allows married couples to file joint returns, and that has all equal-income earners, married or single, taxed equally.

For years, single people paid proportionately somewhat higher taxes than married couples filing jointly. Then, in 1969, Congress switched things, and now married couples pay higher taxes than singles do. In an effort to offset this, the Economic Tax Recovery Act of 1981 allowed married couples in which both parties work to take as a deduction 10 percent of the earned income of the spouse with lower earnings, for a maximum deduction of $3,000. Couples must file jointly to take this deduction, using Schedule W, Form 1040.

See also Section II, "Tax Savings."

MasterCard 1) a popular bank credit or credit/debit card; 2) the name of traveler's checks and other services marketed through MasterCard. Local banks act as franchisees in offering this card, and charge slips are sorted and assessed on a national basis.

See also *credit card; debit card; VISA;* Section II, "Bank Accounts."

mature to become payable. Thus, an endowment that has matured is payable to the insured person; a loan that has matured must be paid by the borrower; or a bond that has matured is payable to the owner or bearer.

maturity the date on which an obligation becomes payable.

mechanic's lien See *lien.*

Medicaid federal/state medical assistance for the needy, operated under guidelines set up by the Department of Health, Education and Welfare. In general, Medicaid is available to those who qualify for public assistance or Supplemental Security Income (SSI).

See also *health insurance; Supplemental Security Income (SSI).*

Medicare See *health insurance.*

medium of exchange any commodity generally accepted as payment for goods or services or in payment of debts. One of the necessary characteristics of money is that it be a medium of exchange; obviously, unless money is universally accepted, it is worthless.

See also *money.*

megabucks once, $1 million; now, a slang term meaning a lot of money. "John is making megabucks," has meaning only in relative terms. Thus, if a child says it, megabucks may mean $25 a week; if Mr. Gotrocks says it, megabucks may mean $5 million a year.

member bank a bank that belongs to the Federal Reserve System. All national banks must be members and any state bank may join. At one time, it was an advantage not to be a member because nonmember banks did not have to maintain as much money in reserves. Now there is little difference, so more banks will probably join.

member firm   a securities brokerage house that has a partner who is a member of a stock exchange. Usually, the firm will list itself as "Member New York Stock Exchange" or some similar title.

merger   the combining of two or more companies. This is usually accomplished by one firm buying a controlling interest (more than 50 percent) of the common stock of the other.
See also *takeover.*

Michigan roll   also *Philadelphia roll;* a roll of $1 bills with a $20 bill wrapped around it to create the impression that the owner is carrying a lot of money.

MICR   magnetic ink character recognition. The dull black numbers printed at the bottom of checks are MICR numbers, and automatic sorterreader machines at banks use them to expedite check clearing. The numbers include the bank's routing symbol and transit number, the checking account number, and the number of the check. They are always dull black because they contain iron filings. In fact, shiny numbers may indicate that the check is counterfeit.
See also *check.*

microeconomics   the study of individual economic units or firms in an economy as opposed to *macroeconomics,* which is the study of the economy as a whole.
See also *macroeconomics.*

MID   the Midwest Stock Exchange.
See also *stock exchange.*

Midwest Stock Exchange (MID)
See *stock exchange.*

milling   the serrated edge found on the rims of all American coins, except pennies and nickels. Milling was originally used to prevent crooks from shaving bits of gold and silver from the edges of coins; the smoothness of a shaved coin would show. Now that American coins have no real intrinsic value, the milling is decorative.

Mini-Keogh Plan   See *Keogh Plan.*

minimum wage   the rate set by the Fair Labor Standards Act (the federal Wage and Hours Law), below which a person may not be legally paid. The minimum wage has increased several times, and in 1984 is $3.35 per hour.

mint   a factory at which coins are manufactured. In the United States, there are mints in Philadelphia, San Francisco, and Denver, the largest of which is in Philadelphia. In addition to U.S. coins, the mints also make coins for several foreign nations for a fee.

mixed fund   See *mutual fund.*

MMDA   See *money market deposit account.*

mobile home loan   a loan for the purchase of a mobile home that is not secured by a real estate mortgage. A mobile home loan is usually a *chattel mortgage.* Until the 1970s, this was the most common way to finance mobile homes. The advantage was that a low down payment was required. The disadvantage was the relatively short term for repayment, causing high monthly payments. Now mobile homes qualify for government-approved financing, and standard real estate mortgages are usually used.

See also *chattel mortgage*.

M1A; M1B; M2; M3   See *money supply*.

money   the coin and currency of a nation that is used as a medium of exchange. Money must have certain characteristics, including the following:

- Be acceptable to everyone.
- Be easily recognized.
- Be difficult to counterfeit.
- Be uniform in quality.
- Allow for simple calculations, hence our decimal system of money.
- Have a reasonably high face value.
- Be legal tender.

The United States issues currency as *Federal Reserve Notes* in the following denominations, each of which bears the portrait of a posthumous famous American:

$1 bills —— George Washington
$2 bills —— Thomas Jefferson
$5 bills —— Abraham Lincoln
$10 bills —— Alexander Hamilton
$20 bills —— Andrew Jackson
$50 bills —— Ulysses Grant
$100 bills —— Benjamin Franklin

Bills of $500 to $100,000 are used strictly for transactions between the U.S. Treasury and the Federal Reserve.

In addition to Federal Reserve Notes, the Treasury issues *United States Notes* (called *greenbacks*) in the $100 denomination. Less common, these contain a red seal and the words "United States Note" instead of the green seal and the words, "Federal Reserve Note." Incidentally, the United States Notes were first issued during the Civil War to help finance that war and were originally meant to be retired. They remain in circulation.

American coins, bearing the following portraits are:

Half-dollar ——John Kennedy
Quarter   ——George Washington
Dime   ——Franklin Roosevelt
Nickel   ——Thomas Jefferson
Cent   ——Abraham Lincoln

At present, no dollar coins are being minted, though some of the smaller Susan B. Anthony dollar coins (popularly called *sufferin' Suzies*, or *Tonies*) and the large Dwight Eisenhower dollar coins (popularly called *cartwheels* or *Ikes*,) are still around.

Not all money is issued by the government, however. Some is created by banks exercising a loan function. Here's an example: Suppose a person applies at his or her bank for a loan and gets it. The bank credits the proceeds of the loan to his or her checking account—no cash has changed hands, but the person has spending power. The person then makes purchases and issues checks to pay for them—again, no cash has changed hands. In effect, money has been created.

Banks also create money when they use their customers' loans as collateral for loans from the Federal Reserve. They receive credit from the Fed, then make more loans that they can again borrow against, and so forth. In each case, no cash changes hands, yet the money in circulation through bank credits is increased dramatically.

See also *money supply; numismatics*.

money fund   See *money market mutual fund*.

money in circulation   the total amount of coin and bills actually issued to banks and the public. There is usually about $115 billion in bills and $12 billion in coin in circulation, though the amounts can vary from year to year.

See also *money; money supply*.

money market certificate   originally, a six-month certificate of deposit at a bank or savings institution. These paid interest indexed to the current rate on Treasury securities. Effective October 1, 1983, all certificates of deposit of over 31 days' maturity were deregulated, which means that depository institutions can pay whatever rates they choose on certificates of any size or maturity. So the term money market certificate, if still used, is strictly a local distinction for advertising purposes.

money market deposit account (MMDA)   a bank account authorized by Congress to compete with money market mutual funds. MMDAs have a set legal minimum balance and a limit to the number of checks and/or transfers that may be made, but no legal minimum interest rate and no restrictions on the allowed number of in-person deposits or withdrawals.

The original regulations established by the Depository Institutions Deregulation and Monetary Control Committee called for a minimum balance of $2,500 and allowed six transfers per month, of which only three could be checks. These regulations are subject to change, so check with your banker for current rates and rules.

Consumer tip: MMDAs have a few distinct advantages over money market mutual funds. Like all bank accounts, your MMDA is insured by either the Federal Deposit Insurance Corporation (FDIC), the Federal Savings and Loan Insurance Corporation (FSLIC), or some other authorized agency. And, when you save at a local bank, your money is usually put to use in your community.

See also *money market mutual fund*.

money market mutual fund   a type of mutual fund that specializes in high-quality short-term money market investments, such as Treasury Bills, high-grade bank certificates of deposit, grade A loans to large corporations, and Eurodollars. Usually, the average maturity of the investments in a fund ranges from 30 to 60 days, which means that the administrators can take advantage of changes in money rates and safety factors with great speed.

The money market mutual funds are administered by managements affiliated with the traditional stock and bond mutual funds, and like the traditional mutual funds, charge a management fee. Many money market mutual funds are no-load—there is no sales commission involved. Deposits in these funds are not insured, but the quality of their investments is so good that insurance is almost a moot point. Most money market mutual funds allow their customers to have some check-writing privileges.

Funds are even available that have specialized investment goals. For example, some invest only in Treasury securities, others only in industries that are environmentally sound, and still others invest only in industries involved in nonmilitary production. Money market mutual funds are a relative newcomer to the economic scene, but they're undoubtedly here to stay.

Consumer tip: If you consider a money market mutual fund, look first for security, second for a no-load feature, and third for instant availability of funds. Excellent funds are administered by the major service groups and are advertised regularly in the business section of the Sunday paper, *The Wall Street Journal* or *Money* magazine. The advantages of a money market mutual fund are market-responsive earnings, high liquidity of funds, a high safety factor, and, if the fund is part of a mutual fund group, fast transfer availability to any of several mutual stock or bond funds.

See also *money market deposit account (MMDA); mutual fund.*

money order a draft drawn on a bank or the United States Postal Service that may be purchased by a customer for the face amount of the draft plus a sales and handling fee. The purchaser may designate any desired payee. Money orders are as acceptable as cash or official bank checks and therefore can expedite shipment when ordering goods by mail, because the supplier needn't wait for a check to clear. But they are inconvenient and expensive, with fees for a bank money order averaging about $1 and for a postal money order from 75 cents to $1.55.

Consumer tip: Don't use money orders to pay routine bills; they are ex-

pensive. Instead, open an interest-paying checking or NOW account. It helps to build your credit rating and gives you great convenience. If you must pay in guaranteed funds, ask your bank to issue an official check.

See also *check; official check.*

money supply the total amount of cash and other monies in circulation. M1A, M1B, M2, M3, and L are standard measurements of the current money supply as defined by the Federal Reserve Board. Here's a synopsis:

- *M1A* is the currency in circulation plus checking account deposits at commercial banks.
- *M1B* is the total of M1A plus checking account deposits at all other financial institutions, including NOW accounts at thrift institutions, share accounts at credit unions, and so forth.
- *M2* is the total of M1B plus savings accounts, certificates of deposit under $100,000, overnight repurchase agreements, money market fund deposits, and overnight Eurodollars.
- *M3* is the total of M2 plus all certificates of deposit over $100,000, large-denomination time deposits, and term repurchase agreements.
- *L* stands for "liquid" and includes all of the items of M1A, M1B, M2, and M3, including cash in circulation, money on deposit in banks, repurchase agreements, Eurodollars, large-denomination time deposits, banker's acceptances, commercial bills, Treasury bills and other securities, U.S. Savings Bonds, and other liquid assets.

Experts believe a sharp rise in the money supply forecasts inflation and higher interest rates. It usually has an adverse effect on the stock market and the cost of living.

See also *money*.

monopoly in a pure sense, exclusive control of the production and distribution of a particular good or service by one company that has been granted a government charter for that purpose. There are few pure monopolies in the Unites States today; even the Postal Service has competition from United Parcel Service, Federal Express, and other carriers. Gas and electric utilities are examples of pure monopolies on a regional basis. However, there are many partial monopolies in industries in which start-up or production costs are prohibitive.

Consumer tip: You can fight city hall as effectively as you can fight a monopoly. After all, if you get angry at the electric company, you can't take your business to a competitor. This gives monopolies, even partial ones, great power over consumers. If you have a grievance with a monopoly that you can't settle, your only effective recourse is to contact your state's consumer affairs bureau for help.

See also *laissez faire; oligopoly*.

monthly investment plan a method of investing in common stocks that works like the bond-a-month plan. Under this plan, an investor selects his or her stock or stocks, then invests as often as once a month or as infrequently as once every three months, for a minimum of $40 per period or a maximum of $1,000 per period. This plan was popular in the 1950s when stock prices were stable, but is not as common today.

Consumer tip: If you want to invest regularly in small amounts, buy a no-load mutual fund with monthly or quarterly payments. Why pay brokers' fees for small lots of common stocks? It can take years to recoup these transaction charges.

See also Section II, "Investments."

Montreal Stock Exchange (MSE) See *stock exchange*.

Moody's Bond Yield an index that measures the return on investments made in bonds, which averages 12-month yields based on market price, coupon rate, and on being held to maturity.

Moody's ratings stock and bond ratings by Moody's Investor Service, a highly respected firm.

Stocks, both common and preferred, are rated:

- *High quality*—excellent by all standards.
- *Good quality*—have many favorable high-grade investment qualities.
- *Medium quality*—medium-grade securities.

Bonds are rated:

- *Aaa*—best quality.
- *Aa*—high-grade bonds.
- *A*—have many favorable investment qualities and are considered high medium-grade bonds.
- *Baa*—Lower medium-grade bonds.

There are lower ratings for both stocks and bonds, but those above are the only ones the average investor should consider.

See also *Standard and Poor's bond ratings;* Section II, "Investments."

mortgage   a legal document pledging property as security for a debt. *Real estate mortgages* are used to finance homes and other real property purchases, while *chattel mortgages* are used to finance the purchase of personal property.

See also *chattel mortgage; real estate mortgage;* Section II, "Home Financing."

mortgage-backed securities   See *Federal Home Loan Mortgage Corporation (Freddie Mac); Federal National Mortgage Association (Fannie Mae); Government National Mortgage Association (Ginnie Mae).*

mortgagee   the lender who makes a loan secured by a mortgage.

See also *mortgage; mortgagor.*

mortgage life insurance   decreasing term insurance written against the life of the principal breadwinner to cover the balance due on a mortgage loan.

Consumer tip: People buying homes are setups to be sold storm windows, swimming pools, and mortgage life insurance. Mortgage life is an expensive addition to a life insurance plan. It is far better to protect the family against any outstanding debt by writing a simple term policy, that is, if extra insurance is needed at all.

See also Section II, "Life Insurance."

mortgage loan   a loan secured by a mortgage.

Also see *chattel mortgage; real estate mortgage;* Section II, "Home Financing."

mortgagor   a debtor whose loan is secured by a mortgage. To avoid getting mortgagee and mortgagor mixed up, it helps to remember that mortgagor has an "o" in it because he or she "owes" the money.

See also *mortgage; mortgagee;* Section II, "Home Financing."

MSE   the Montreal Stock Exchange.

See also *stock exchange.*

municipal bond   also *municipals.* See *bond.*

mutual association   a savings and loan association owned by its depositors.

See also *bank.*

mutual fund   an *open-end investment trust* in which investors' money is pooled to buy common stocks, bonds, or other investment vehicles. The open-end feature means that people may invest more or liquidate their investment in it at any time at the going market rate. Mutual funds are set up to meet specific investment goals. Some specialize in tax-free investments, some seek growth, some look for high current income, and some, called *mixed funds,* seek growth plus income. Most mutual funds are common stock funds. Many are managed by investment groups with several funds available, which makes switching from fund to fund easy for the investor.

In addition to being classified by investment objective, funds also break down into *load*, *low-load*, and *no-load* funds. On load funds, a transaction charge is made, usually on the purchase. This may be as little as 3 percent, but is more commonly 6 or 8 percent. All funds charge a management fee, ranging from a modest .5 percent per year of total assets to 1.5 percent. Funds offer the safety of diversity and reduce the expense of brokerage fees.

Consumer tip: Mutual funds offer small investors an excellent way to make market investments. With very few exceptions, the investor should always choose no-load funds; they have just about as good earnings records as the load funds and save a great deal in fees.

Especially interesting are some of the new retirement funds restricted to Individual Retirement Account (IRA) or Keogh Plan investors, which specialize in seeking short-term capital gains investment opportunities that most funds overlook. Since the investments are tax-deferred, you gain the advantage of a fast-moving short-term investment situation without a tax burden.

See also *load; low-load; money market mutual fund; no-load;* Section II, "Investments."

mutual savings bank   See *bank*.

mutual will   See *will*.

NASD See *National Association of Securities Dealers.*

NASDAQ See *National Association of Securities Dealers Automated Quotations.*

National Association of Securities Dealers (NASD) the organization of brokers that, by federal law, self-polices the over-the-counter securities market.
See also *over-the-counter stock.*

National Association of Securities Dealers Automated Quotations (NASDAQ) a computerized system of trading over-the-counter (OTC) stocks. Years ago, trading in OTC stocks was cumbersome, which meant that investors faced certain additional risks because of possible delays. With automation, NASDAQ has a system that is the envy of every conventional exchange, and OTC stocks

have been opened up to many more investors.
See also *over-the-counter stock;* Section II, "Investments."

national bank See *bank.*

National Credit Union Administration (NCUA) the federal agency that charters, supervises, and insures all federal credit unions and state credit unions that are members. The NCUA insurance coverage and regulatory authority is similar to that which the Federal Deposit Insurance Corporation (FDIC) exercises over commercial banks.
See also *Federal Deposit Insurance Corporation (FDIC); Federal Savings and Loan Insurance Corporation (FSLIC).*

national debt the debt incurred by the federal government to cover its operating deficits. In 1910, the national debt amounted to $12.41 for every man, woman, and child in America; by 1982, the figure had risen to $4,909.87 per person, for a total of $1,142,035,000,000.

national income the total income received by all Americans over a one-year period.

nationalization takeover of property by a national government with or without compensation to the owners. The danger of nationalization of industries is a factor that keeps many people from investing in companies that do much business in countries where a takeover is a possibility.

negative income tax an alternative system of public welfare that would require the filing of tax forms by everyone. Under this system, the Internal Revenue Service would make cash distributions, instead of collections, to those below a certain level. The negative income tax has been proposed from time to time by various politicians, but has never won widespread approval.

negligence legally, failure to do what a reasonably prudent person would do; or the reverse, doing what no reasonably prudent person would do. Negligence is a factor in many civil lawsuits.

See also *contributory negligence; prudent-man rule.*

negotiable a term that describes property, the ownership of which may be transferred from one person to another.

negotiable instrument commonly, a check, trade acceptance, sight draft, or promissory note that must, as defined by the Uniform Negotiable Instruments Act, ". . . conform to the following requirements: (a) be in writing and signed by the maker or drawer; (b) contain an unconditional promise or order to pay a certain sum in money; (c) be payable on demand, or at a fixed or determinable future time; (d) be payable to order or to bearer; and (e) where the instrument is addressed to a drawee, he must be named or otherwise indicated therein with reasonable certainty."

See also *check; draft; drawee; promissory note; trade acceptance.*

negotiable order of withdrawal (NOW) originally, a sight draft drawn on a commercial bank through a savings bank. Now, a check drawn on a special type of savings account called a NOW account.

See also *NOW account.*

nest egg money saved as a nucleus around which, it is hoped, other savings will grow by additional deposits and earned interest.

See also Section II, "Savings."

net money remaining after certain deductions have been made.

net assets the property owned by an individual, family, business, or estate after all debts have been paid.

net-asset value the amount each shareholder in a mutual fund would receive if its assets were sold, its bills were paid, and the remainder were divided equally on a per-share basis. Mutual funds compute this figure at least daily, and many more often than that. For a no-load fund, the net-asset value is the price at which shares are bought and sold; for a load fund, a commission charge is added.

See also *load; mutual fund; no-load; offering price*.

net balance the payoff balance; the amount due on a loan or bill after all refunds have been deducted.

Consumer tip: When paying off a loan in advance, it's always a good idea to ask for the net balance and pay that amount. You may get a rebate of any overpayment of interest, but, then again, you may not. It's best to be sure by taking the refund off at your end.

See also Section II, "Debt Management."

net capital assets less liabilities less any assets that cannot be quickly converted into cash at their full value; net worth less illiquid assets. In other words, net capital is the cash that could be easily raised if all assets were quickly liquidated and all debts paid.

See also *illiquid asset*.

net cost the actual cost of a good or service, calculated by taking the price and deducting any earnings produced by the property. Thus, the net cost of an insurance policy, for example, would be the premium total less all dividends paid.

net earnings gross earnings less gross operating expenses (*operating earnings before taxes*) less taxes. This figure is of special interest to stock mar-

ket investors. Comparisons with previous years' earnings can show important trends.

net estate the value of an estate after all obligations and administrative expenses have been deducted.

net income profit after all costs and expenses have been paid and allowances for depreciation and possible losses have been set aside.

See also *net profit*.

net income after dividends net income less declared dividends on common stock and dividends due on preferred stock.

See also *net income*.

net loss loss remaining in a certain time period if expenses during the period exceed income received.

net price the price after all discounts.

net profit profit during a certain time period after deducting all expenses; the gross profit less sales, administrative, and other costs, but before taxes. Net profit after taxes is the final income figure. Net profit (before taxes) is the figure that is usually shown on corporate profit and loss statements.

See also *gross profit*.

net sales gross sales less returns and allowances during a specific time period.

net surplus profit left after deducting all operating expenses, taxes, and dividends.

net worth total assets less total liabilities.

See also *accounting*; Section II, "Family Accounting."

net yield the profit or loss from an investment, calculated by deducting all costs from all income.

new high the new all-time high price of a security.

new issue a stock or bond offered by a corporation for the first time. Money raised by new issues may be used to expand production facilities or to retire old debts.

New York Stock Exchange (NYSE) See *stock exchange*.

next of kin a person next in blood relationship to another person. The next of kin inherit the property of a person who has died without a will, and distribution is determined by state law.

night depository a vault inside a bank building with locked access from the outside through which certain customers may make deposits at any time. Merchants apply for special keys that open a door in the vault through which they may drop special locked deposit bags of cash and checks. Many night depositories also feature an unlocked envelope drop through which any customer may make deposits. Bank personnel prove the deposits on the next business day and either mail the customers receipts or give them to them when they come in if they are regular visitors to the bank.

Consumer tip: Most bank depositors are unaware of the small envelope slot in many night deposit vaults. Ask if your bank has one, and, if it does, use it. It is cheaper, safer, and faster than making deposits through the mail. Also, it is the only safe way to deposit cash during nonbanking hours, since the mails should never be used in this way.

See also Section II, "Bank Accounts."

NINOW See *noninterest-paying NOW account.*

no account a common reason for a bank to return a check to the last holder in due course. It means just what the term says—the person writing the check has no account with the bank. To write such a check is a crime.

See also *holder in due course; insufficient funds.*

no funds a common reason for a bank to return a check to the last holder in due course. It means that the maker of the check has no funds left in his or her account at all.

See also *holder in due course; insufficient funds.*

no-limit order an order to buy or sell a stock with no limitation on price.

no-load the absence of a charge to cover the sales commission at the time a securities transaction is made, especially one involving mutual funds. Unfortunately, more and more mutual funds are charging such fees, though they vary widely, ranging from 3 to 8 percent.

See also *load; low-load; mutual fund;* Section II, "Investments."

nominal asset any asset of questionable value. Nominal assets are often carried on the books with a "nominal" value of $1.

nonassessable stock securities, the owners of which cannot be assessed for additional payments should the company become insolvent. Almost all stock is nonassessable.

noncompetitive tender an offer to the Federal Reserve Bank to buy Treasury securities directly, at the average price offered by those who bid on the issues. Treasury securities are sold at auctions by the Federal Reserve, with huge institutional investors bidding millions of dollars. A small investor may not be in a position to bid, but may make a noncompetitive tender or offer to buy at the going price. This is usually done through his or her bank or broker, but a service charge may be saved if buying is done directly through the nearest Federal Reserve Bank.

noncontributory policy a group insurance policy on which the employee pays all of the premiums, with no share being paid by the employer.

nonconvertible preferred stock See *stock, preferred.*

noncumulative preferred stock See *stock, prefered.*

nonforfeiture provisions the options under a cash-reserve or ordinary life insurance policy that exist when the policyholder fails to pay a premium and after sufficient reserves have built up. They include surrender for cash value; a loan for the cash value; purchase of a paid-up policy for the amount that the cash value, as a single premium, will buy; and purchase of term insurance for the face value of the original policy for as long as the cash value will pay the premiums.

Too often, the consumer has these options in name only—they're written in the fine print that no one reads. The rule at many insurance companies seems to be, "Never give back the money!" Almost one-quarter of all ordinary life policies written in the United States are lapsed (cancelled) within two years, a primary reason being that the policyholder was oversold and cannot afford the payments. In such cases, the consumer may really need whatever money he or she can get back, but all too often the cash value is used to buy extended term coverage.

Consumer tip: If you must lapse a policy and need the coverage while you get reestablished, ask the agent to buy extended term with the cash reserves. But if you really need the cash, demand it. And don't be surprised if the cash value isn't nearly as much as you had hoped for.

See also *life insurance;* Section II, "Life Insurance."

noninterest loan a loan on which the borrower doesn't pay any interest. This is usually a private loan between family or friends.

noninterest-paying NOW account (NINOW) a NOW account that pays no interest. They are no longer used because the passage of the Depository Institutions Deregulation and Monetary Control Act of 1980

121

made interest-paying NOW accounts legal in every state.

nonmember bank a state-chartered bank that is not a member of the Federal Reserve System. Non-membership in the Federal Reserve is chosen for various reasons and is in no way a reflection of the stability of a bank.

nonmember firm a brokerage firm that is not a member of a stock exchange.

nonpar check also *no-par item;* a check that cannot be collected at face value. All checks drawn on banks that are members of the Federal Reserve System or clear checks through that system must pay their checks at *par*, or face value. However, in a very few rural regions of the United States, some small banks make a small collection fee against each check they pay for their depositors.

All checks bear American Bankers Association (ABA) transit numbers and most bear Federal Reserve routing symbols. The number appears on the face of the check and is printed as a fraction. The bottom number is the Federal Reserve routing symbol. All checks with such a bottom number are payable at par because that number indicates that they can clear through the Federal Reserve.

Also see *check*.

nonpar life insurance See *nonparticipating life insurance*.

nonparticipating life insurance also *nonpar life insurance;* ordinary life insurance that does not participate in

dividend distributions. Nonpar policies are usually issued by stockholder-owned insurance companies, whereas participating policies are issued mainly by mutual companies. The initial premium cost on nonparticipating policies is lower than on participating ones, but dividends usually lower the cost on participating policies substantially so that they may be less costly in the long run.

See also *ordinary life; participating life insurance;* Section II, "Life Insurance."

nonpayment failure to pay on time and in full.

nonperformance failure to live up to a contractual obligation.

nonprofit corporation an organization designed for social, religious, or community service rather than for profit. Such organizations are often incorporated to enable them to take advantage of the legal benefits granted to corporations, especially the right to make contracts.

nontaxable income income not subject to taxation. The most common use of the term applies to federal tax exemption of income from bonds issued by state and local governments. Because of the separation of powers under the Constitution, income paid by such bonds is nontaxable by the federal government.

Consumer tip: As a general rule, it pays to invest in municipal securities if your marginal tax bracket is 35 percent or higher.

See also *bond; tax-free income;* Section II, "Money Math," "Tax Savings."

no-par item See *nonpar check.*

no-par-value stock common stock with no designated face value. Much stock is of the no-par variety, which makes little difference for ordinary investment purposes.

See also *book value;* Section II, "Investments."

no-passbook savings account
also *statement savings account;* a savings account that operates under the same rules and interest regulations as a passbook account, but for which a periodic (usually quarterly) statement of account is issued instead of the traditional passbook.

See also *passbook savings account.*

notary public a minor public official with a state commission to administer certain oaths and to certify documents.

Consumer tip: In some states, it is customary for some bank officers to be notaries public. They perform their duties as a bank service at no charge. Should you need a document notarized, ask your banker first; it may save you a fee.

note the written, legal evidence of a debt. A note is a negotiable instrument, signed by the maker, bearing a date on which a certain sum of money is due and specifying where and to whom it is due. The rights under a note may be transferred to another person.

See also *negotiable instrument;* Section II, "Borrowing."

note notice a reminder of a payment soon coming due that is sent to a borrower by his or her bank.

note payable a loan payable to a person, firm, or bank.

note receivable a loan payment due from a person or business.

notice of dishonor also *protest;* a written statement asserting that a check has been returned for a reason that indicates an inability to repay (obviously, not for a missing endorsement). A check is usually dishonored when it is for a large amount, has been unsuccessfully presented for payment one or more times through normal channels, and when the person holding the check intends to take legal action against the person who issued it and is seeking evidence to bolster his or her case. The check may be protested by having a notary public present it for collection, and, should payment be refused, having him or her issue the notice of dishonor or *protest.*

Consumer tip: Having a check protested is a serious business. In every state, it is a criminal offense to issue a check with no funds or insufficient funds to cover it. If you do issue a bad check, try to make it good as soon as you learn that it has been returned; if you get a bad check for a large enough amount, ask your banker about a protest.

notice of withdrawal notification by a customer to a financial institution that he or she intends to withdraw funds from a savings account. Under the law, banks may require such notice, except for certificates of deposit, which, of course, have maturity dates. However, the rule is seldom applied.

Consumer tip: If your bank asks for

notice of withdrawal from a passbook savings account, look for another bank. This may indicate that the bank is having liquidity problems.

notice to creditors   the posting of legal notification to creditors, usually through newspaper ads, stating that the settlement of an estate is about to begin and that any creditors should present their claims to the executor or administrator of the estate.

not sufficient funds (NSF)   See *insufficient funds*.

NOW   See *negotiable order of withdrawal*.

NOW account   technically, a savings account from which withdrawals can be made with a type of sight draft called a *negotiable order of withdrawal*. This is strictly a legalism to avoid the sanctions of the Banking Act of 1933, which stipulated that interest could not be paid on checking accounts.

NOW accounts look and work like interest-paying checking accounts, and NOW drafts look and work exactly like checks. Interest, which was set by law at 5.25 percent under Federal Reserve Regulation Q, will, by Congressional direction, be unregulated by 1986.

Consumer tip: Be sure to use a NOW account; it's a good way to make *float* work for you. Usually, you should keep a balance in the account that is just enough to cover your outstanding checks and to pay any service charges, investing the difference between your balance and the bank's required minimum in a higher-paying account.

See also *negotiable order of withdrawal*

(NOW); Section II, "Bank Accounts," "Cash Management."

NSF   not sufficient funds. See also *insufficient funds*.

numismatics   collecting money, especially coins, for its value as a collectible. Coin collecting is a good hobby if certain rules are followed. The collector should:

1. Try to buy silver or gold coins when bullion prices are low.

2. Collect as many items as possible at no premium charge by checking his or her pocket change or coins received from banks and stores. An interested person should buy a coin collector's guidebook to see what has value.

3. Learn the different grades of coins—they will be described in that same guidebook—and then try to save only quality coins.

4. Also think in terms of percentage return. For example, pre-1953 pennies bore a wreath on the reverse side. These pennies, millions of which are still in circulation, are sold for a minimum of 2 cents each by dealers. If you find one, that could be a 100 percent profit. Pre-1981 pennies were pure copper; as the new, cheap alloy coins replace them, they too will be worth a premium.

nuncupative will   an oral will spoken before witnesses that is later written down.

See also *will*; Section II, "Estate Planning."

NYSE   New York Stock Exchange. See also *stock exchange*.

NYSE Common Stock Index a composite index based on all common stocks listed on the New York Stock Exchange. Like the Dow Jones Averages, it is a valuable tool for stock-market watchers. The NYSE index is based on every stock listed on the exchange, whereas the Dow is based on a small percentage of those listed. See also *Dow Jones Averages*.

OASI   See *old age and survivors insurance*.

obligation   the legal responsibility to pay a debt when due.

obverse   the front of a bill, coin, or note.

odd lot   See *lot*.

odd-lot dealer   a member firm of an exchange that deals in odd lots for other brokers.

offer   the asked price; the price at which a person is willing to sell a stock. See also *bid and asked price*.

offering   an issue of stocks or bonds placed on public sale.

offering price   the price at which new issues of stock are placed on sale. It is usually the net-asset value per share plus underwriting fees and the sales commission.
See also *net-asset value*.

official check   a check issued by a bank. At a state-chartered bank, this is called a *treasurer's check;* at a national bank, it is called a *cashier's check*. Many banks will provide a depositor with an occasional official check at little or no charge for special uses.
Consumer tip: If you have an obligation that must be paid with an official check or money order, try for an official check first. Chances are, it's the less expensive route to go. But remember, it's the bank's check, not yours, so you won't get it back after it's paid. Make a photocopy of it before you send it, so that, in case of any mixup, you'll have proof that it was issued and when.
See also *money order*.

off-line   a computer system that processes previously collected data. An *on-line* computer posts each transaction as it is made.

See also *on-line.*

old age and survivors insurance (OASI) Social Security basic benefits, excluding Medicare and disability coverage.

See also *Social Security;* Section II, "Retirement Planning."

Old Lady of Threadneedle Street slang for the Bank of England.

oligopoly an industry in which a small number of firms supply all of a certain good or service. An example is the automobile industry. In an oligopoly, there are many buyers and few sellers, which means that sellers have an advantage in setting prices.

oligopsony the opposite of oligopoly; a situation in which there are many sellers but few buyers, which means that buyers have the advantage in setting prices.

See also *oligopoly.*

on account a partial payment to reduce a debt.

one-bank holding company See *holding company.*

one-stop banking full-service banking; being able to do all of one's banking business with one bank.

on-line a computer system in which transactions are posted to a customer's account as they are made. Many banks now have their teller stations on line,

so that, when a customer makes a deposit or a withdrawal, it is instantly credited or deducted.

Many banks hope to eventually have point-of-sale (POS) on-line terminals in most retail establishments so that debit cards will be able to access customers' accounts to pay for purchases at once.

See also *debit card.*

on-us check a check drawn on the bank where it is presented for collection. If there are adequate collected funds in the account on which the check is drawn, it may be cashed on the spot or deposited for immediate credit.

open-end credit also *revolving credit;* a loan agreement under which a lender establishes a maximum amount the borrower may draw upon. Each time the borrower makes a payment, he or she then may borrow any amount up to the difference between the amount owed and the credit limit. Bank credit card or automatic overdraft checking accounts are both examples of open-end credit.

See also *overdraft checking account.*

open-end fund a mutual fund that issues new shares as new capital is received or redeems shares for investors at their net-asset value. The vast majority of mutual funds are open-end.

See also *closed-end fund; net-asset value.*

open-end investment trust See *mutual fund.*

open-end mortgage a type of mortgage agreement, written in some states, that allows the borrower to re-borrow money paid against the principal without the filing of new papers.

Consumer tip: If possible, choose an open-end mortgage because it makes later refinancing much easier and less costly. Open-end mortgages are especially useful for home repairs or modernization, or even for tapping your equity for educational or other expenses.

opening price the price at which the first transaction of a stock or bond takes place on a given day.

open mortgage a mortgage with no *prepayment penalty clause.* This means that such loans may be paid off at any time prior to maturity without a prepayment fee.

operating earnings before taxes
See *net earnings.*

opportunity cost the extra cost of a good or service computed on the basis of a lost investment opportunity. Thus, for example, if a new car sells for $10,000, the opportunity cost might be stated as $1,067 per year because, had that $10,000 been invested instead at 10 percent interest compounded daily, it could have earned $1,067. Or if a person financed a car with payments of $200 a month for four years, the opportunity cost in terms of interest lost would total $1,887.90, because $200 a month at 10 percent compounded daily would have earned that amount in four years.

Consumer tip: Figuring opportunity cost on necessities is a waste of time; no one wants to be a recluse living without a car, clothes, or any form of

entertainment. But in some cases, it makes good sense to figure it out. Figuring in the opportunity cost on luxuries is always smart; that $2,000 stereo, for example, doesn't cost just $2,000—it also costs the potential income that $2,000 could have earned if it had been wisely invested.

See also Section II, "Money Mistakes."

option a privilege to buy or sell property. In investment terms, options exist in three main cases:

1. *Real estate.* If an owner is having trouble selling, he or she may be willing to rent with an option to buy, for which there may or may not be a charge. In turn, from the renter's viewpoint, it is hoped that all or part of the rental payments will, under the option agreement, be applied to the purchase price. This is one kind of creative financing that makes good sense.

2. *Commodities.* Commodity options are of two types, calls and puts, which are sold on commodity futures. Under a *call option,* the investor buys the right to purchase a contracted amount of the commodity at a certain price on a certain date. If the commodity goes up in price, he or she may sell the option contract and pocket the profit; there is no need to buy the actual product. If the commodity goes down in price, the investor loses all or part of the cost of the option. Under a *put option,* the investor buys the right to sell a contracted amount of a commodity at a certain price on a certain date. If the commodity goes down in price, the investor sells the option contract and gets his or her profit; if the commodity goes up in price, he or she may lose all

or part of the cost of the option contract. Commodity options are perhaps the most speculative of all investments.

3. *Stocks.* Options on some common stocks are available through any broker and are traded on several exchanges. Like commodity options, they are sold as call or put options. There are also mutual funds that specialize in investments in stocks on which options are traded. In addition to dividends, mutual funds make considerable amounts of money on premiums from expired option contracts.

See also *calls; commodities; puts;* Section II, "Investments."

oral will   See *will.*

ordinary income   for tax purposes, income that does not include long-term capital gains. Short-term capital gains are taxed as ordinary income.

See also *capital gains.*

ordinary life   also *whole life; straight life; cash-reserve insurance; cash-value insurance; permanent insurance; level-premium insurance;* a life insurance policy that continues in force as long as premiums are paid and the insured person lives. Premiums are the same throughout the life of the policy. There are many variations of ordinary life, including executive life, life paid up 65, 10-payment life, and 20-payment life.

The theory life insurance companies use to explain ordinary life is that higher premiums are charged than are necessary during the early years so that a cash reserve is built up that will keep premiums level during later years. Other experts point out that this accruing cash reserve becomes part of the possible death benefit, and that the insurance portion of the death benefit is actually reduced by being augmented with savings—which usually earn at a very low rate. In this sense, they argue, ordinary life is simply an expensive version of decreasing term, similar to mortgage insurance, with an inferior savings plan tacked on.

Ordinary life is sold vigorously by almost all insurance companies and accounts for about 75 percent of all insurance purchased by · individuals. When sold by mutual companies, it is usually sold as *participating*, which means that it pays "dividends"; when sold by stock companies, it is usually, but not always, *nonparticipating*, in that it earns no "dividends." Hence, participating policies usually have a higher initial cost, but the "dividends" reduce that cost to the point where they are often lower than the rates for nonparticipating policies. Incidentally, insurance "dividends" are nontaxable; the IRS views them not as earnings but as refunds of premium overcharges, hence the quotation marks around the word as used in this paragraph.

Consumer tip: Ordinary has a limited place in your insurance portfolio. It is a good idea to have enough in ordinary life to cover final illness and burial expenses, but to buy remaining insurance as term. Then, as your needs change, you can add to or delete the term coverage. If you invest the difference in cost between ordinary and term, you'll come out way ahead. And when the insurance salesperson asks, "But what will you do when you're 75 and you can't renew the term?" say, "I'll have burial insurance in my small amount of ordinary life, and my earnings on the savings will have taken away the need for any other insurance."

See also *life insurance; limited-payment life; term life insurance;* Section II, "Life Insurance."

origination fee   a charge made by a mortgage lender for processing a mortgage loan.

See also *closing costs;* Section II, "Home Financing."

orphan's court   See *probate court.*

OTC stock   See *over-the-counter stock.*

out of the money   a term relating to stock options in which the *striking price*, the price at which the option takes effect, is higher than the current market price for a call option and below the current market price for a put option. When an option is out of the money, it is the time to buy it because the goal for which the option would be purchased has not been reached.

See also *calls; in the money; option; puts.*

outstanding   1) an unpaid debt; 2) in the stock market, stock that has been issued by a corporation and sold to investors.

overdraft   a check for which there are insufficient funds on deposit but that is still honored and paid by the bank. Banks have no obligation to overdraw an account; in fact, they usually mark the check "NSF" and return it to the last holder in due course. However, for very valued customers, banks will often honor overdrafts and simply notify the customer to make a covering deposit. Banks usually charge an overdraft fee to cover their book-keeping costs.

Consumer tip: An occasional over-draft is not serious, but a number of them can reflect negatively on your credit rating. If you are careless, or often short of ready cash, open an overdraft account rather than risk un-authorized overdrafts or returned checks.

See also *insufficient funds; overdraft checking account; returned check.*

overdraft checking account also *automatic overdraft account;* a line of credit extended by a bank that au-tomatically covers any checks drawn for which there are insufficient funds on deposit. Thus, to create a loan, the customer simply writes checks for more than he or she has on deposit and overdrafts are automatically covered by that loan balance. Often, overdraft checking account privileges are in-cluded in the line of credit extended for a bank credit card. In this case, the amount of the overdraft is charged to the credit-card account.

Consumer tip: An overdraft account, if not used carelessly, is a great safety net. With it, you can write checks right up to your credit limit, and that means emegency funds are on tap at any time. Do beware of using an overdraft ac-count for everyday purchases; you not only pay a lot more because of the in-terest charges, but also deplete your emergency reserve as well.

See also *check;* Section II, "Bank Ac-counts."

overdraw   to write a check against insufficient funds and thus draw into a nonexistent balance.

See also *insufficient funds.*

overextended   loan balances that are beyond the borrower's ability to repay.

· **over-the-counter stock**   also *OTC stock;* securities not listed or traded on a stock exchange, but bought and sold through dealers who specialize (make a market) in such stocks. With automation, over-the-counter stocks are traded as readily as those listed on exchanges.

Consumer tip: The more speculative stocks tend to be traded over-the-counter, but so are many excellent issues. The OTC market offers many good investment opportunities and should not be overlooked.

See also *National Association of Securities Dealers Automated Quotations (NASDAQ);* Section II, "Investments."

owner financing   a method of real estate financing wherein the seller either assumes the entire mortgage or a second mortgage for a portion of the debt. Owner financing is especially common in land purchases because many banks and other lenders tend to shy away from straight land deals.

Consumer tip: If you're a buyer, owner financing is fine if your rate is as low or lower than that charged at a bank and if the total payments are not so high that you can't comfortably make them. If you're a seller, you should realize that if the loan goes sour you might get hurt, and badly. Assume the mortgage yourself only as a last recourse, unless you have sufficient means so that a loss won't hurt you too much.

See also *creative financing;* Section II, "Home Financing."

P

Pacific Stock Exchange (PSE)
See *stock exchange*.

paid check 1) a check that has been charged against the account of its maker; 2) a legal receipt for paid obligations.

paid-up additions a dividend option of ordinary life insurance under which the policyholder may elect to have his or her dividends purchase additional ordinary life insurance. There are no recurring premiums charged for this insurance, and, because the underwriting has been done on the base policy and because there are no sales charges, the rates are low. By selecting this option, the policyholder can substantially add to the death benefit over the years. Both insurance dividends and death benefits are tax-free, as long as the benefits go to a named beneficiary. By choosing the paid-up additions option, the policyholder can get a very attractive and legal tax-free pyramid scheme, because the paid-up additions also earn dividends, so the long-term profit potential is attractive.

Consumer tip: Allowing the dividends from your ordinary life policy to buy paid-up insurance is a great advantage in some cases. Younger people who need maximum protection should usually opt for additional one-year term insurance; but if you can afford it, paid-up ordinary additions add substantially to your eventual death benefits with a totally nontaxable asset, since insurance proceeds are not subject to estate taxes if there is a named beneficiary.

See also *dividend options;* Section II, "Life Insurance."

paid-up insurance a life insurance policy on which all premiums have been paid. A policy may be paid up when a consumer buys a one-premium policy. Although this is very rare, it can be done when a person wants to take advantage of a financial windfall.

palimony   See *alimony.*

P&L statement   profit and loss statement.
See also *income and expense statement.*

panic   a sudden and often irrational fear of the collapse of all or part of the economy. A panic may lead to a mass attempt to convert assets into cash, which can cause huge losses in the stock market and runs on banks.

paper hanger   slang for a person who passes forged or worthless checks; usually, a professional criminal who makes a very lucrative business of paper hanging.

paper profit or loss   capital gains that have not actually been received, resulting from an increase in the price over what the investor paid for the property or security. Paper profits are worth only the paper they're written on—until the property or security is resold for the higher price.
See also *capital gains.*

par   1) face value; 2) an abbreviated term for participating life insurance.
See also *nonpar check; par value.*

par item   a check that is payable at face value.
See also *nonpar check.*

participating life insurance   a life insurance policy under which the policyholder is entitled to dividends. These dividends are not based on investment earnings, but are a partial refund of the premium based on the difference between the company's income and cost of operations. The IRS holds that dividends are a refund of excess premiums; because they aren't technically earnings, they are not taxable. All mutual insurance companies issue participating policies as do some stock companies.
Consumer tip: In general, the net cost of insurance tends to be less with participating policies than with nonparticipating. The lowest cost of all may be realized by buying term insurance and putting the difference in cost between that and ordinary life in a higher-yielding investment.
See also *nonparticipating life insurance; ordinary life;* Section II, "Life Insurance."

participating preferred stock
See *stock, preferred.*

participation certificate   See *pass-through certificate.*

part payment   a fractional payment of a total obligation, often made to show good faith toward paying the entire debt.

par value   *face value;* 1) the principal amount of a legal instrument, such as a check, note, or bond; 2) the stated value of a stock on its date of issue. The par value of a stock is completely unrelated to its market value.

passbook   a booklet issued by a bank in which a record of deposits, withdrawals, and additions of savings interest is kept.

passbook loan   a loan for which a savings account is pledged as collateral. In years past, interest was posted only periodically, so passbook loans were made to allow the customer's interest to continue accruing until that posting. Now, computers post interest on a daily basis, so passbook loans are much less common. The interest rate charged is very low because the loan is secured by cash in the bank.

Consumer tip: If you find saving money difficult, consider a passbook loan rather than a savings withdrawal. While you may not repay yourself, you will repay the bank. On the other hand, if you can discipline yourself to save, make a withdrawal rather than a loan, then rebuild your balance with regular deposits. You'll come out ahead this way.

See also Section II, "Borrowing."

passbook savings account also *regular savings account;* a savings account for which the customer's copy of the records of transactions made is kept in a passbook. With automation, more and more banks are switching their regular accounts to *no-passbook savings,* in which a computerized statement is issued to the customer periodically, usually quarterly. Passbook accounts technically require a possible 30 days' notice for withdrawals; but, as a practical matter, no bank has enforced this rule since the Great Depression.

Regular savings are among the last to still have regulated rates, but under Congressional orders, these regulations must be phased out by 1986.

Passbook accounts pay the lowest savings rates and are therefore mainly useful for accumulation rather than for earnings. Despite this, it is not unusual for banks, especially the smaller thrift institutions, to have as much as 50 percent of their deposit base in passbook accounts.

Consumer tip: Use a passbook account as a place to allow regular deposits to build into a worthwhile balance; but as soon as a reasonable level is reached (perhaps $1,000), switch that amount to a high-yield CD or money market mutual fund or enjoy whatever you saved for. Then start building up the passbook balance again.

See also Section II, "Savings."

passing papers closing a mortgage loan; a term for the actual mortgage settlement, at which time the buyer receives the deed to the property and the mortgage loan is issued. The word "passing" is appropriate because there is, indeed, a great passing back and forth of papers.

See also *closing.*

pass-through certificate a bond issued by the Government National Mortgage Association (Ginnie Mae). It is termed "pass-through" because both principal and interest payments are made monthly to investors. Federal Home Loan Mortgage Corporation (Freddie Mac) and Federal National Mortgage Association (Fannie Mae) securities are *participation certificates* for which regular principal repayments are not guaranteed, although ultimate payment is.

See also *Federal Home Loan Mortgage Corporation (Freddie Mac); Federal National Mortgage Association (Fannie Mae); Government National Mortgage Association (Ginnie Mae).*

past due also *due and unpaid;* a loan payment, full or partial, not made on the specified date is said to be past due.

See also *delinquency.*

pay-by-phone a bank service through which depositors may, over the telephone, instruct their bank to pay their bills. Pay-by-phone has worked well in some parts of the country and has failed in others. As postal rates have risen, it has often become cheaper to use pay-by-phone than the mail. But there is something of a psychological barrier to phone payment. Many people like the satisfaction of writing checks and putting them in the mail. As time goes by, pay-by-phone will undoubtedly be replaced by computerized bank-at-home systems.

Consumer tip: Investigate pay-by-phone if it is offered in your area. It is a way to get bills paid on time, regardless of weather conditions or transportation problems. Check the cost versus the cost of mailing checks before you sign up.

See also *home banking.*

payee the person, company, or organization to whom a check, note, or other instrument is payable. The payee's name follows "Pay to the order of" on the instrument.

See also *payer.*

payer also *maker;* the person, company, or organization who must pay a check, note, or other instrument. The payer is the person who signs the instrument.

See also *payee.*

paying bank the bank at which a check is payable.

payroll savings plan any of various plans whereby employees may instruct an employer to deduct a certain amount from each paycheck to go into savings. In some companies, management matches all or part of the employee's deposits as an incentive to save. The bond-a-month plan is a savings plan in which U.S. Savings Bonds are purchased; the mutual fund payroll deduction plan makes investments in stock funds chosen by the employee; the traditional payroll savings plan allows an employee to make deposits in a bank or thrift institution.

See also Section II, "Savings."

P/E See *price-earnings ratio.*

pegging setting the price of something by manipulating the market. Thus, the price of wheat may be stabilized by the government's buying of enough to control the price.

penalty clause a clause in a certificate of deposit specifying that "substantial penalties may be imposed for early withdrawal." These penalties are set by federal regulation at loss of one month's interest for early withdrawal of CDs with a maturity of one year or less and three months' interest for CDs with a maturity of over one year. There is also a clause in installment-loan agreements that allows late penalties to be assessed for payments not made on time.

Consumer tip: Penalties for early withdrawal of CD savings and loan late charges are both deductible from federally-taxed income on Form 1040. In general, it pays to cash in a CD early and take the penalty if the yearly interest rate for your new investment is 2 percent or more higher than that of the CD and if the CD has six or more months to go before it matures. Ask your banker to compute the exact costs and advantages before you act.

See also *late-payment penalty.*

penny stock   generally, a speculative stock selling for less than $3 or so a share. The key word here is "speculative," since some nonspeculative stocks also sell for low prices. There is widespread interest in penny stocks, and, especially in the Far West, many brokers are making markets in them. They are sold over-the-counter and are not listed on the National Association of Securities Dealers Automated Quotations (NASDAQ).

Buying penny stocks is a comparable investment to playing the horses; it is a gamble, pure and simple. Best-selling weekly papers feature articles and ads about these low-priced stocks.

Consumer tip: A survey conducted in 1983 by *Venture* magazine indicated that as many as 45 percent of issues of penny stocks were tainted with real or potential fraud. Because of this and because they are highly speculative, penny stocks, as a rule, are very risky. If you wish to deal in low-priced issues, fine; there are many good reasons for doing so. For one thing, when the market goes up, the low-priced stocks often have disproportionate price increases; for another, by buying low-priced stocks in round lots, you can save money. But there are excellent low-priced stocks listed on the American Stock Exchange and even a few on the New York Stock Exchange. Investigate these before you buy penny stocks. Or, if you must buy penny stocks, look on it as a day at the races—and be prepared to lose.

See also Section II, "Investments."

pension   a sum received by a person who has retired from a company or organization. Retirement monies are accumulated in a *pension fund* and are distributed under a *pension plan*, which defines the benefits available. Unfortunately, only about one person in seven in the United States ever gets the pension he or she expects, either because the person is eventually ineligible or because the pension fund fails.

Consumer tip: Don't count on your pension or Social Security for your retirement; if you haven't done so, open an Individual Retirement Account.

See also *Pension Benefit Guaranty Corporation (PBGC); vesting;* Section II, "Retirement Planning."

Pension Benefit Guarantee Corporation (PBGC)   a federal agency established under the Employee Retirement Income Security Act (ERISA) of 1974 that insures some pension plans against loss. Only defined benefit plans (plans that promise employees certain benefits) are covered. Plans financed by union dues are not covered; neither are plans in companies with fewer than 25 employees, such as law firms, medical practices, or professional art groups.

See also *Individual Retirement Account (IRA);* Section II, "Retirement Planning."

pension fund   See *pension.*

pension plan   See *pension; Pension Benefit Guarantee Corporation (PBGC).*

per capita   per person. Thus, per-capita output is the gross national product divided by the number of people in the population; a per-capita tax is a head tax assessed on each person; per-capita expenditures are total expenses divided by the number of people in the population.

percent   per hundred.
See also Section II, "Money Math."

per diem   each day. Thus, per diem expenses refers to a flat allowance for expenses incurred on a daily basis.

perfect title   a title to real estate that is not questioned because it is complete in every way. When a perfect title exists, a *warranty deed* is used to transfer title.
Consumer tip: Never buy real estate unless you get a perfect title and a warranty deed to prove it.
See also *warranty deed*.

performance fee   a bonus paid by some mutual funds to their management groups when the earnings they achieve by wise investment policies exceed those indicated by predesignated market averages. In other words, if a fund's asset growth is 40 percent for a year and the Dow has grown 20 percent for the year, the management group may be entitled to a performance bonus. Any performance fees must be disclosed in the prospectus for the fund.

perk   short for *perquisite;* a benefit given in addition to income. This was originally a British term that is now popular in the United States. Top executives commonly receive such perks as company cars, paid membership in country clubs, special stock bonuses,

and so forth. Perks prove the adage, "Them that has, gets."

permanent life insurance   See *ordinary life*.

perquisite   See *perk*.

personal check   a check drawn by an individual as opposed to a check drawn by a business or organization.

personal income   the total income received by individuals and non-profit institutions during a given period of time. A statistical measure used by the U.S. government, personal income is calculated by taking national income and subtracting undivided profits, corporate taxes, Social Security taxes, and transfer payments received by the needy.

personal loan   See *installment loan; loan*.

personal property   nonbusiness property other than real estate.
See also *chattel; real estate*.

personal unsecured loan   See *installment loan; loan*.

petition in bankruptcy   the legal form used to declare voluntary bankruptcy.

phantom stock   an executive perk whereby the executive, at a future date, receives as a bonus the amount by which a set number of shares of stock has risen in value over a fixed time. It works like a call option except that there is no charge to the executive, and no possible loss for him or her.

Philadelphia-Baltimore-Washington Stock Exchange (PHLX)
See *stock exchange.*

Philadelphia roll   See *Michigan roll.*

PHLX   the Philadelphia-Baltimore-Washington Stock Exchange.
See also *stock exchange.*

phony dividends   dividends paid from additional stock sales rather than from earnings. This practice is illegal. Phony dividends are rarely issued for listed securities or those supervised by the Securities and Exchange Commission.
Consumer tip: Buying penny stocks or other unsupervised securities is always risky. Stick with reputable brokers and listed issues for safety.

piece rate   a sum of money paid for each item produced. This is an alternative method to an hourly wage. Sometimes a piece rate may be used as a bonus to an hourly wage.
See also *salary; wage.*

pink sheets   the papers on which were listed the price quotations on over-the-counter stocks before the introduction of the National Association of Securities Dealers Automated Quotations (NASDAQ) system.

pit   the trading area of a stock exchange; an area in the middle of the floor of the exchange.

plunger   a speculator who takes great investment risks that may result in huge profits or losses.

point   1) the unit of price used in stocks; a point equals one dollar. Also, 2) a one-time charge of 1 percent made by a lender as a condition of granting a mortgage loan. Typically, mortgage loan points range from 1 to 3 percent of the total of the loan.
Consumer tip: Points charged by a mortgagee are an extra finance charge. For this reason, it makes sense to pay them at the time of settlement with a separate check so as to have proof of payment, and then to show that amount as a tax deduction in the interest section of Schedule A, Form 1040. If you prorate them over the life of the loan, you lose this large one-time tax advantage.

point-of-sale (POS)   the physical spot at which transactions are made. There is a great deal of interest in locating bank terminals at points-of-sale in retail stores and other places where money changes hands.
See also *electronic funds transfer system (EFTS).*

policyholder   a person who owns an insurance policy. Note that in life insurance the policyholder may not be the same as the person insured.
Consumer tip: Sometimes there is an estate tax advantage to having a person other than the insured own the policy. Check with a competent tax accountant or attorney before you make this move because there can be tricky complications.
See also Section II, "Tax Savings."

policy loan   a loan from an insurance company using the cash value of a policy as collateral. A policy loan can be an excellent way to borrow, especially if the policy is an old one and the loan rates are set at 5 or 6 percent annual interest.

See also Section II, "Borrowing."

Ponzi scheme   a pyramid-type consumer fraud perpetrated by Charles Ponzi in the 1920s, in which investors were paid "earnings" based on the money received from new investors. Obviously, this is a house of cards that eventually falls—and it did.

See also *chain letter; pyramid scheme;* Secton II, "Consumer Frauds."

POS   See *point-of-sale.*

postal money order   See *money order.*

post-dated check   a check payable at a future date. Some courts have ruled that a post-dated check is not a check at all, but a promissory note until the date it bears arrives, at which time in may be handled as a check. In any event, post-dated checks are legal and may be endorsed from one person to another. A post-dated check cannot be considered invalid because there are insufficient funds on deposit to cover it; in fact, a Pennsylvania court ruled that the fact that a check is post-dated implies that there are insufficient funds until the date specified arrives.

Consumer tip: Issuing a post-dated check to show intention to pay at a future date is a common practice. Some people will accept a post-dated check because, should the date payable arrive and the check prove to be no good, they then have legal recourse against the issuer. If you are pressed to the wall by a creditor, don't issue a post-dated check—your ship might be late in coming in and you could face both civil and criminal penalties.

See also *check; stale-dated check;* Section II, "Debt Management."

power of attorney   a legal document giving authority to another to perform certain acts on behalf of the issuer. A power of attorney may be full or limited, and must be executed before a notary public. Typically, a power of attorney is given to a trusted relative or friend during the issuer's long absences or incapacity.

Consumer tip: Be extremely careful before giving anyone power of attorney. Many people have been financially ruined by "trusted friends" who emptied their bank accounts. However, using a power of attorney as an alternative to a joint account makes sense in some cases. To put certain accounts—a safe deposit box, for example—in a wife's name with the husband having power of attorney, keeps that box from being sealed pending probate in the event of the death of the husband. Ask your attorney for applicable state laws.

See also Section II, "Money Mistakes."

preemptive right   the right of a stockholder to buy new shares of stock in an equal ratio to his or her present holdings.

preferred stock   See *stock, preferred.*

premium 1) an extra charge made; also, 2) the periodic payment due for an insurance policy.

See also *insurance*.

premium loan a life insurance policy loan made to pay a premium. Many policies feature automatic policy loans that go into effect if there is sufficient cash reserve as soon as a premium goes unpaid.

prenuptial agreement also *antenuptial agreement*; a legal agreement made prior to marriage defining the property rights of each party in the event of a divorce or the death of either spouse. Prenuptial agreements are common among the very rich and in the case of a second marriage when one spouse wishes to protect the property rights of any of his or her children by a first marriage.

Consumer tip: When in doubt, put it in writing. In the event that you wish to remarry, if you're afraid that a child may not get his or her due should you die, see a lawyer about a prenuptial agreement.

prepayment clause a section in a mortgage agreement that gives the borrower the right to prepay any or all of the mortgage without incurring penalty charges.

See also *prepayment penalty clause*.

prepayment penalty clause a section in a mortgage agreement that gives the lender the right to assess a penalty should the mortgage be paid before it comes due.

Consumer tip: Don't accept a prepayment penalty clause in any mortgage you sign.

See also *open mortgage; prepayment clause;* Section II, "Home Financing."

presentation the delivery of a check or other negotiable instrument to the paying bank for payment. Presentation is normally a routine matter, with checks being handled electronically and in huge batches. The only time a formal presentation is made is when it is necessary to dishonor a check for legal reasons.

See also *notice of dishonor*.

present value also *present worth;* the discounted value of a specific amount due on a specific future date. As an example, .9091 cents will be worth $1 exactly one year from now at 10 percent interest compounded annually. So the present value of the dollar is .9091 cents. This is useful for the investor who seeks to have a certain amount by a certain date. He or she may ask, "How much must I invest at X percent today to have a certain amount of money in so many years?" Thus, the investor who uses present-value formulas can calculate how much money he or she must save today to grow in the future to a desired goal.

Consumer tip: Learning the concept of present value can help to encourage you to become very well off someday. For example, at 10 percent annual interest compounded annually, $57.30 saved today becomes $1,000 in 30 years if you don't add one cent to it! The secret is to start saving when you are young, no matter how little you save, and to save regularly.

See also *future value;* Section II, "Money Math," "Money Mistakes."

present worth   See *present value.*

price-earnings ratio (P/E)   the current price of a share of stock divided by the annual earnings per share. As a rule, the lower the P/E ratio, the better the buy, since it is more likely that the stock will yield reasonably high dividends in this case. Traditionally, income stocks have relatively low P/E ratios whereas growth-type stocks, on which investors seek capital gains instead of dividends, have high P/E ratios. If a stock sells for $10 a share and has earnings of $1 a share, the P/E ratio is 10:1, or, as quoted in the financial pages, simply 10.

See also *earnings yield;* Section II, "Investments."

price index   a relative measurement of the purchasing power of the dollar as of a specific date. Price indexes are used to determine the rate, if any, of inflation or deflation. The most commonly quoted index is the *Consumer Price Index.*

See also *Consumer Price Index (CPI).*

price stabilization   keeping prices for certain goods at a level set by governmental authority, a tactic sometimes used to curb inflation.

price support   a subsidy given by the government to the producers of certain goods in order to keep the prices for these goods above a minimum level.

primary beneficiary   See *beneficiary.*

prime   See *prime rate.*

prime rate   also *prime;* the interest rate charged by a bank to its commercial borrowers with the best credit ratings. Much is made of the current prime rate as set by major New York banks; but, in fact, a small business in a rural or outlying area often can borrow at rates below New York prime.

Consumer tip: Commercial-type loans tend to be tied, at least loosely, to the prime rate, whereas personal installment loans tend to have much higher rates that often bear little relation to the prime rate; competition tends to be a more important factor. Therefore, it usually pays to shop for credit on a business-loan basis. If you have a good credit record and adequate deposit accounts, you can often borrow in this way and save a lot of money in finance charges.

See also Section II, "Borrowing."

principal   1) a major party to a business transaction; 2) the face value of an investment or instrument; 3) the basic amount invested, not counting any earnings.

principal beneficiary   primary beneficiary.

See also *beneficiary.*

prior lien   a lien that has precedence over another.

See also *lien.*

private enterprise   an economic system in which the means of production and distribution are owned and managed by individuals willing to assume risk for potential profit.

See also *capitalism.*

private mortgage insurance insurance against loan default issued by a private insurance company, as opposed to that issued by the Federal Housing Authority (FHA) or the Veterans Administration (VA). The coverage is usually for 20 to 25 percent of the mortgage loan, and the borrower pays the premiums. This kind of mortgage insurance may induce a lender to take a questionable risk.

private property real estate not owned by a government unit.

private trust a trust not operating under an order from a court.

probate 1) the act of certification by a court of law that a document purporting to be the will of a deceased person is genuine; 2) where necessary, the action taken to see that the instructions in a will are enforced.

probate court also *orphan's court; surrogate's court;* a court in which wills are probated, under which the estates of those who die without wills are settled, and, in some jurisdictions, a court where guardianships, adoptions, and even divorce suits are administered.

See also *probate.*

proceeds 1) the actual amount of money given to a borrower after deduction of any prepaid interest, fees, or other charges; 2) the monies received from a sale after the payment of all charges and commissions.

proceeds-left-with-the-company *See settlement options.*

profit the amount of income remaining after a business has paid all of its bills.

See also *gross profit; net profit.*

profit and loss a firm's total income and expenses during a specific period.

profit and loss (P&L) statement See *income and expense statement.*

profit sharing a fringe benefit received by some employees whereby they share in the profits of the company for which they work according to a prearranged formula. These payments, which are in excess of regular salaries and wages, may be in cash, in company stock, in various savings plans, or even in retirement fund contributions.

Consumer tip: Profit sharing is great, *if . . .* you do not get promises of bonuses instead of better pay; if the plan has reasonable vesting requirements; and, most of all, if it doesn't lock you into an undesirable job. Profit sharing has been called the "golden crutch" or the "golden chain," because it can make an employee dependent on a certain job or hold him or her to it when he or she really should leave.

profit taking the selling of securities in a rising market in order to realize gains that have been made. Profit taking is often the excuse for a sudden drop in the market; perhaps it is sometimes even responsible for that drop.

progressive income tax See *tax.*

promissory note a negotiable instrument that is evidence of a debt owed. Like all negotiable instruments, it must be for a certain sum in money, include a date that it is payable, be signed by its maker, be payable to a named person or to the bearer, and be payable at a named place.

Most people do not realize when they borrow that they sign a note that is negotiable—i.e., the lender may sell or assign the note to another person or firm. For example, many banks that make mortgages later sell those mortgages to other investors and then simply act as collectors; some retail stores sell their accounts receivable to finance companies; all banks that issue credit cards buy the receivables of the merchants who sold the goods. There is no problem in this as long as the goods purchased are acceptable; when they are not, there are certain rules that must be followed in order for the borrower to avoid problems. These rules are outlined under the *Fair Credit Billing Act.*

See also *Fair Credit Billing Act; holder in due course.*

property things that are legally owned by a person, persons, or company that may be disposed of as the owner sees fit.

property insurance coverage against losses that may be caused to property owned by the policyholder or against losses that may be caused to the persons or property of others, for which the policyholder may be liable. The most common type of property insurance is the homeowner's or tenant's policy.

See also *homeowner's insurance.*

property tax a tax that is based on a percentage of the assessed value of the property. Property taxes are the most common source of revenue for local governments in the United States.

Consumer tip: Property taxes can be very high and are sometimes extremely unfair. Inequities can result from personal favoritism on the part of the assessor; but, more likely, they result from the fact that property more recently transferred is often valued at closer to market value than property that hasn't changed hands in many years. State laws usually require that taxes be equitable, whatever the base, so if you are overassessed in relation to your neighbors, see a lawyer about seeking an abatement. The few dollars you spend may save you thousands over the years.

See also *tax abatement.*

property tax lien See *lien.*

proprietor a person who owns a business as a single individual. Thus, a *sole proprietorship* is a business owned by one person.

Consumer tip: There can be one big tax advantage to a sole proprietorship. For a married couple, if a business is in the name of one spouse and the other works in the business without pay, that person need not pay any Social Security taxes.

pro-rata cancellation a method of rebate of unearned premiums made by an insurance company when a policy is cancelled. The pro-rata method is normally used when the return premium is for a period of a year or more. Under the pro-rata method, the company calculates refunds by simply charging a proportion of the total premium and returning the difference. Thus, if a two-year premium is $500 and the insured cancels after one year, the pro-rata cancellation rebate will be $250.

See also *short-rate cancellation*.

pro-rata rebate a refund of prepaid loan interest based on the actual number of days remaining on the contract, as opposed to a short-term rebate, which is based on the Rule of 78.

See also *Rule of 78; short-term rebate*.

prospectus a written offer to sell a security that provides the information an investor must have to make an informed decision. By regulation of the Securities and Exchange Commission, a prospectus must meet certain requirements to ensure fair statements and accuracy. Prospectuses are most commonly read by investors who are interested in new stock issues or in mutual funds.

protest See *notice of dishonor*.

prove 1) to show the accuracy of the total in a financial transaction by relisting and calculating each item; 2) to balance, as in "to prove an account."

proxy a limited power of attorney given by a stockholder that authorizes someone else to vote his or her stock on all or some issues at a corporate meeting.

prudent-man rule a rule, restricting trustees in some states, that requires that trust funds be invested

only in such securities that would be purchased by a "prudent man." In other states, banking authorities simply issue a list of approved securities in which banks and other trustees may invest.

PSE the Pacific Stock Exchange. See also *stock exchange*.

public offering a new issue or an additional issue of corporate stock offered for sale to the public.

purchase and sale statement a notice, sent to commodities investors when their futures positions have been reduced or sold out, that shows the amount involved, the original price, the final price, the gross profit or loss, the commission charged, and the net profit or loss.

purchase-money mortgage a so-called "creative-financing" option whereby a home seller offers a buyer a short-term second mortgage so that the buyer can meet the terms of a regular mortgage lender for the primary portion of the sale price.

See also Section II, "Home Financing."

purchasing power the current value of the dollar based on consumer items it can purchase.

See also *Consumer Price Index (CPI); cost of living*.

put options See *puts*.

puts also *put options;* options that give the buyer the right to sell a number of shares of stock at a certain price on a set date. Put options are purchased in anticipation that a stock will drop in value. They are the exact opposite of call options and are similar to selling short, except that options rather than shares of stock are involved. A put option contract is for 100 shares.

By purchasing options rather than the stock itself, the investor has great leverage, since an option will invariably sell for a small fraction of the cost of the stock itself. Thus, if an investor buys puts on a stock for $1, he will pay $100 for the contract, plus commission. If the stock drops in price, the put option rises in price proportionately, so he or she may simply sell the option at a profit.

Consumer tip: Put options are sophisticated investments. Like selling short, they call for real skill. Before you consider buying options, study the market carefully—and get the advice of an astute broker.

See also *calls; option; sell short; spread;* Section II, "Investments."

pyramid scheme   a common consumer fraud, ostensibly offering quick riches, based on the idea of the chain letter. Pyramid schemes are of many types, but they all require each participant to recruit additional participating contributors in increasing numbers. Unlike chain letters, pyramid schemes avoid the mails; they replaced chain letters when chain letters were made illegal and postal inspectors began cracking down on them. The mathematical odds against winning anything in a pyramid scheme are extremely remote.

Some legal, if financially questionable, pyramid-type operations do exist, the most common of which are the sales organizations that reward their representatives more for lining up additional salespeople than for selling products.

Consumer tip: If someone from such an organization tries to sell you its products, check comparative prices—chances are, you can do better elsewhere. And if he or she tries to sign you up as a distributor or salesperson, be aware that it may cost you time and money and that you can probably do much better elsewhere to earn additional income. Although some people do make money with pyramid-type distribution companies, they are a very small percentage of those who try.

See also *chain letter; Ponzi scheme.*

qualified endorsement   See *endorsement*.

qualified retirement plan   a private retirement program that conforms to the regulations of the Internal Revenue Service. Contributions are almost always tax deductible and earnings are tax-deferred until retirement.
   Consumer tip: If you are employed, you are qualified to open an Individual Retirement Account; if you are self-employed, you may have a Keogh Plan account. Both are excellent ways to reduce current taxes, and both defer taxes until you retire, when you will probably be in a lower marginal tax bracket, with higher personal deductions. In addition, you'll probably be paying today's taxes, not only at a lower rate, but in tomorrow's inflated dollars.
   See also *annuity; Individual Retirement Account (IRA); Keogh Plan;* Section II, "Retirement Planning."

quick asset   an item of value that can be immediately converted to cash without loss.
   See also *asset; liquid asset*.

quitclaim deed   See *deed*.

raised check a criminally altered check on which the amount has been increased. This is an extremely common type of forgery. Many crooks simply change the figures on the check, making a 1 into a 7 or 9, a 6 into an 8, or adding a 1 before another number, and so on. But some crooks are more clever and overwrite the amount written in words as well, making "four" into "forty," "five" into "fifty," etc.

Consumer tip: Protect your checks against raising by starting the amount written in figures as close to the printed dollar sign as possible, without leaving adequate space for the insertion of numbers. Also, begin writing the amount written in words as far to the left as possible, filling in any blank space to the right with a line. And never write a check with an erasable pen. Best of all, type your checks, using a typewriter without the lift-type correctible feature.

See also *forgery*.

RAM See *reverse annuity mortgage*.

random walk an investment term based on the title of a book, *A Random Walk Down Wall Street* by Burton Malkiel, a professor at Princeton. The random-walk theory holds that the stock market is efficient in that new information is immediately discounted by investors, that on any given day a common stock is as likely to go up as down and, further, that the future price of a stock cannot be predicted on the basis of its past history. The random-walk theory, if carried to the extreme, would mean that an investor could choose worthwhile stocks as accurately by throwing darts at the market pages as by careful analysis.

Consumer tip: Even the book's author admitted he was not a complete random walker, because he felt that the theory was largely but not totally right. The main point to be learned is that

jumping quickly from stock to stock seldom justifies the commission costs.
See also Section II, "Investments."

ratable distribution the reapportionment of an estate by percentage, which occurs when legacies are for specific amounts but cannot be paid in full, so each is reduced by the same percentage.

rate of exchange in foreign exchange, the amount of one nation's currency that may be obtained for that of another nation.

rate of inflation the annual percentage rate of the increase of the price of money, which causes a proportionate decrease in the real value of money. Most economists agree that, in an expanding economic system, a small annual rate of inflation is not only beneficial but normal. It is when the inflation rate becomes excessive that it becomes dangerous. Most economists agree that an annual rate in excess of 4 or 5 percent is too high.

ratio the proportional relationship between two things expressed in numbers. Many ratios are used by financial analysts to determine the health of a particular industry or firm.

real earnings income that has been adjusted to allow for the effects of inflation.

real estate land and any property that is physically attached to the land, including buildings, trees, and fences. Parts of buildings are also included, such as furnaces; kitchen stoves, sinks, and cabinets; and other built-in necessities of life.
See also *personal property*.

real estate investment trust (REIT) an unincorporated trust that pools funds for real estate investment. REITs have centralized managements and get 90 percent or more of their income from real estate rentals, dividends, or gains and must distribute 95 percent or more of that income to their shareholders. They must meet very strict IRS requirements.
Consumer tip: REITs seem to offer a way for small investors to enjoy the benefits of diversified investments in real estate. But beware: many investors lost a lot of money in REITs during the 1970s. Management fees can be high, and frequently the price of a share in a REIT has little relationship to the actual real estate-backed asset value of the share.
REITs can be good investments, but they can also be a haven for people who make a living by rooking small investors. Before you invest, get the advice of a really competent attorney who knows something about REITs.

real estate mortgage a legal document setting forth the terms and conditions of a mortgage loan and pledging the property involved as security for the loan. In common usage, a mortgage refers to the loan itself, although this is technically incorrect.
See also *conventional mortgage; creative financing; graduated-payment adjustable mortgage; rollover mortgage; second mortgage; variable-rate mortgage (VRM);* Section II, "Home Financing."

real estate tax See *property tax*.

real property   See *real estate*.

Realtor   a real estate agent who is a member of the National Association of Realtors. The word "Realtor" is a registered trademark.

realty   real estate.

rebate   a reduction or refund from a payment or charge; a return of a portion of prepaid interest to a borrower whose loan is paid in full before its due date.

recap   See *recapitulation*.

recapitulation   also *recap;* a brief review or summary of figures or other facts.

receipt   a written acknowledgement of payment made.
Consumer tip: Save your receipts. You may need to return the product or complain about the service for which you paid. Or you may be rebilled for something for which you have already paid. One way to assure having receipts is to pay bills by check and to write the purpose of the check on the memo line.

receivable   See *accounts receivable*.

receiver   a neutral party appointed by a court to direct the affairs of a person or firm in bankruptcy or to manage property that is the subject of a lawsuit.

recession   a time period in the economic cycle during which production lags and unemployment rises. During a recession, inflationary trends may continue, whereas during a depression, prices will drop as well.
See also *depression*.

recompense   payment made to compensate for loss or damage.

reconciliation   calculations done by a checking-account customer to prove that the figures on a bank statement agree with those in a checkbook. Differences may arise because the checkbook is in ongoing usage; thus, there are almost always checks written that have not yet been deducted by the bank. The easiest way to reconcile a statement is to add any uncredited deposits to the bank's balance, deduct all outstanding checks from that figure, then deduct any bank charges from the checkbook balance. At that point, the adjusted bank balance should agree with the adjusted checkbook balance.
Consumer tip: Always reconcile your bank statement as soon as you receive it. By law, you must notify the bank of any errors on its part within a reasonable time—usually 90 days—or you may lose the right to have them corrected.
See also Section II, "Family Accounting."

recourse   the right of a holder in due course of a negotiable instrument to go back to prior holders in due course if the maker of the instrument fails to pay it as agreed.
Consumer tip: Never accept a check that is endorsed, "Without recourse." By so doing, you give up any rights to collect from the person who gave you the check if it bounces.
See also *endorsement*.

redemption the paying off of a debt.

rediscount a loan made by a Federal Reserve Bank to a member commercial bank in which the collateral involved is a promissory note issued by a customer of the commercial bank. By controlling the *rediscount rate*, the Federal Reserve can control the rates of interest that banks charge and, to a degree, the money supply. If the rediscount rate is low, loans are stimulated and the money supply increases.

rediscount rate See *rediscount*.

redlining the discriminatory practice of some mortgage lenders of not making loans in certain neighborhoods that are supposedly outlined in red on a map. These areas are, of course, in slum or ghetto neighborhoods. Redlining is illegal but hard to prove.
See also *greenlining*.

refinance 1) to revise a payment schedule on a loan; 2) to borrow additional funds against an open-ended mortgage or to write a new mortgage.

registered bond See *bond*.

registered check a type of bank money order.
See also *money order*.

registered representative See *customer's representative*.

Reg Q See *Regulation Q*.

regular dividend earnings on a stock paid at regular intervals and usually at established rates.

regular savings account See *passbook savings account*.

Regulation Q (Reg Q) the Federal Reserve Board regulation establishing savings interest rates that may be paid by banks and other depository institutions. Under the Depository Institutions Deregulation and Monetary Control Act, Regulation Q is to be completely phased out by 1986, and all savings interest rates are to be set by individual banks and thrift institutions. As of early 1984, Reg Q applies only to passbook savings, NOW accounts, and certificates of deposit with maturities of 31 days or less and balances of $2,500 or less.

Regulation T the Federal Reserve Board rule regulating the amount of credit that stockbrokers may advance to customers who buy securities on margin.

Regulation U the Federal Reserve Board regulation governing the amount of credit that a bank may give a customer for the purchase of listed stocks when the collateral for the loan is to be listed stocks. The purpose of this regulation is to attempt to prevent the investment pyramiding that helped lead to the Great Depression.

Regulation Z the Federal Reserve Board regulation implementing the so-called "truth-in-lending" provisions of the Consumer Credit Protection Act. This regulation, details of which

change from time to time, stipulates the forms and information that borrowers must be given so as to be able to make informed borrowing decisions.
See also *Consumer Credit Protection Act.*

reinstatement   reactivation of an insurance policy by paying a past-due premium and being accepted for reinstatement by the company. Also, in property insurance, after a claim has been paid, the amount of insurance coverage may be reduced by the amount of the claim; in this case, reinstatement involves bringing the insurance coverage back up to its prior limits, which may or may not require an extra premium.

REIT   See *real estate investment trust.*

remittance   payment of all or part of an obligation.

remuneration   payment in the sense of wages or salary for employment.

renegotiable-rate mortgage   See *rollover mortgage.*

rent   income received from the leasing of real estate.
See also *lease.*

reorganization   the changing of the capital structure of a company that affects the rights and responsibilities of the owners. Reorganizations are usually undertaken to make a business more efficient, to avoid bankruptcy, or both.

replacement value   the amount of money that would be needed to replace property should it be totally destroyed. This is the figure for which houses and other valuable property should be insured.
See also *actual cash value;* Section II, "Property and Liability Insurance."

replevin   a legal remedy under the common law giving the person who has title to personal property the right to possess it. If, for example, a buyer pays for something but the seller fails to turn it over to him, the buyer may ask the court for a writ of replevin to obtain possession of the item.

repo   See *repurchase agreement.*

repossession   the taking back of an item bought under a conditional sales contract when the buyer is past due on his or her payments.
Consumer tip: A creditor has the right to take back any item you have purchased under a conditional sales contract if you do not meet the repayments exactly as agreed. Automobiles are commonly repossessed. If your car is repossessed, it will probably be sold at auction, and should the price it brings be insufficient to repay the balance of the loan, you will be responsible for any amount that is still owed. The answer is to buy only from reputable dealers, never taking on more monthly payments than you can handle. If you do begin to have money troubles, however, don't let debts become delinquent without talking to each of your creditors. Reputable firms use repossession only as a last resort, so if you contact them early enough,

they will almost always help you to work out a reasonable repayment schedule.

See also *conditional sales contract;* Section II, "Debt Management."

representative money paper money that is fully backed by gold or silver in a national depository. U.S. dollars are not representative money.

repurchase agreement also *repo;* an investment device whereby a person "lends" a bank money for a short time—usually less than 90 days—and the bank promises to repay the money plus interest when the repo matures. The advantage is that there is no penalty for early withdrawal; the disadvantage is that repos are not insured because they are technically not deposits.

Some banks still market so-called *sweep accounts,* in which excess funds in a checking account are automatically invested in short-term repos, thus giving the customer earnings on inactive money reserves. As a matter of practical fact, with the deregulation of certificates of deposit, repos have become less common and have little interest to the average consumer.

Consumer tip: It is usually wiser to keep a minimal deposit in an interest-paying NOW account and to invest the excess in short-term CDs or money market funds. In this way, your liquidity level is still high, your earnings are usually better, and with bank CDs, your funds are insured up to the legal limit.

See also Section II, "Cash Management."

restrictive endorsement See *endorsement.*

retail sales index an economic indicator issued monthly by the U.S. Bureau of the Census that measures retail sales throughout the nation. It is most useful as an indication of shifts in consumer preferences and buying patterns.

retained earnings See *surplus.*

retirement paying off a debt.

retirement plans See *Individual Retirement Account (IRA); Keogh Plan; pension.*

returned check also *return item;* a check the drawee bank has refused to pay that will be sent back to each successive holder until it reaches the original person to whom it was payable. Checks may be returned for many reasons, some technical, some serious.

Technical reasons include informality, which means that the amount written in figures does not match the amount written in words; a missing endorsement; an improper endorsement; and the absence of a maker's signature. Each of these things can easily be corrected, with a new check if necessary.

Serious reasons include no account, which indicates that the issuer's account was closed since the check was issued or that he or she never did have an account; insufficient funds; no funds; or, less serious, uncollected funds.

Consumer tip: If a check of yours is returned for any reason, take corrective action immediately. If the reason was because of a lack of funds, be aware that to deliberately issue a bad check is a crime in every state, so take steps to make it good at once. If you get a bad check, it is usually permissible to take any action necessary, such as adding an endorsement, and to redeposit it and see if it will clear the second time. If it again bounces for lack of funds, see an attorney.

See also *insufficient funds; notice of dishonor*.

return item See *returned check*.

return premium the amount refunded to a policyholder if his or her property insurance policy is reduced or cancelled or if the policyholder has taken some action to lower the premium.

Consumer tip: You can often lower your premiums by taking small corrective actions. For example, installing smoke or burglar alarms may result in a return premium and subsequently lowered premiums. Nonsmokers also often qualify for lower premiums.

See also Section II, "Property and Liability Insurance."

revenue sharing the return of some taxes collected by a larger unit of government to a smaller unit of government. Such funds must almost always be used for specific purposes.

revenue stamps a form of taxation consisting of stamps sold by the federal or a state government that must be affixed to certain documents, especially to deeds. Duck stamps, sold at post offices, must be affixed to hunting licenses to permit people to shoot

ducks; some states issue property excise tax stamps that must be affixed to deeds before they are registered. Revenue stamps are similar to the stamps over which the American colonies fought the English, but they are still very much in use.

reverse annuity mortgage (RAM) one of a variety of plans that allows homeowners to borrow the equity in their property to ensure a decent lifestyle during retirement years. A typical plan allows homeowners in areas where property values tend to rise to receive a monthly income that accumulates as a debt against their property. When the homeowner dies or sells the property, the mortgage loan, which consists of the total of all of the amounts advanced plus interest, becomes payable. Also, there is usually a sharing of any increase in the value of the property between the homeowner or his or her estate and the lender.

Consumer tip: Reverse annuity mortgages are the most exciting thing to happen to the elderly since Social Security. They can easily provide an income of $200 to $500 a month to augment pensions or Social Security, and need not be repaid until the title to the property is transferred. They do, of course, reduce the amount that a homeowner can leave to his or her heirs, but that usually is better than living in penury. There are many types available, so shop for the best deal. Although RAMs are not legal in every state, it's only a matter of time before they will be.

See also Section II, "Retirement Planning."

reverse split a reduction in the number of shares of stock outstanding, that is, stock actually issued and owned by persons or institutions other than the corporation itself, as opposed to an increase, which is more common.

reversionary trust See *Clifford Trust*.

revocable beneficiary a beneficiary under an insurance policy whose rights may be cancelled by the policyholder at any time. Most beneficiaries are revocable, which means that the policyholder may designate a new beneficiary at any time.
See also *beneficiary*.

revolving credit See *open-end credit*.

right of recision under the Consumer Credit Protection Act and also under the laws of many states, the right to cancel a contract within three business days without penalty and with full return of any down payment made. This right applies to any credit purchase made for which the borrower's home is used as collateral, and, under a Federal Trade Commission (FTC) ruling, to any sales made by door-to-door salespeople. This right is the reason borrowers must wait for three days to receive the proceeds of a second mortgage loan after the loan has been finalized. In addition, consumers who have been high-pressured by encyclopedia salespeople or home improvement peddlers can take a couple of days to cool off and change their minds and say, "I want my money back!"

Consumer tip: Keep in mind that your home is used to secure loans quite often. Since that is so and, realizing that you must be given a right of recision document at the time the sale is made, don't be afraid to change your mind within the three-day period and get your money back. Also, while it is not required under the right of recision laws, life insurance companies also give you a few days after you receive your policy to change your mind. So if you've been high-pressured, don't be afraid to ask for the return of your money.
See also Section II, "Debt Management," "Money Mistakes."

right of survivorship the automatic inheritance by the remaining party of property that is jointly owned upon the death of one of the parties.
See also *joint property*.

rights a privilege granted by a company to its shareholders to buy additional stock before it is offered to the general public and, usually, at a reduced price. The stockholder may exercise the rights, ignore them, or sell them.
Consumer tip: Never allow rights to simply expire; either use them or sell them.
See also *warrant*.

risk capital common stock investments in a new business.
See also *venture capital*.

risk management the balancing of risks in terms of personal financial management by means of various types of insurance.

See also Section II, "Health Costs," "Life Insurance," "Property and Liability Insurance."

rock bottom   the lowest price at which goods or services may be obtained.

roll over   1) renewing a loan agreement to extend the term. This is common in unsecured time loans, for which the bank may simply wish to review a company's financial status after a period. It is increasingly common in the newer mortgage loans. 2) Also, transferring assets from one investment vehicle to another.
See also *loan; rollover mortgage.*

rollover mortgage   also *renegotiable-rate mortgage*; a mortgage loan under which the unpaid balance is rewritten periodically, usually every three or five years, with an adjustment in rates being made that is indexed in some way to the cost of living.
Consumer tip: Rollover mortgages scare most consumers, but they can be a viable way to buy a home. In the first place, the average family moves every five years or so. In such a case, the rate adjustment feature is meaningless. In the second place, rates may be adjusted downward as well as upward, as many homebuyers learned during the latter part of 1982 and early 1983.
See also *conventional mortgage; graduated-payment adjustable mortgage; variable-rate mortgage (VRM);* Section II, "Home Financing."

round lot   See *lot.*

routing symbol   See *check.*

royalty   payment for the use of the property of another person based on a percentage of the income generated by that property. For example, the authors of books usually receive royalties on their sales.

rubber check   a check that is returned for one of the following reasons: no funds, insufficient funds, or no account with the bank.
See also *bounce; insufficient funds; returned check.*

Rule of 116   See *Rule of 72.*

Rule of 78   the sum-of-the-digits method of calculating installment loan interest rebates. The name comes from the fact that, if the number of the months in one year are added together, the sum equals 78 (12 + 11 + 10 + 9 + 8 + 7 + 6 + 5 + 4 + 3 + 2 + 1 = 78). This fact is important because, throughout the period of a loan, even though the payments are all the same, the portions that are interest and principal are very different.
The calculations are extremely complicated, and lenders use charts to figure rebates. Using such a chart for a one-year loan shows that, in the first payment, 15.38 percent of the interest due is paid off and, by the sixth month, 73.08 percent of the interest is paid off. This means that, if a person makes a one-year loan with a total interest charge of $100 and pays the loan off in full with the sixth payment, he or she will not get an interest rebate of $50, but only $26.92, since $73.08 of the interest has been paid.
Consumer tip: More and more lenders are using simple interest for loan rebates, and the unfair Rule of 78 is going

its well-deserved route into oblivion. Check loan agreements before you sign if there is any chance you can prepay in order to avoid this de-facto prepayment penalty.

See also *pro-rata rebate*.

Rule of 72   a formula stating that the number of years it will take compounded interest to double the amount of the principal investment can be approximately calculated by dividing the interest rate into the number 72. Thus, if interest is compounded at 6 percent per year, the principal invested will double in 12 years. An extension of the Rule of 72 is the *Rule of 116*. This tells the number of years it takes for the principal to be tripled, and is determined by dividing the annual interest rate into 116.

These formulas are very handy for figuring the growth of funds saved. They can also be used in reverse, that is, to calculate at what rate of interest money must be invested to double or triple in a certain number of years. For example, to determine the interest rate

required to double an investment within eight years, the investor should simply divide 8 into 72, which would indicate that a rate of 9 percent per year is necessary to reach this goal.

runaway inflation   inflation at such a high level that it cannot be controlled by governmental action.

runoff   the last transactions of the day at a stock exchange, which are reported only after the exchange closes. In years past, the runoff could be hours late when the market had a heavy day. Computers have speeded things up considerably.

run on a bank   a panic situation in which large numbers of people, fearing that a bank may fail, that is, be unable to meet its short-term obligations, line up to demand immediate withdrawal of their funds. Naturally, banks do not keep everyone's funds available in cash, so a run may actually cause a bank to fail when it otherwise wouldn't.

S

safe deposit box a metal box that the bank rents for the safekeeping of valuables that is locked in an individual section of a bank vault. No one, not even the bank, has access to the contents of a safe deposit box without the permission of the renter, except under court order or legal procedures to settle the estate of the renter. Safe deposit boxes are commonly thought of as providing secure storage for jewelry and coin collections, but the safeguarding of papers that are difficult or impossible to replace is equally important.

Safe deposit rentals are deductible from federal income taxes on Schedule A, Form 1040, if any of the contents are used to produce income or safeguard tax records; almost every renter meets this requirement for a deduction.

Consumer tip: Use a safe deposit box for storing obvious valuables and important papers and for copies of treasured family pictures and other mementos. With vandalism on the increase, a safe deposit box is a must. Two warnings: First, the contents of safe deposit boxes are not insured, so be certain that your homeowner's or tenant's policy covers yours. And second, do not keep a will or life insurance policies in a safe deposit box; both may be needed quickly in the event of death.

See also Section II, "Bank Accounts."

safekeeping a service some but not all banks offer to customers who want bulky valuables stored, whereby they are placed in the vault on a permanent or temporary basis. Many urban banks use old vaults for this purpose that are unsuitable for modern cash storage. With safekeeping, customers may store paintings or silver while vacationing, or even gun collections. In at least one urban bank, a man's ashes perpetually rest in the safekeeping vault.

safety of principal the main goal of a conservative investment policy, which endeavors to prevent the loss of the basic amount invested.

salary income at a fixed rate, either weekly, monthly, or yearly. The word comes from the Latin *salarium* or "salt money," which is a reference to the days when salt was valuable and Roman soldiers were paid with small bags of it.
See also *wage*.

sales agreement a legal document whereby a seller agrees to deliver property to a buyer at a set price if certain conditions are met.

sales charge the commission fee on a securities transaction.
See also *load*.

sales tax a tax placed by a state, city, or town on some or all goods at the time they are purchased. There is as yet no federal sales tax, though one has often been proposed, sometimes as a value-added tax. A sales tax is regressive in that in impacts most on those least able to afford to pay it.
Consumer tip: Sales tax payments are deductible from your federal income tax; you can use the IRS table to come up with a fair estimate, or you can detail your own. The main thing to remember is to deduct additional amounts for very large purchases, such as a new car.
See also *tax; use tax; value-added tax;* Section II, "Tax Savings."

Sallie Mae See *Student Loan Marketing Association*.

S&L savings and loan association.
See also *bank*.

S&P 500 See *Standard and Poor's Composite Stock Index*.

satisfaction of judgment a document certifying the paying of a court-imposed judgment.
Consumer tip: When such a payment is made, be sure it is entered in the court records.

satisfaction of mortgage the document issued by the lender certifying that a mortgage loan has been fully repaid.
Consumer tip: Don't burn your cancelled mortgage or the satisfaction certificate. Put it in your safe deposit box in case you need to prove that you did pay it. Celebrate by burning a symbolic piece of paper instead.

savings account a time deposit account at a bank or savings institution. At insured institutions, the balances in savings accounts are insured up to the legal limits by various federal or state agencies. Checks may not be drawn on these accounts.
See also *certificate of deposit (CD); passbook savings account;* Section II, "Savings."

savings account loan See *passbook loan*.

savings and loan association (S&L) See *bank*.

savings bank See *bank*.

Savings Bank Life Insurance (SBLI) life insurance that is sold over-the-counter in Massachusetts, New York, and Connecticut savings banks. SBLI offers eligible people a chance to really save money on life insurance costs. The insurance plans offered cover about the same range as those offered by the traditional insurers; but because there are no agents—and hence no commissions—the cost is much lower, especially in Massachusetts.

To qualify for Massachusetts SBLI, you must live or work in Massachusetts; to buy New York SBLI, you must live or work in New York or have a close relative who is a resident of New York apply for you; to qualify in Connecticut, you must live or work in Connecticut or have a depository relationship with the savings bank through which you apply for insurance. Unfortunately, the three state legislatures, under pressure from the insurance industry, have restricted the amount of SBLI that an individual may have.

Consumer tips: If you live or work in an SBLI state, buy all of your permanent insurance through SBLI, then add whatever term you can up to the allowable limit before buying any insurance from a regular insurance company.

If you send a child to a college in Massachusetts, New York, or Connecticut, see that he or she gets life insurance while a resident. The child can keep it forever, even after he or she moves.

Savings Bond   See *bond; U.S. Savings Bonds.*

savings certificate   See *certificate of deposit (CD).*

savings rate   on a national basis, the percentage of income saved out of total income. The savings rate in the U.S. is traditionally the lowest of all Western industrialized nations, usually ranging between 4 and 8 percent. In Japan, the rate averages about 25 percent, and in the European nations, it is about 12 percent. In the U.S., with most savings income taxed as regular income, there is no government-supported incentive to save. In most Western nations, a substantial portion of savings interest—often the first $1,000—is excluded from taxation each year as an incentive to save.

See also *dividends.*

SBLI   See *Savings Bank Life Insurance.*

scavenger sale   a public sale of the property of tax delinquents held by a state to recover back taxes that are due.

search   See *title search.*

SEC   See *Securities and Exchange Commission.*

secondary market   the market that exists for a stock issue after its initial distribution to the public. Few transactions are made in the primary market, which is where new venture capital is raised by the issuance of new stock. All transactions made on exchanges or over-the-counter are secondary market transactions. The purpose of the secondary market is to support the primary market; in other words, investors buy new issues only because they hope to sell those shares someday, for a profit, on the secondary market.

second mortgage a mortgage on real estate that already has a first mortgage outstanding. Years ago, second mortgages were looked on as the last resort of desperate people, but times have changed. With real estate equities at an all-time high, a second mortgage gives many people an easy and often less expensive way to borrow money for home repairs, college costs, or whatever.

Consumer tip: If you consider a second mortgage, discuss it with the lender from whom you got the first mortgage, then shop around. Rates are competitive, so you can save money. Your first mortgagee may offer to refinance your original loan; but if that means giving up a really low rate, it could be a big mistake.

See also *first mortgage; reverse annuity mortgage (RAM);* Section II, "Borrowing," "Debt Management."

Section 403(b) plan the portion of the Internal Revenue Code that allows teachers in public schools and employees of certain charitable groups to establish retirement plans through tax-deferred annuities.

secured loan a loan backed with collateral.

secured time loan See *loan.*

Securities and Exchange Commission (SEC) the federal regulatory agency that oversees all securities traded on stock exchanges and over-the-counter stocks for which issuing companies have at least $1 million in assets and more than 500 shareholders. The SEC was established in 1934 to correct the abuses that contributed to the Great Depression.

Securities Investor Protection Corporation (SIPC) a nonprofit corporation created by act of Congress to insure the cash and securities of the customers of a brokerage house in the event the firm fails.

Consumer tip: If you maintain a cash account at a brokerage house or keep securities there in street name, be sure the house is a member of SIPC.

See also *street name.*

securities trading the buying or selling of stocks or bonds through a stock exchange or over-the-counter.

security exchange See *stock exchange.*

security interest a claim that a lender has against some property of the borrower to insure payment of the debt.

seignorage the difference between the cost of the metal used for making coins and the face value of the coin when issued. Until 1965, except for pennies and nickels, U.S. coins were made of silver and the seignorage was quite low. With the new "clad" coins, the value of the metal is much less than the face value of the coin, so the seignorage is quite high.

self-insurance a system of establishing one's own insurance fund as opposed to paying premiums to a company.

Consumer tip: Total self-insurance is impossible, except for the very rich, but most people can profit from partial self-insurance simply by taking the maximum deductibles on all property, casualty, and liability insurance and maintaining a savings fund to cover the amount of the deductible. For example, if you elect to take a $500 deductible on your auto insurance, you may save $100 or more a year in premiums. If you cover that risk with $500 in a money market fund paying 9 percent interest, you will earn about $47 a year in interest. Your net gain will be about $150 a year, so that, if you have no claims on that policy for four years, you will be ahead of the game.

See also Section II, "Property and Liability Insurance."

sell and leaseback   a real estate deal whereby an owner/occupier of a building sells it to an investor, then rents it back under a long-term lease, usually with an option to buy when the lease expires. This gives the seller immediate cash and the buyer a tax-advantaged income source.

seller's market   the situation under the law of supply and demand in which demand for a product or service is greater than the supply. Thus, sellers may set prices and other conditions of sale to a great degree.

See also *buyer's market.*

selling climax   the dumping of large quantities of stocks at the termination of a declining or bear market. Following a selling off, there is usually a strong rally in prices of stocks for a short period.

Also see *bear market; blowing off.*

selling off   the selling of securities when there are few offers to buy and many to sell. Under these circumstances, the price of a stock—or more typically, of the market as a whole—tends to drop temporarily.

sell short   also *short;* to sell a borrowed stock in anticipation of a drop in its price, at which time it will be repurchased, returned to its owner, and the short seller will have gained a profit. Stocks for this purpose are routinely lent by brokers, for a fee, to short sellers. Selling short is a very risky business for all but the most sophisticated investors. To short a stock, you must have a margin account with the broker—that is, a loan account. And the brokerage house must have a sufficient supply of the stock to lend it to you.

Consumer tip: Selling short requires a constant watch on the market, since the time in which you can profitably cover your short position may be very brief. If you are really convinced enough that a stock will fall in price, consider put options if they are available on that stock. Then you will at least have limited your possible losses.

See also *margin; puts; spread.*

SEP   See *Simplified Employee Pension.*

sequestered account   also *frozen account;* an account impounded by process of law pending court action.

serial bond   a bond that is part of an issue in which some bonds are retired at regular intervals. The purpose is to have the outstanding bond indebtedness decrease periodically. In this way, as the objects purchased with the funds raised by the issue depreciate in value, the bond indebtedness decreases proportionately.

serial numbers identifying numbers appearing on currency, bonds, and some other negotiable items that are printed on each in a series in sequential order. Serial numbers are used as a means of helping to detect counterfeits and to keep track of circulation.

Series EE bonds See *bond; U.S. Savings Bonds.*

Series HH bonds See *bond; U.S. Savings Bonds.*

service charge a fee imposed by banks for certain activities in connection with accounts. Checking account service charges are the most common and typically include an account maintenance fee, check printing costs, a per-check handling fee, a return item fee, and stop-payment charges.

Consumer tip: Service charges may be all or partially offset by keeping large balances on deposit; but, as a rule, it is wiser to pay the fees, which may be tax deductible anyway, and to invest the funds needed to offset the fees at a higher rate of return. When possible, use a NOW account instead of a checking account.

See also *NOW account;* Section II, "Cash Management."

service counter terminals point-of-sale computer terminals that are located in retail stores and connected to a bank's central computer, through which customers may have instant access to their money on deposit, make credit purchases, or even make deposits and withdrawals.

See also *point-of-sale (POS).*

service credit an extension of credit allowing a bill to be paid at the end of a period for service previously rendered. A phone bill is a typical example.

settlement 1) the balancing of an account; 2) the meeting between a buyer of real estate, the seller, and the mortgage lender, at which time title to the property is passed to the buyer, payment is made, and the mortgage loan is finalized; also, 3) settlement refers to the final distribution of the estate of a deceased person or the property distribution arrangement between a husband and wife at the time of their separation or divorce.

See also *balance.*

settlement costs See *closing costs.*

settlement day the day on which an investor must pay for his or her stock purchases. Normally, an investor has five days after a buy order has been executed to pay for a stock purchase, but he or she must pay for options the next day.

See also Section II, "Investments."

settlement options the provision in a life insurance policy for an alternative method of payment of the policy to the beneficiary. The option for settlement may be chosen by the owner of the policy at the time the coverage is purchased or by the beneficiary at the time a death claim is made.

The options include:

1. *Lump-sum payment.* With this choice, the beneficiary gets the proceeds of the policy in one check.

2. *Limited-installment payments.* With this choice, the beneficiary receives periodic installments for a specified number of years.

3. *Life-income.* With this option, the beneficiary receives an annuity, which may either be paid in installments for life or as *life-income-with-installments-certain.* This means that, if the beneficiary dies soon after the original policyholder, at least a certain amount goes to another named beneficiary for a period of time.

4. *Proceeds-left-with-the-company.* With this option, the face of the policy remains with the insurance company, which pays interest on the amount to the beneficiary. At a later date, the principal amount goes to another named beneficiary.

Consumer tip: Take the cash. Insurance companies like the last three options because they retain the continued use of the money; but they are notorious for low investment interest rates, so always opt for the lump-sum payment. A better course of action than choosing a settlement option for your heirs if they are incapable of handling their own financial affairs is to set up a life insurance trust at a bank with a good track record in investments, and let it administer the proceeds. Your heirs will be better off.

See also *dividend options;* Section II, "Life Insurance."

shading   giving a small discount in price.

shake out   changes in the stock market that force speculators to dispose of their shares.

share   a unit of stock.
See also *stock, common; stock, preferred.*

share account   a regular- or passbook-type savings account at a credit union; also, but not too often a savings account at some savings and loan associations is called a share account. The word "share" is used because the saver is not making a deposit but is buying shares—an unimportant technicality if the account is insured by the National Credit Union Administration (NCUA) or the Federal Savings and Loan Insurance Corporation (FSLIC). With uninsured accounts, should the credit union or savings association fail, savers, because they are shareholders, would not have a primary claim on its assets.

Consumer tip: Always save in insured banks, savings and loan associations, or credit unions. Whatever the technical legal status of depositors, don't risk money in uninsured institutions.

shared-appreciation mortgage
one of the many mortgage loan schemes to come out of the lending crisis of the early 1980s. With this plan, the borrower receives a mortgage with the interest rate set substantially lower than the prevailing conventional loan rate, but he or she agrees to give the lender a share of any profit from the eventual sale of the house.

Consumer tip: Stay away from this type of mortgage. The long-term trend in real estate is toward increasing values. As Will Rogers said, "Buy land;

they ain't making no more of it."
Agreeing to a shared-appreciation feature in a mortgage is a costly lien on future potential profits.

See also Section II, "Home Financing."

share draft a negotiable instrument drawn on a share account at a credit union. Share drafts look and work like checks, so for all practical purposes, they are checks.

See also *NOW account.*

shareholder a *stockholder;* a person who owns one or more shares of stock in a corporation.

share loan a passbook loan made at a credit union and at some savings and loan associations.

See also *passbook loan; share account.*

shares outstanding the number of shares of stock issued by a corporation that are actually in the hands of the public.

short See *sell short.*

short certificate an abbreviated version of letters testamentary or a certificate of administration, issued by a representative of a probate, orphan's, or surrogate's court, testifying to the authority of an executor or administrator to settle an estate. Short certificates must be filed with every bank and other institution with which the deceased person had accounts or other business so that the assets may be released into the estate.

See also *letters testamentary;* Section II, "Estate Planning."

shortcut foreclosure clause a clause in a mortgage agreement that allows the first mortgage lender to sell the property without public notice after foreclosure. With this clause, there is little incentive for the first mortgage holder to sell the property for more than the balance due on the first mortgage loan, so the holders of second or third mortgages often lose out because there are no residual funds to pay their claims.

See also *foreclosure.*

short position the amount of stock an investor has sold short as of a certain date.

See also *sell short.*

short-rate cancellation a method of computing the portion of a casualty, liability, or property insurance premium to be returned when a policy is cancelled, which is usually used when the remaining term is less than one year. The short-rate cancellation method is somewhat similar to the Rule of 78 method of rebating unearned interest that is used by some lenders, in that it penalizes the policyholder for cancelling.

Consumer tip: Always try to avoid a short-rate cancellation, because you get back much less of the premium than under the pro-rata method.

See also *pro-rata cancellation; Rule of 78.*

short sale See *sell short.*

short term in financial dealings, usually a period of a year or less. There are a few exceptions, however. A short-term trust (*Clifford Trust*), for example, has a period of at least 10 years.

See also *Clifford Trust*.

short-term capital gains See *capital gains*.

short-term rebate a refund of unearned interest calculated by the Rule of 78.

See also *pro-rata rebate; Rule of 78*.

side collateral security pledged to induce a lender to make a loan, but which does not have sufficient value to cover the loan. As an example, a borrower with marginal credit might pledge $2,000 in securities against a $5,000 loan. Side collateral, which is common in loans to small businesses, is rare in personal loans.

sight draft See *draft*.

signature card the basic document used to open a personal checking or savings account at a bank or savings institution. The signature card is used to identify the customer and often contains the rules of the bank in relation to the account, to which the signer agrees.

Consumer tip: Your signature is valuable; treat it carefully. With bank accounts, this means never using a rubber-stamped signature or allowing anyone else to write your signature. If you need another signer, have him or her authorized on the signature card. Also, update your signature card occasionally. In many cases, especially with the elderly, difficulties may arise with bank transactions when a signature has changed radically. Since banks do not routinely check signatures because of the volume of their work, a major change may not be noticed. Also, banks rely on their customers to examine their cancelled checks and to report forgeries.

See also *forgery*.

silver certificate a United States bill that was redeemable for silver by the bearer on demand. From 1873 to 1968, much U.S. currency consisted of silver certificates.

Consumer tip: Occasionally a $1 silver certificate will still turn up. You can spot it because the Treasury seal is blue (on Federal Reserve Notes it is green; on United States Notes, it is red). It bears the words, "This certifies that there is in the Treasury of the United States one dollar in silver, payable to the bearer on demand." You can no longer trade silver certificates for silver, but they are collectors' items, so hang on to them.

See also *money; numismatics*.

simple interest interest only on the principal with no compounding of interest on the interest. For example, simple interest on $100 at 6 percent for one year is $6; if the interest is compounded daily, it totals $6.183124.

Consumer tip: Obviously, it pays to borrow at simple interest and to save at compound interest. More and more banks are now making true simple interest loans because computers have made it easy to charge for money for the exact number of days it is borrowed. Shop for loans on a simple interest basis; it can save you money.

See also *add-on rate method; annual percentage rate (APR); discount rate method*.

Simplified Employee Pension (SEP) a retirement plan, similar to an Individual Retirement Account (IRA) to which both the employee and the employer contribute. The employer must contribute to all employees at an equal percentage rate of their salaries. If an employer establishes an SEP, the employee pays no taxes on the portion contributed by the employer; the employee's own contributions are subject to the same tax deduction rules that apply to an IRA.

The employer may contribute up to $15,000 or 15 percent, whichever is less, of an employee's salary to his or her plan, and the employee may contribute up to $2,000 or 100 percent, whichever is less. In addition, the employee can set up his or her own IRA. Should the employee die, any undistributed funds are exempt from federal estate taxes if they are distributed to heirs in installments over a period of 36 months or more.

SEPs, unlike most pension plans, are fully vested immediately, which means the employee gets all that has been deposited in his or her name if he or she leaves the job, with no time-on-the-job requirements. The one negative feature of SEPs is that they can discriminate in favor of highly paid executives, because the employer may deduct the amount he pays for Social Security from the amount contributed to an SEP. Since the more highly paid people pay proportionately less for Social Security, this means they get proportionately more in an SEP.

Consumer tip: If your employer offers you a chance to participate in an SEP, take it. Like an IRA or Keogh Plan, it is one of the best tax deferrals available to average people.

See also *Individual Retirement Account (IRA);* Section II, "Retirement Planning."

Simultaneous Death Act a law in many states that allows a clause to be included in wills that establishes the order of death in the event of a mutual disaster of people whose wills are interdependent. The purpose is to allow the parties involved to instruct the courts or those who settle estates in deciding how to make distribution of the estates. In such a *common disaster clause*, it is usually specified that, in case of the simultaneous death of the parties, it is to be assumed that a certain party lived longer than the other. This establishes the rights of heirs as desired by the persons making the wills.

Consumer tip: Every married couple should ask their attorney about including such a clause in their wills. With auto accidents and other disasters such a frequent cause of death, it is not uncommon for a husband and wife to both be fatally injured in the same catastrophe. If this happens, what becomes of their property? If they have no children, or if the children are also killed, and the doctors testify that the husband outlived his wife by a few breaths, his relatives may inherit their property—yet that may not be what the couple wishes. Decide whom you wish to outlive the other for legal reasons, then see your lawyer.

See also *will;* Section II, "Estate Planning."

single-premium deferred annuity See *annuity.*

sinking fund an account in which cash is accumulated to pay off an obligation that will come due at a future date. Companies that issue corporate bonds often set up sinking funds to which they make regular and carefully calculated deposits to pay off those bonds when they mature. A bond issued by a corporation that has established a sinking fund for its retirement is obviously safer than a bond with no such backup fund.

See also *bond*.

sin tax   a tongue-in-cheek term for sales or excise taxes on products or services that are legal but that are deemed by some not to be in the public interest. This includes taxes on tobacco, alcoholic beverages, and entertainment. The ideas behind sin taxes are twofold: Because they are not taxes on necessities, they don't impact on people who can't afford them; and many people they do affect won't complain too loudly because they won't wish to appear to be in favor of the activities or products taxed.

SIPC   See *Securities Investor Protection Corporation*.

skip   a person who owes money and then moves, leaving no forwarding address.

skip-payment privilege   a clause in some loan agreements that allows a borrower to skip a payment under certain conditions. These clauses aren't as common as they were in the 1950s, because credit cards have given almost everyone a revolving line of credit under which people may, if strapped, simply make a minimum payment.

slow pay   a credit rating term used to describe a person with a history of more than a few late payments.

Consumer tip: Slow pay is a good description to avoid. Make payments before they are overdue and you'll protect your credit record. Some people rationalize, "They know I'm good for it," but the fact is, a potential lender sees a slow-pay borrower as one from whom it is costly to collect, because he or she must be sent late notices.

See also Section II, "Debt Management."

Small Saver Certificate   a certificate of deposit issued to encourage average savers. Under the regulations for these certificates, there were no deposit minimums, but there was a voluntary floor on interest that banks or thrift institutions could pay. Small Savers Certificates were the most popular of all certificates of deposit, but were phased out beginning in October 1983, when all CDs with maturities of over 31 days were completely deregulated.

See also *certificate of deposit (CD)*; Section II, "Savings."

smart card   a plastic credit and/or debit card in which tiny computer chips are impregnated, giving the card a memory. This means that banks and other issuers can use smart cards to retain and update transaction records on the spot. Popular in Europe, these cards are slower to catch on in America.

smart money   wealthy inside investors. Knowing what the smart money is doing in the market can theoretically make any follower rich. However, by the time such information filters down to the less affluent, it is almost always worthless.

See also Section II, "Investments."

smokestack industries   firms that produce traditional products, such as steel or glass, through traditional means. Some experts feel that smokestack industries are declining in importance in the economy of the United States as technology becomes more important.

See also *sunrise industries.*

socialism   an economic system under which the means of production and the distribution of goods and services are largely owned and controlled by the government.

See also *capitalism; communism.*

socialist   a person who advocates socialism as an economic system.

See also *capitalist; communist.*

Social Security   a government administered pension system that covers old age assistance, disability payments, and other programs. People who are employed have a substantial percentage of their earnings in Federal Insurance Contributions Act (FICA) wages on which Social Security taxes are paid. In fact, over half of all taxpayers pay more in Social Security taxes than in federal income taxes.

Contrary to common belief, taxes paid to Social Security do not accumulate in some huge trust fund; benefits are paid out of current revenue. Thus, as life expectancies have risen and birth rates have declined, the Social Security system has been under great economic pressure. Congress has made some attempts to salvage it, but bar-

ring a major funding program, all such efforts must eventually fail.

Social Security taxes are unfair to people in the middle and lower classes, because only income from employment is taxed and because there is a cut-off level above which even employment income is not taxed. Thus, in 1983, for example, a person earning $35,700 a year paid Social Security taxes on all of it, whereas a person who earned $357,000 a year paid taxes on only 10 percent of it.

Beginning in 1984, some people who receive Social Security will pay federal income taxes on their benefits. For more details, see Section II, "Retirement Planning."

Consumer tip: Look on Social Security as what it was originally designed to be—a supplemental source of retirement income, period. If you plan to retire on Social Security alone, learn to like being poor well in advance. Otherwise, save for your own retirement. The younger you start, the better.

See also Section II, "Retirement Planning."

sole proprietorship   See *proprietor.*

solvent   the condition that exists when assets exceed liabilities. If a person or firm is solvent, it means it has the ability to meet debts as they come due.

special dividend   See *extra dividend.*

special endorsement   See *endorsement.*

specialist   a member firm of a stock exchange that buys and sells a certain stock. If necessary, the specialist will buy or sell shares to or from his own account so that transactions may be promptly made. This is known as *making a market* in that particular security.

special warranty deed   See *deed.*

specie   coin.

specific performance suit   a legal action made to require a person or firm to perform an action specified in a contract. A specific performance is required in cases in which monetary damages would not compensate the injured party. For example, suppose an art collector wishes to buy a specific painting and the owner agrees to sell it. The collector orders it, gives a down payment, and the owner promises to deliver in a week. Two weeks pass, but no delivery is made. The buyer complains, and the seller tells him that he has changed his mind because he's received a better offer; he says he'll refund the down payment. But the buyer doesn't want the money; he wants the painting. Thus, he may sue for specific performance to force the seller to live up to the original contract.

Specific performance suits cannot be brought for personal services. If a professional football player agrees to play for a team and then refuses, the courts will not try to force him to do so. However, they may grant an injunction forbidding him to play for another team.

speculator   a person who buys and sells securities, options, commodities, or other investment vehicles and who is more interested in increasing his or her capital than in earnings or, in many cases, than in safety of principal. A speculator is willing to take fairly large risks. One who both buys and sells in a very short time period for a quick profit is called a *trader.*

See also Section II, "Investments."

spendable earnings   take-home pay.

See also *disposable income.*

split   See *stock split.*

split commission   the sharing of fees or sales commissions between two or more agents or brokers who have sold an account.

split deposit   also *cash-back deposit;* a deposit that calls for a portion of a check or checks being deposited to be credited to the account and a portion to be paid to the depositor in cash. Some banks will not accept split deposits because they are a major source of teller or depositor error.

Consumer tip: To protect yourself from possible loss due to error, it's a good idea to deposit the total amount of a check or checks, then write your own check for cash or, in the case of a savings account, make a withdrawal. If you do make a split deposit, double-check the figures.

spot market   also *commodity cash market;* a place where a commodity is sold for cash and promptly delivered. A food chain, for example, might buy corn on a spot market. Many people buy gold and silver on the spot market.

spot price   the cash price for which a specific commodity is selling. For most investors, spot price relates to the daily cash price for gold or silver.

spread   also *straddle;* 1) the difference between the bid and asked price; 2) in options trading, the practice of writing (or selling) a call and buying a call on the same stock; 3) in commodities trading, a spread refers to the purchase of a futures contract for delivery in one month and the sale of a futures contract in the same commodity in another month, whereas a straddle 4) is the practice of trading in two different markets for diversification, such as in soybeans and corn. Using a spread reduces risk either by diversification or by holding opposing positions in the same investment.

spurt   a short, fast rise in price.

squeeze   a period when interest rates are high and money is tight, making it hard and/or costly to borrow.
See also *tight money.*

SSI   See *Supplemental Security Income.*

stable currency   See *hard money.*

stagflation   a recessionary period in the economic cycle during which the economy is sluggish yet inflation persists. During stagflation, the cost of living continues to increase while production, employment, and capital investment stand still or even decline.

stale-dated check   a check bearing a date that is considerably past that on which it is presented to the paying bank. Bank policies differ, but checks may be considered stale 30, 60, or 90 days or even six months after the date of issuance.
Consumer tip: If you have a stale-dated check to cash or deposit, ask at your bank if it will clear; if it seems advisable, your bank may call the paying bank to be sure it will accept it. If the issuing bank won't pay it, ask the maker to issue a replacement. Having a check go stale doesn't make the check worthless, just a bit harder to collect.
See also *check; post-dated check.*

stamp tax   See *revenue stamps.*

Standard and Poor's bond ratings   the best known of all safety ratings for these securities. Standard and Poor's rates bonds from triple-A through D, as follows:

- AAA—the issuers' ability to pay the interest and principal on the bond is excellent.
- AA—almost as good as AAA; the rating is very strong.
- A—the rating is strong, but the issuer is somewhat subject to adverse reactions from changes in the economy.
- BBB—the rating is adequate, but the issuer is even more subject to economic influences than those with an A rating.
- BB, B, CCC, and CC—these bonds are considered speculative, with BB being the least risky and CC the most.
- C—issuers of these bonds agree to pay interest only when they have earnings. A current rating of C means that a bond is not paying interest.

- D—bonds with this rating are in default and are not currently paying either interest or principal.

Consumer tip: Remember this rule of thumb: any rating with a "B" in it means "beware"; and a "C" or lower means to avoid the investment "Completely."

See also *Moody's ratings.*

Standard and Poor's Composite Stock Index (S&P 500) a daily
index of common stock prices based on 425 industrial firms, 50 utility companies, and 25 railroads. Similar to but not quite as well known as the Dow Jones Industrials Average, the S&P 500 is an indicator of general stock market trends. Speculators can buy both call and put options on the S&P 500 index itself; this is simply gambling on the future of the market as a whole, since no securities can actually be involved in these transactions.

See also *averages; Dow Jones Averages; stock market index futures; stock market index options;* Section II, "Investments."

standard mortality table the
common name for the Commissioners 1958 Standard Ordinary Mortality Table, which is used by life insurance companies as the basis for premium computations. This table shows the death rate per thousand and the expectation of life for Americans at every age level. The figures are based on vital statistics collected from 1950–1954 and have a built-in safety factor designed to create extra reserves.

A new table has been developed, based on death rates from 1970–1975, which may now be used by any company choosing to do so; this has been mandated for use by 1989. However, with the Supreme Court ruling that voided sexual distinctions in premium levels, it is probable that a totally new table will be developed and that, in the meantime, most companies will continue to use the 1958 table.

See also *insurance;* Section II, "Life Insurance."

standard of living a measure of
the material wealth of the economy based on the production of goods and services; also, the economic lifestyle level of a person, family, or group.

star notes currency printed to re-
place bills that are damaged in production and then destroyed. These notes bear a star before the serial numbers. Because they are quite common, they have no value as collectors' items.

state bank See *bank.*

statement a financial record. Banks
issue statements to their customers on checking, savings, and loan accounts; businesses issue statements to their customers of accounts due; and individuals and businesses prepare financial statements showing their net worth and relative financial strength in order to obtain credit.

See also Section II, "Family Accounting."

statement of condition a bal-
ance sheet showing the financial strength of a person or firm as of a certain date. A statement of condition "balances" because the sum of the liability and net worth totals must equal the assets.

See also Section II, "Family Accounting."

statement savings account   See *no-passbook savings account.*

sterling silver   silver that is at least 91.9 percent pure silver and no more than 9.1 percent alloy. Pure silver is soft, so a hardening alloy, often copper, is usually added to protect it from being dented. U.S. silver coins issued before 1965 were 90 percent pure silver.

Consumer tip: Silver coins are often sold as investments through newspaper and magazine ads, so the unwary investor might pay quite a premium. Actually, the best way to invest in silver is to buy sterling bars or to buy "junk" silver coins in bulk.

stock   shares in the ownership of a corporation.

See also *stock, common; stock, preferred.*

stockbroker   a person or firm that buys and sells stocks on behalf of others.

stock certificate   a legal document providing proof of ownership of shares of stock. Many investors do not bother to actually acquire stock certificates.

See also *street name.*

stock, common   stock in which each share represents one part ownership in a corporation and the right to receive one part of the earnings distributed by that corporation. When most people speak of buying stock, they mean common stock. Common stockholders not only have the right to share

in profits, they may vote at shareholders' meetings.

See also *stock, preferred;* Section II, "Investments."

stock dividend   a dividend that is payable in fractional shares of stock to existing shareholders. Obviously, stock dividends dilute the per-share value of stock because the net result is more shares with no more corporate assets or earnings. Stock dividends are sometimes used as a goodwill gesture when cash dividends cannot be afforded.

stock exchange   a place where stocks and other securities are traded. The exchanges in the United States and Canada are:

- The *New York Stock Exchange (NYSE),* the largest of all exchanges. The most prestigious company stocks are traded on the NYSE, which has the strictest requirements for listing.
- The *American Stock Exchange (AMEX),* formerly called the Curb Exchange because originally shares were traded, literally, on the sidewalk. The shares traded on the AMEX tend to have lower prices than those on the NYSE. Also, options of stocks listed on the NYSE are traded on the AMEX.
- The *Boston Stock Exchange (BOX).*
- The *Midwest Stock Exchange (MID).*
- The *Montreal Stock Exchange (MSE).*
- The *Philadelphia-Baltimore-Washington Stock Exchange (PHLX).*
- The *Toronto Stock Exchange (TSE).*
- The *Pacific Stock Exchange (PSE).*
- The *Chicago Board of Options Exchange (CBOE).*

See also *National Association of Securities Dealers Automated Quotations (NASDAQ); over-the-counter stock.*

stockholder   See *shareholder.*

stockholder of record   a stockholder whose name is listed on the official records of the corporation.
See also *street name.*

stock market   the combined trading in securities done on all exchanges and over-the-counter. In common usage, the term refers to the New York Stock Exchange, as in the question, "How is the market today?" which usually means, "What is the Dow Jones Industrial Average doing?"
See also *stock exchange.*

stock market index futures contracts sold on some exchanges in which the buyer agrees to deliver an agreed amount of cash that is tied to the value of the market index on a certain date. The amount of cash is often 500 times the index value. Most futures contracts are sold on *margin,* which means that the investor may put up a percentage and carry the balance on credit.
Consumer tip: Be careful. If you must play the stock market indexes, choose the options. They're far from safe, but they don't have the risk of margin calls that futures do.
See also *calls; margin; puts; stock market index options.*

stock market index options increasingly popular option contracts based on the common stock market indexes. These offer people who want to bet on a market trend a chance to do

so. Thus, if a person wishes to speculate that the market, as a whole, will advance in value, he or she may buy call option contracts on any of several market indexes; if he or she thinks the market, as a whole, will drop, the speculator may buy puts.
Consumer tip: In a changing market situation, stock market options contracts offer a fairly safe way to speculate, since the risk is diversified over many securities issues. If you can afford risk and are convinced that the market, overall, is going up, gamble on a call; if you think it's going down, buy a put. But be aware of your risk. Options are a fast way to make a profit—or a loss.
See also *calls; puts; stock market index futures.*

stock option   See *option.*

stock, preferred   corporate stock, the owners of which have special privileges. Preferred stockholders usually have no right to vote on corporate affairs unless the dividends on the preferred stock are in default. Owners of preferred stock are assured precedence in dividends and, should the company be liquidated, in a share of the assets after all bondholders are paid but before the common stockholders.
Preferred stock may be *cumulative,* which means that, if a dividend is skipped, it must be paid before a common stock dividend, or *noncumulative,* which means that dividends skipped are gone forever. Or it may be *participating,* which means that it receives a guaranteed dividend and may, in some cases, share in dividends voted on common stock. It may also be *convertible,* which means that it can be

switched for common stock; or *nonconvertible*, which means that it cannot.

Preferred stock is a cross between common stock and bonds because it earns set dividends, offers some security in case of liquidation, offers some rights of ownership, but has no voting rights or, usually, rights to extraordinary profits.

Consumer tip: Some preferred stocks pay very high yields. And they are usually very safe investments. Preferred stock is an excellent choice for older people who wish high income and little risk. A favorite way to buy is to invest in mutual funds specializing in preferred stock. Most preferred stock is owned by corporations or organizations that qualify for the 85 percent dividend exclusion from federal taxes. For most consumer investors, however, common stocks offer the better buy because they hold out hope for capital gains as well as income.

See also *stock, common;* Section II, "Investments."

stock proxy　a limited power of attorney that allows a designated person to represent the owner in voting on affairs of the corporation.

stock split　a division'into a greater number of shares of corporate stock outstanding. A stock that is split two for one, for example, would double the number of shares held by each stockholder and theoretically halve the per-share price. Splitting is done to encourage trading in that security. When prices are above a certain level, some people shy away from stocks. Thus, a split makes a stock more accessible to more people and usually has the effect of raising its relative value.

stock transfer　upon the sale of stock, the cancelling of a stock certificate and the issuance of a new one in the name of the new owner.

stock-transfer agent　a bank appointed by a corporation to act as its agent in doing the actual paperwork involved in stock transfers.

stock yield　the dividend earnings of a stock versus its market price, expressed as a percentage. Thus, a stock selling for $100 and paying $5 in annual dividends has an annual stock yield of 5 percent.

stop order　an order to buy or sell a security at a price that will limit losses. A stop order goes into effect when the market price reaches that specified price. Stop orders to sell at a price above the current market are used to limit losses on short sales, and stop orders to sell at a price below the current market are used to limit losses on regular investments.

See also *stop price.*

stop payment　an order given by a depositor to a bank not to honor a check he or she has written. Stop-payment orders may be given orally, but must be confirmed in writing.

Consumer tip: Stopping payment on a check is serious business. In the first place, it costs money—often as much as $10 or more. In the second place, it may give the person to whom the check was issued grounds for action against you. Don't just stop payment out of spite. Do so when a check is lost or stolen, and notify the payee in case it turns up and he tries to collect it.

stop price   the price at which a stop order is to be executed.
  See also *stop order*.

straddle   See *spread*.

straight annuity   See *annuity*.

straight life   See *ordinary life*.

straight-line depreciation   the rate of decline in the value of an asset calculated by dividing its anticipated number of useful years into its cost. As an example, if an asset costs $10,000 and has an expected life of 10 years, it may be depreciated at a rate of $1,000 a year under this method.
  See also *depreciation*.

straw man   a person who buys real estate on behalf of someone else, but does not reveal the identity of the true buyer. Straw men commonly buy property in situations in which, if the real buyers were known, the sellers would raise the prices unfairly. A typical situation in which this may occur is when a major company decides to move into a new area.

street broker   a broker who deals over-the-counter as opposed to on an exchange.

street name   the designation given to stock certificates that are held in the name of the broker rather than that of the buyer. Most people who frequently buy stocks do so in street name; in this way, the stocks are in the broker's possession, and when a sale is made, there is no necessity to deliver the actual certificates. This expedites trading by telephone. Stocks held in street name do not belong to the broker; they are similar in that respect to escrow funds held by an attorney.

striking price   the price at which an option may be exercised.
  See also *in the money; out of the money*.

Student Loan Marketing Association (Sallie Mae)   a private corporation sponsored by the federal government that purchases student loans from banks and other lenders, thereby making additional funds available to lend. Sallie Mae is funded by the sale of securities on the open market.

sublease   the renting of a property by the original tenant to a third party, with the original tenant retaining his or her rights and responsibilities under the lease.
  Consumer tip: If you are a tenant and must move, subleasing your apartment or house to another can be risky because you still have legal responsibilities under the lease. Instead, consider assigning the lease, which relieves you of risk. See an attorney for details.
  See also *lease*.

sublet   See *sublease*.

subordinated debenture   a debenture that, because it has a secondary claim to payment should the company fail, offers its owner a higher rate of return than a regular debenture.
  See also *debenture*.

subordinated interest a claim to property that is not as good as the primary claim. A second mortgage, for example, does not have as strong a claim as a first mortgage.

subordination agreement a document signed by a creditor acknowledging that his or her claim is inferior to that of another lender. Banks often require other lenders to sign such agreements before granting a loan.

subscription 1) an offering of securities; 2) an agreement to buy a security.

subsidiary a corporation that has a voting majority of its stock owned by another company.
See also *holding company*.

subsistence theory of wages See *iron law of wages*.

substantial penalty for early withdrawal See *penalty clause*.

subtenant someone who rents under a sublease.

sufferin' Suzy also *Tony*; slang name for the Susan B. Anthony dollar coin issued by the U.S. Treasury in 1979 and 1980. The coin was issued at the behest of vending machine operators and featured Susan B. Anthony on the obverse as a gesture to feminists who had been pushing for a woman to be featured on a coin or bill. The issue was, by any standards, a total flop because the coin was too similar in size to a quarter, so no coins were issued bearing dates later than 1980, except for a few in proof sets in 1981. The Sufferin' Suzy sobriquet was given the coin in testimony to its utter lack of public acceptance and the fact that bankers and merchants disliked it.
See also *money*.

sunrise industries new businesses that offer investors a high degree of risk and great potential profits. Computer and other hi-tech firms are examples.
See also *smokestack industries*.

Supplemental Security Income (SSI) a federal program, administered by the Social Security Administration, to assist those with very limited resources who are elderly, blind, or disabled. The program guarantees a minimum monthly income from the federal government, which, in some cases, may be supplemented by state funds. To qualify, individuals must have cash assets of no more than $1,500 and couples no more than $2,250. They may own their own home, household effects, and an automobile as long as these assets have only a "reasonable" value.
Consumer tip: If you think you or a member of your family might qualify for SSI, get further details from your Social Security office.
See also *Medicaid; Social Security*; Section II, "Retirement Planning."

supply and demand, law of a classical law in economics stating that price is determined by the supply of a product or service vis-à-vis the demand for it. If there is a larger supply than there is a demand, the price will fall. This will reduce profits and lead to a reduced supply. If demand exceeds supply, the price will rise, which will raise profits and encourage businesses to produce a greater supply.

supply-side economics   a school of economics that teaches that supply plays a greater role in encouraging investment and production than does demand. A basic tenet of supply-side economics is the Laffer curve, which shows that, as taxes are increased, fewer dollars are invested in business expansion. The corollary is that, as taxes are reduced, more money will flow into business expansion. When this theory was first tested by the Reagan Administration, in many cases the tax dollars released to businesses were spent on acquisition by merger rather than for true growth. Supply-side economics is essentially the opposite of Keynesian economics; it is a new name for the old trickle-down theory.
   See also *Keynesian economics; trickle-down theory.*

surcharge   an extra charge added onto a basic cost.

surety   1) a guaranty; 2) a person who guarantees to be responsible for the debts of another.
   See also *co-signer.*

surplus   also *retained earnings,* a newer term, since surplus connotes "extra"; the balance-sheet figure remaining after liabilities and capital stock figures have been deducted from total

assets. Surplus plus capital stock equals net worth.
   See also *net worth.*

surrender value   See *cash-surrender value.*

surrogate's court   See *probate court.*

surtax   a tax added onto another tax. A common way of raising revenues in government is simply to add a surtax to a state or local income tax. Surtaxes are almost always introduced as temporary measures, but have a habit of becoming permanent.

survivorship account   a joint account in which the entire balance becomes the property of the living party on the death of the other party.
   See also *joint property; right of survivorship.*

swap   See *barter.*

sweat equity   value added to a property by the labor of the owner.
   Consumer tip: Adding value to your home with do-it-yourself projects or maintenance makes very good sense, because labor invested saves before-tax dollars. Here's why: If you hire a plumber for $20 an hour to fix a drain and you are in the 30 percent marginal tax bracket, that means you must earn about $28.50 before taxes to have $20 left to pay him. So by doing the job yourself, you actually save $28.50 to put into a tax-deferred or tax-sheltered investment.
   See also Section II, "Tax Savings."

sweep account See *repurchase agreement*.

sweeten a loan to pledge additional collateral either to satisfy margin requirements or to calm a nervous banker.
See also *side collateral*.

swindle to defraud.

switch order an order to a broker to sell one security and buy another.

take a bath   slang for suffering great financial losses.

take a flier   take a chance. In investment cliches, to take a flier is to gamble on unknown factors in the hope of making a killing and not "taking a bath."

takeout loan   a long-term real estate mortgage loan used to pay off the initial construction loan.

takeover   the buying out of a company by another company, either through outright purchase or by exchanging stock in the two companies, with or without a cash differential.
  See also *merger*.

T&E card   travel and entertainment card.
  See also *credit card*.

tangible assets   physical assets, such as cash, buildings, and machin-

ery, as opposed to intangible assets, such as goodwill.
  See also *asset*.

tape price   the latest price of a security.

tax   a charge levied by a government that is used for the government's cost of operation. There are many kinds of taxes, among them:

- *Income taxes*, which may be either progressive or fixed. *Progressive income taxes*, like the United States federal income tax, go up in rate as the income rises. *Fixed income taxes*, like those in many states, tax all incomes at the same percentage rate.
- *Property taxes*, assessed by local governments, are levied against real property and in many areas, against personal property as well.
- *Sales taxes*, which may be assessed against all or selected items at the

time they are purchased, are used by state and local governments.

- *Excise taxes* are levied on selected goods or on the right to perform certain acts.

The problem with taxes is that not everyone pays a fair share. It is estimated that people in the underground economy avoid paying almost $100 billion a year in federal income taxes alone. It is estimated, for example, that there are about 500,000 prostitutes in the United States who pay no taxes. Other experts claim that illegal marijuana is the third largest cash crop in America; its growers and sellers pay no taxes. Because churches and educational and charitable institutions pay no property taxes, about $450 a year is added to the tax burden of every American family. These inequities in taxation provide the arguments for a national sales or excise tax, with tax credits available for the poor. Unfortunately, such a tax would impact most heavily on the average middle-class family.

See also *excise tax; property tax; sales tax; sin tax; underground economy; value-added tax.*

tax abatement a reduction in property tax, either on a general basis or as correction of an overassessment of value. For example, some states give all elderly citizens or veterans tax abatements. All states provide a means of relief for unfair charges or assessments.

See also *property tax.*

tax bracket See *marginal tax bracket.*

taxable estate the remaining value of an estate after all allowable deductions have been made.

taxable income See *adjusted gross income.*

taxable value assessed value.

tax deferral the putting off of tax payments until a later date. The most common examples of tax deferrals involve money deposited in Individual Retirement Accounts, Keogh Plans, Simplified Employee Pension plans, and tax-deferred annuities. The idea behind a tax deferral is to avoid current taxes on some income, which will then be invested and allowed to grow, tax-free, until the taxpayer retires. Deferral has three benefits:

1. Without current taxes on the growth, the investment will compound at an accelerated rate. For example, $2,000 saved each year for 20 years at 10 percent annual interest by a taxpayer in the 30 percent marginal bracket will grow, after taxes, to $87,730. Those $2,000 annual deposits, at 10 percent with taxes deferred, would grow in 20 years to $126,000.

2. The withdrawals made after retirement from tax-deferred investments are taxable, but by retirement time, most taxpayers are in a lower marginal tax bracket and usually have extra personal and/or spousal exemptions for being over 65.

3. Assuming that inflation continues, if only at a modest rate, the taxes on the withdrawn sums will be paid in the inflated dollars of that time.

Consumer tip: The big argument against tax-deferred savings is, "So I'll be a millionaire! And a loaf of bread will cost $100,000." This is a foolish excuse for not being willing to save money. Here's why: Interest rates in high-yield CDs or money market mutual funds tend to outpace inflation by four to five percentage points per year. Some mutual stock funds do much better. You will always be better off with tax-deferred savings, unless one of two things happens—if you become filthy rich and are in a much higher tax bracket after retirement (in which case the few extra dollars you'll have to pay in taxes won't matter), or if the economy should be in a sustained deflation and you have to eventually pay taxes in dollars that have greater purchasing power than current ones, which is very unlikely.

See also *annuity; Individual Retirement Account (IRA); Keogh Plan; Simplified Employee Pension (SEP); tax shelter.*

tax-deferred annuity   See *annuity.*

tax evasion   an illegal attempt to avoid payment of income or other taxes. With income taxes, the most common tax dodges are understatement of income or overstatement of deductions. Some people, for example, deliberately encourage cash payment in order to avoid leaving an audit trail through which income can be verified.

With sales taxes, the most common dodge is to purchase goods in another jurisdiction that has no sales tax or a lower sales tax. In some states, if people pay for goods with credit cards issued by out-of-state banks and use an out-of-state address, merchants will not collect sales taxes. In such cases, the buyer is supposed to pay a use tax to his home state, but usually fails to do so.

tax-exempt bond   a bond issued by a state or local government, the income from which is exempt from federal income taxes and, in some cases, from state income taxes as well.

Consumer tip: As a general rule, if you are in the 35 percent marginal tax bracket or higher, tax-exempt bonds make good sense as investment vehicles.

See also *bond.*

tax exemption   an allowed deduction that reduces taxable income. Exemptions are made by taxing authorities for specific classes of people or for specific reasons. For example, personal exemptions are allowed for an individual taxpayer and his or her spouse, with additional exemptions if either or both are over 65 years old or blind. In addition, those dependent on the taxpayer for support may qualify him or her for dependency exemptions if they meet the required standards of relationship, income, degree of dependency, citizenship, or residency and if the dependent has not filed a joint return except for the purpose of obtaining a refund.

Consumer tip: Know who your dependents are and be sure to claim them. This sounds basic, but many people fail to take a few simple steps to have elderly parents, for example, qualify as dependents. Also, don't forget that, while children under 19 are automatically considered dependents, so are children of any age if they are full-time students. While a spouse must live with you to be claimed as a dependent, many other relatives, by blood or marriage, need not physically live with you. Ask a tax accountant for advice if you think you are missing out on a dependency exemption.

tax foreclosure   the taking of real estate or personal property because of past-due taxes.

tax-free income   interest paid on a tax-exempt bond.
   See also *tax-exempt bond.*

tax lien   a claim filed by a government body against real estate for unpaid taxes.
   Consumer tip: It is extremely easy for a government or even a private lender to place a lien on real estate. If you're not sure your tax payments have been properly credited, ask the tax authorities. And if you have any reason to think that a lien may have been placed on your property, visit the county courthouse or registry of deeds to find out. Don't wait until you try to sell the house or to get another mortgage to find that your title is not clear.

tax penalty   a punitive payment required for failure to pay taxes on time. With federal income tax, penalties and interest are assessed for late payment of taxes, for underpayment of taxes, and for failure to file estimated taxes when required. Here are the penalty and interest rates:

- If less than 80 percent of the final tax for the year is paid, interest due is calculated by multiplying the difference between the amount prepaid and the total tax due times

the number of days late times the prime rate (adjusted by the IRS twice annually).
- For underpayment due to negligence or disregard of IRS rules, the penalty is 5 percent of the underpayment plus 50 percent of the interest due on the underpayment, as figured above.

Penalties paid to the IRS are not tax deductible because they are held to be additional taxes and not interest, as on a loan.
   Consumer tip: It used to cost less to "borrow" from the government by not paying estimated taxes when due instead of taking out a loan for that money. But the recent pegging of penalty interest to the prime rate plus the negligence penalty have combined to make this a very expensive way to get an unauthorized loan. Pay your taxes, including the estimates, on time, even if you have to borrow money from a bank to do so, because the bank interest, unlike that charged by the IRS, is tax deductible.
   Also see Section II, "Tax Savings."

tax rate   the percentage at which a tax is assessed. Thus, a tax rate of 2.5 percent on property valued at $100,000 means a tax of $2,500.

tax reform act   any of a number of federal laws with various titles enacted for income tax reform, simplification, or economic recovery. By and large, however, because there are always special interest groups to serve, these laws have done little to reform or simplify income tax procedures and little to aid the economy. There is a serious move afoot to eliminate all tax shelters, deductions, and other measures that lead to abuses and to substitute a simple, basic tax—such as a flat 10 percent of income.

tax roll   in real property taxation, an official listing of properties taxed along with their respective valuations, current assessed taxes, and owners.

Consumer tip: If you are not familiar with your local tax roll, take the trouble to examine it personally. The only way to tell if you are being fairly taxed is to compare your property assessment with that of similar homes in the community. If you are being overtaxed, consider filing for an abatement.

See also *tax abatement;* Section II, "Tax Savings."

tax shelter   a means of legally avoiding the payment of federal income taxes by manipulation of personal finances. Tax shelters are made possible because Congress builds incentives for specialized investments into the tax laws. In theory, this is to stimulate disadvantaged areas of the economy; but in the past, it has primarily helped very wealthy individuals who had a great deal of political clout. However, lowering the maximum tax rate to 50 percent has eliminated the advantages of some of the classic shelters, so that the best shelters are real estate, which can now be depreciated in 15 years (especially favored is the rehabilitation of slum buildings); oil and gas; energy properties; and, in some cases, research and development.

People of more modest means have one big tax shelter available to them— the ownership of a primary residence. If capital gains on the sale of a residence are reinvested in a more costly home within two years, taxes on those gains are deferred. This rollover can continue until the homeowner reaches age 55, after which time, if the principal residence is sold, the first $125,000 of profit is tax-free. Another tax shelter commonly available is the custodial account under the Uniform Gifts to Minors Act.

Consumer tip: If you're looking for a tax shelter, be wary. Sometimes the management and investment fees are so high that the tax advantage is dubious. But do try to take advantage of the tax-sheltering features of home ownership.

See also *Clifford Trust; tax deferral; Uniform Gifts to Minors Act (UGMA);* Section II, "Tax Savings."

T-bill   Treasury bill.
See also *Treasury securities.*

teller   an employee of a bank or savings institution who handles the routine money transactions, such as deposits, withdrawals, and check cashing. The word comes from the Dutch *tellen,* to count.

The more mundane bank transactions are rapidly being turned over to computer-based *automatic teller machines (ATMs),* which, in some cases, can do everything but make business loans, and can do so every hour of every day. These machines may be located on the outside wall of the bank or savings institution or in an offsite location. They are accessible both during and after regular banking hours.

As ATMs do more of the routine tasks, many tellers' jobs are being upgraded to that of *customer service representative,* which involves personal account supervision as well as transaction handling.

See also Section II, "Bank Accounts."

tenancy by the entirety See *joint property.*

tenancy in common See *joint property.*

tenant's insurance a type of homeowner's insurance that covers a renter's personal belongings against such things as fire, flood, vandalism, and theft. Such a policy may also provide liability protection. Expensive riders that cover jewelry and other valuables are available as well.

See also *homeowner's insurance.*

tender to offer legally authorized money in payment of an obligation.

tender offer 1) an offering by a corporation to buy its own stocks or bonds; 2) a bid by a person or corporation to buy controlling interest in another company.

10-year trust See *Clifford Trust.*

term the length of time required for the maturity of a contract.

term life insurance life insurance protection written for a specific time period, usually one, three, or five years. With term insurance, the policyholder buys protection only, that is, no savings feature is involved. The advantage of term insurance is that during the insured's younger years, it is inexpensive; the disadvantage is that

during his or her older years, it may become prohibitively expensive.

Consumer tip: Agents don't like to sell term insurance because both the premiums and the commission rates are much lower than those on cash-value insurance. This could be an excellent reason for you, as a consumer, to buy it. Numerous studies have proved that a person makes out much better by buying term insurance for needed protection and by investing the difference in cost between term and cash-value premiums in high-yield certificates of deposit, money market mutual funds, or common stock mutual funds. It is said frequently that the cost of term insurance is too high in old age. But if a person has accumulated any savings at all, and if he or she has enough permanent insurance for final expenses, the term insurance can then be allowed to lapse.

See also *ordinary life;* Section II, "Life Insurance."

term loan a loan with a fixed maturity, as opposed to a demand loan, which is payable at any time. Extended term loans may have maturities of up to 10 years.

testament See *will.*

testamentary trust a trust established under terms of a will. A trustee, usually a bank, is appointed to collect the deceased person's property and then to invest or manage it on behalf of the trust beneficiary.

See also *trust.*

testate having a legally valid will.

third-party check   a check given by the maker to the payee who endorses it to a third party. A typical example is a paycheck endorsed by a person to a supermarket. Many check-guarantee systems will not accept third-party checks because of the danger of accepting checks that have been stolen from mailboxes.

third-party credit transfers   a deposit made to a bank account by a third party. Typical examples are the direct deposit of Social Security and payroll checks.

thrift   1) the practice of saving; 2) the term for a *thrift institution*.
See also *thrift institution*.

thrift institution   also *thrift;* a mutual savings bank, a savings and loan association, a building and loan association, or a cooperative bank.
See also *bank*.

ticker   a machine that prints out transactions made on stock exchanges on a continuous paper tape.

tickler   a dated file that shows the maturity dates of financial documents. A note tickler in a bank, for example, shows loans coming due in the near future so that customers may be billed, as well as loans due on their maturity dates.

tight money   a scarcity of money in the credit markets resulting in high interest rates and making it much more difficult to get loans.

time deposit   a savings account or a certificate of deposit; technically, money on deposit for a specific period of time or for which notice may be required for withdrawal. Under the law, banks and thrifts may require a month's notice for withdrawal of regular savings, but these institutions have not exercised this right in many years.
See also *demand deposit*.

time draft   See *draft*.

time loan   See *loan*.

title insurance   insurance that is intended to reimburse a buyer of property from loss should the legal ownership, or title, later prove defective. Title insurance is required in some states and not in others. If it is purchased, the one-time premium is paid at the time of the closing or settlement.

Title I FHA loan   a home improvement loan made through a bank or lender but guaranteed by the Federal Housing Administration (FHA), a division of the Department of Housing and Urban Development. Because of the federal guarantee, these loans are somewhat less costly than other home improvement loans, but they do require a great deal of paperwork and a fairly long wait for approval. Also, Title I FHA loans can usually be written for longer terms than conventional loans. However, they may not be made for luxury additions to property, such as swimming pools.
Consumer tip: A Title I FHA loan can save you quite a bit of interest if you don't mind the hassle. They are most advantageous for people who are marginal credit risks because the govern-

ment guarantee greatly enhances their chances for loan approval.

title search an investigation of the legal right to the possession of real estate prior to the transfer of the property. The title search is usually routine, requiring only a simple search of the records in the county courthouse or registry of deeds office. It is usually done by an attorney.

tombstone ad a slang term describing a newspaper ad for a new security that lists all of the brokers participating in the offering. The name comes from the fact that the ads tend to be stark in layout and list pertinent data, much as a tombstone lists data about the deceased.

Tony See *money; sufferin' Suzy.*

Toronto Stock Exchange (TSE) See *stock exchange.*

tort under civil law, a wrongful act committed by a person against another person or his or her property. A tort occurs when someone injures another person, hurts his or her property, attacks his or her reputation without just cause, or deprives him or her of freedom of action without just cause. A crime is an offense against the public at large; drunken driving is an example. But a tort occurs when that drunken driver smashes into another person's car. So a crime may or may not involve a tort.

Employers are liable for the torts committed by their employees if the action takes place during the course of their employment; children or men-

tally incompetent people may be liable for their torts. If the person who commits a tort does so with the consent of the injured party, either expressed or implied, there is no recourse under the law; if he or she acted in self-defense, there is no recourse; or if he or she acted to maintain law and order, there is no recourse.

Consumer tip: You may inadvertently commit a tort; someone may trip on a sidewalk you neglected to repair, or you may have an accident that causes injury or damage of some kind. To protect yourself, it is imperative to have adequate liability insurance.

See also Section II, "Property and Liability Insurance."

total debt to tangible net worth a ratio calculated by dividing a business's total of all debts by its tangible (excluding goodwill) net worth. If the ratio exceeds 100 percent, the claims of creditors against the assets of the business exceeds the equity of the shareholders or owners.

total of payments the sum of all payments necessary to repay an installment loan. Thus, a loan of $5,000 for five years with an annual percentage rate of 12 percent will have a total of payments of $6,374 (60 monthly payments of $106.24).

Consumer tip: Most borrowers overlook the total of payments. You might say, "I paid $6,000 for that new bathroom." But if you put $1,000 down and financed the $5,000 balance as above, you really paid $7,374. And if you want to be really technical and add in opportunity cost, you can add about $650 in savings interest lost on the

$1,000 down payment for a true total cost of about $8,024.

See also *opportunity cost;* Section II, "Borrowing."

Totten trust   a trust for the benefit of another person that is set up by a person who deposits his or her money and names himself or herself as trustee. During the life of the person establishing the trust, it may be revoked at any time; but after his or her death, a new trustee is named and the trust continues for the benefit of the beneficiary. Such trusts offer a viable way to protect incompetent heirs both now and in the future.

trade   acceptance   a negotiable instrument executed to facilitate trade. It is drawn by the seller of a product at the time of the sale and accepted by the purchaser. Trade acceptances are common when auto dealers buy new cars from the factory. They are cleared through banks as collection items.

See also *draft.*

trader   See *speculator.*

trading post   a location on the floor of a stock exchange at which specific securities are bought and sold.

transaction   a contractual agreement between two parties resulting in a legal obligation. Buying, selling, making deposits, or making withdrawals are all common transactions.

transfer   See *wire transfer.*

transfer agent   a person, or, in the case of a large business, usually a bank, appointed by a corporation to keep the official records of outstanding stock, by owners' names and the number of shares each owns. The transfer agent also cancels old certificates and issues new certificates when a person sells or buys stock.

transfer payment   a bureaucratic term for transfers of money from a business or person to another person through taxes. Welfare benefits are prime examples of transfer payments. Transfer payments add nothing to the gross national product, but simply shift wealth. The concept of improving the economy via transfer payments is primarily that of economic liberals, who reason that when people receive money to spend, it not only benefits them but stimulates business. The transfer-payment theory is in essence the opposite of the trickle-down theory.

See also *trickle-down theory.*

transfer tax   a tax imposed when a security is transferred either by sale or gift from one person to another. The tax is paid by the seller or giver.

transit number   See *check.*

travel and entertainment card (T&E card)   See *credit card.*

traveler's check   a sight draft that is sold through a bank or other agency, payable by the issuing company, and used when traveling in place of cash. These "checks" are signed by the purchaser when bought and countersigned when cashed or spent, which helps to protect the issuer and the traveler's checkholder from possible loss. Traveler's checks are universally acceptable, are insured against loss or theft, and are fairly easy to replace, even when traveling.

Consumer tip: Never carry more cash than you can afford to lose; use traveler's checks and credit cards when you're on the go. But don't keep an extra $20 traveler's check tucked into your wallet as emergency money at all times. Just think—if only 100,000 people did that, each buying the same kind, the issuing company would have the use of $2 million interest-free on a very long-term "loan." And do shop for traveler's checks—some banks issue them with no service charge to regular customers.

treasurer   a person appointed to receive, disburse and safeguard money on behalf of a company or organization.

treasurer's check   See *official check.*

Treasuries   See *Treasury securities.*

Treasury bill   See *Treasury securities.*

Treasury bond   See *Treasury securities.*

Treasury certificate   See *Treasury securities.*

Treasury note   See *Treasury securities.*

Treasury securities   also *governments; Treasuries;* any of various obligations of the U.S. government that are offered for sale to the public through the Federal Reserve Banks. Treasury securities have the highest credit rating of any investment in the world, and

the yield is competitive with that on many other investments. Since 1950, common stocks and real estate have outperformed treasuries, and treasuries have outperformed both fixed corporate and municipal bonds. Treasury securities include:

- *Treasury bills (T-bills),* with maturities of 91 to 182 days.
- *Treasury bonds,* with maturities of over five years.
- *Treasury certificates,* with maturities of one year.
- *Treasury notes,* with maturities ranging from one to five years.

Consumer tip: You may invest in Treasuries through your local bank, for which you will pay a fee, or you may buy them directly from the nearest Federal Reserve Bank and pay no fee.

See also *Federal Reserve Banks (FRBs); noncompetitive tender.*

treasury stock   stock in a corporation purchased on the market or donated to the company, which is held by the corporation. The ownership of such stock decreases the number of shares outstanding and thus increases the relative value of each share held by the public.

trial balance   a list of the total of account debits against a list of the total of account credits. If they are the same, it is an indication that no accounting errors have been made in posting the books. A trial balance does not indicate financial strength as a balance sheet does.

trickle-down theory   the concept holding that reduced tax burdens on capital investment result in increased savings and investment, and that the benefits of these increases will then seep down to every level of the economy. Trickle-down is the favorite economic theory of fiscal conservatives who espouse supply-side economics.

See also *supply-side economics*.

truncation in modern banking, the "cutting off" or stopping the practice of returning a customer's paid checks with his or her statement. Banks do this to avoid handling and postage charges. Under a truncation system, the bank keeps the checks and provides the customer with copies should proof of payment be needed. As an inducement to accept truncation, customers sometimes receive statements that list checks paid by number and leave spaces where checks written have not cleared, which supposedly makes the statement easier to reconcile.

The problems with truncation are these: People have been conditioned, by years of bank advertising, to count on their cancelled checks as legal receipts. In addition, there is some question as to how many creditors will accept a photocopy of a check as final proof of payment. Also, most banks will give a few free photocopies, but if a depositor needs hundreds, such as for a tax audit, the charges can be high.

Consumer tip: If you write a lot of checks and need them as receipts, avoid using a truncated checking account. But you should be aware that eventually everyone will have to accept this type of account.

trust a fiduciary relationship between one person and another person,

bank, or company under which property is entrusted for the benefit of someone else. The basic types of trusts are as follows:

- *Investment trusts* exist when a group of people pool their resources so that they can diversify their holdings and maximize their profits. Mutual funds and money market mutual funds are examples of typical consumer investment trusts.
- *Bank trust accounts*, administered by a trust department, include living trusts, guardianships, life insurance trusts, charitable trusts, accumulation trusts, Totten trusts, and *testamentary trusts*.
- A combination of companies doing business in the same industry that attempt to control production and set prices is a type of trust that was banned by the Sherman Anti-Trust Act.

See also *money market mutual fund; mutual fund; testamentary trust*; Section II, "Estate Planning," "Investments."

trust agreement a legal contract between a person establishing a trust and the trustee, or administrator. When establishing a trust, the trust agreement is drawn up by the attorney who represents the person establishing it.

See also Section II, "Estate Planning."

trust company See *bank*.

trust department the operating section of a bank responsible for its trust accounts. The trust department usually has two major subdivisions, one concerned with estate planning and one concerned with trust administration.

trustee   a person, bank, or company that holds the title to property and administers that property for the benefit of someone else under a legal agreement.

trustee in bankruptcy   a trustee appointed by a court to administer the affairs of a company undergoing bankruptcy.

trust instrument   a will, agreement, or court order that creates a trust.

trust officer   a person who administers trust accounts on behalf of a bank where he or she is employed.

Truth-in-Lending   See *Consumer Credit Protection Act.*

TSE   the Toronto Stock Exchange. See also *stock exchange.*

turnover   1) the volume of business in a securities exchange on a given day; 2) the annual rate of employee replacement in a company or industry.

twisting   a sales attempt made by a life insurance agent to induce a person to cancel an existing policy and to buy a policy from him or her so that the agent can get a commission. Twisting is unethical and illegal, but very common.

Consumer tip: Any agent worth his or her salt can take any policy and "twist" some facts so that a policy his or her company offers looks better. A common way to do this is to overstate anticipated dividends. If you are being pressured to switch policies, check the latest insurance company comparisons made by *Consumer's Reports;* then ask the agent for a copy of his or her policy and projected figures and show it to a representative of the company that now insures you. He or she can quickly spot any phony figures. And you can save hundreds or thousands of dollars in possible added charges. This is not to say that switching never pays—it does. But often it does not.

See also *churning.*

twofer   1) two-for-one; 2) getting a real or apparent bargain.

UCC   See *Uniform Commercial Code.*

UGMA   See *Uniform Gifts to Minors Act.*

ultimate beneficiary   the person or institution named to receive the residue in a trust after all other beneficiaries' rights have been exhausted.

uncollected funds   checks deposited to a bank account that have not yet been paid by the bank on which they were drawn. Here's the way it works: If John, who lives in Histown, deposits a check written by Jane, who lives in Hertown, in his account at Histown Bank, his bank must send that check for payment to Hertown Bank, which must then send the money back to Histown Bank. In actual fact, this is done either through local clearing-houses, the Federal Reserve Banks, or correspondent banks; the process is automated, and payment to the bank is made through immediate bank credits. But it still usually takes at least a few days, even for banks in the same town. So although John has written "Deposit—$100" on his checkbook stub on June 1, the check may not be paid until June 5. Therefore, he can't write checks on the money until that date. Uncollected funds cause more bank/customer misunderstandings than any other situation.

Consumer tip: If you make a deposit and need to draw checks on it, ask someone at the bank how long it takes for deposited checks to clear (be paid). Then wait until that date to write your check. That's the safe way. If you just go ahead and write a check immediately, you're asking the bank to make you an interest-free loan until your deposit clears, and chances are it will return your check and charge you a return-item fee. Best of all, open an automatic overdraft account—then if the deposit hasn't cleared, you can just create a short-term loan at a modest charge.

See also *returned check*.

underground economy those people who either earn a living illegally or whose business activities are strictly cash and carry and who do not report their incomes to the Internal Revenue Service. It has been estimated that if those in the underground economy were to begin paying income taxes, they would add almost $100 billion a year to the federal revenue, thus reducing either the deficit or the taxes of others.

See also *tax*.

underwrite 1) to share an insurance risk; 2) to guarantee the sale of a new issue of securities. This word has an interesting history. In the late seventeenth century, businessmen gathered at Edward Lloyd's coffeehouse in London, where it became a custom for them to share the risks on merchant vessels. In those days, one businessman would agree to insure a ship and its cargo, but if it were lost, he would be wiped out. So he would list the ship and the terms of the insurance on a paper tacked to the coffeehouse wall, sign his name as insurer, and then draw a line across the paper. Those who wished to share in his risk—and potential insurance profit—would write their names and the amount of risk they assumed under the line. Thus, they were "underwriting" him.

underwriter an expert who rates risks for an insurance company. In life insurance, the underwriting function is performed by an actuary.

See also *actuary*.

undivided profit earnings not distributed to shareholders and often intended for special purposes, such as future dividend payments or the charging off of bad debts.

undivided right the rights of a part owner of property that cannot be separated from the rights of the other party. Such rights exist under joint tenancy and for tenants in common.

See also *joint property*.

unearned income income received before a good or service is delivered. Examples are an advance paid to an author under a book contract and rental for an apartment that is received a month in advance.

unearned interest loan interest prepaid but not yet earned. When interest is "discounted," it is paid when the loan is made and is gradually earned as the loan matures.

See Section II, "Borrowing."

unemployment compensation insurance against a loss of income caused by job layoffs. Unemployment compensation is paid through the states and funded by premiums assessed against employers. Benefits vary widely from state to state.

unfunded debt corporate obligations not covered by a bond issue.

Uniform Commercial Code (UCC) the laws governing business activities, which are essentially the same in each of the states (hence the "uniform"), except Louisiana. The laws that most affect consumers are those relating to negotiable instruments and contracts. All states require that contracts for the sale of goods worth more than $500 be in writing, and most require that leases of more than one year be in writing. (Some states specify three years, some revert to common law, and a few require that all leases be in writing.) In addition, most require that contracts to be performed in over one year must also be in writing.

See also *holder in due course; negotiable instrument; notice of dishonor; returned check.*

Uniform Gifts to Minors Act (UGMA) a law, adopted by most states, that allows income from irrevocable gifts to minors to be taxed to the minor and not to the donor. Such accounts are *custodial accounts*, and should be titled, "(Adult's name) as custodian for (child's name) under the (state's name) Uniform Gifts to Minors Act." The gifts are irrevocable, which means that the child, upon reaching his or her majority, may use the money at his or her discretion and that, in the meantime, the custodian cannot touch the money except for the benefit of the child—and that means for strict necessities only. Because most children do not have enough income to be federal taxpayers, using a UGMA account means that the income can grow tax-free.

Consumer tip: If you have small children, begin saving for college costs under the UGMA immediately, even if it amounts to only $5 a week per child. As an example, if an account is opened for a one-year-old child and regular $5 weekly deposits are made until the child's eighteenth birthday, and if the money earns an average of 10 percent per year, the child will have

a fund of about $11,600. If the parents are in the 30 percent tax bracket and save that same sum in their own names, the annual income taxes will reduce the sum to $8,580. That's a total gain of about 35 percent because of the use of a UGMA account.

See also *gift tax*, Section II, "College Costs," "Tax Savings."

unissued stock stock authorized by a corporation but as yet not sold to the public.

United States Note See *money.*

universal life insurance a type of life insurance, developed in the late 1970s by a stock brokerage house, which was an attempt to break the hold of ordinary life on the market. Under universal life, there is an insurance feature and a savings feature, and both are variable as the needs of the insured/investor change.

Universal life was immensely popular when introduced, but as interest rates fell, the savings portion became about as exciting as that under ordinary life. The positive thing about universal life is that it clearly separates the insurance from the savings aspects. The negative factors are that a front-end load (a sales commission) is charged on all premiums, very low interest is paid on the first $1,000 or so of cash reserve, and the Internal Revenue Service has limited any tax advantages on the savings portion by restricting the cash-value limits to 60 percent of the face value of the policy. About 10 percent of all insurance sold is universal life.

Consumer tip: Before jumping into universal life, wait a while. Chances are that newer and better plans will be introduced. In general, though, you're better off buying term insurance at the lowest possible rate and making your own investments.

See also Section II, "Life Insurance."

unlimited mortgage   an open-end mortgage not limited to a fixed amount.
See also *open-end mortgage*.

unloading   selling securities quickly to cut losses.

unpaid balance   the amount outstanding on a loan or credit account. An unpaid balance may either be current (paid up-to-date) or past due.

unrealized profit or loss   See *paper profit or loss*.

unsecured loan   See *loan*.

unsecured time loan   See *loan*.

up tick   a stock transaction made at a higher price than the transaction immediately preceding. By Securities and Exchange Commission (SEC) rules, a short sale must be made on an up tick.
See also *down tick*.

use tax   a type of sales tax that is imposed on goods purchased outside of a sales-tax state and then brought into that state. The use tax is designed to discourage residents of sales-tax states from shopping across state lines.

U.S. Savings Bonds   nonnegotiable obligations of the U.S. government issued in denominations attractive to people of moderate means. These securities come in two varieties:

- *EE bonds* are variable-rate bonds sold at a 50 percent discount. This means that no interest is paid until the bonds mature, at which time the maturity value includes the earnings. The maturity dates vary with the interest rates, so that, as interest rates rise, the maturity becomes shorter. The purchase price is always one-half the maturity value. EE bonds are issued with maturity values of $50, $75, $100, $200, $500, $1,000, $5,000, and $10,000.

- *HH bonds*, which are variable-rate bonds on which interest is paid to the owner every six months by government check. The bonds are sold at full face value and mature in 10 years. They are issued in denominations of $500, $1,000, $5,000, and $10,000.

There are two big advantages to Series EE savings bonds: Income is tax-deferrable until the bond is finally cashed. In the meantime, the proceeds from matured bonds may be used to buy more bonds as many times as the saver wishes. Thus, for example, a saver, age 35, may buy bonds, roll them over at age 45 into new savings bonds, roll them over again at age 55 into new bonds, and then, at age 65, after the saver has retired and is in a lower marginal tax bracket with extra exemptions, use them for retirement income. Also, income from both Series EE and HH is exempt from state and local income taxes.

Consumer tip: If you are putting all you legally can into an Individual Retirement Account (IRA), Keogh Plan, or Simplified Employee Pension (SEP) program, make bonds your next tax-deferred investment choice. Unless the bonds are used for your IRA or Keogh Plan, you can't deduct your annual savings from your income, but the interest does grow tax-deferred.

See also *bond*.

usury originally, any payment of interest to borrow money; now, interest charged in excess of legal rates. During the Middle Ages, Catholic theologians taught that the charging of interest was sinful, so all interest was considered to be usury. For this reason, Christians were forbidden to become bankers; hence many of the early, famous banking families were Jewish. Today, usurious rates are usually associated with loan sharks.

utter to put counterfeit money or forged, worthless, or counterfeit checks into circulation. As commonly used, uttering is the crime of issuing a forged or worthless check. If someone writes a check that is returned for lack of funds and does not make it good, he or she can be charged with uttering.

VA See *Veterans Administration.*

validation verification, often by a second person. Thus, a teller validates a deposit by adding together the items deposited. In financial transactions, when items are validated, this is often indicated by a validation stamp, bearing the date and initials of the person who checked the items.

valuation appraisal.

value-added tax a type of sales tax that is added to manufactured goods at each stage of production and that some experts are proposing as a federal tax to supplement or even replace the income tax. A tax is imposed on the value added as each producer processes the products. With such a tax, there is a great advantage in buying products requiring as little processing as possible. Value-added taxes are popular in Europe, but though proposed, have never been used in the United States. See also *sales tax; tax.*

variable annuity an annuity plan that is designed to protect against inflation by the investment of a substantial portion of the principal in common stocks. The annuitant is guaranteed a basic income from the plan, but if the stock investments pay off, he or she will receive extra payments based on the profits.

Consumer tip: If you really want an annuity, the variable variety makes sense, as long as you are convinced that common stocks will prove anti-inflationary over the long term.

See also *annuity.*

variable life insurance a cash-reserve type policy in which the basic death benefit is guaranteed, but in which additional benefits may be added if the investments underlying the policy increase in value. The policy is tied to the stocks, bonds, or money markets in which the cash reserves are invested. In an inflationary economy, such a policy offers some protection against devalued dollars.

Consumer tip: Chances are good that you'll still make out better by buying the cheapest term insurance you can find and investing the difference in cost between that and an ordinary life policy in bank CDs, a good mutual fund, and money market mutual funds.

Because consumers should need less coverage as they grow older and as their assets grow, the basic flaw in variable life insurance is that it gives low death benefits during the years of maximum risk and high death benefits during retirement years when children are grown and mortgages are paid off.

See also *universal life insurance;* Section II, "Life Insurance."

variable-rate loan an installment loan under which the initial interest rate is usually a bit below the rate for fixed-percentage loans, but the rate for which may be increased or decreased every six months as the cost of living changes. The basis for the rate adjustment varies, sometimes being tied to the going rate for Treasury securities, sometimes to the cost of money as determined by a government index, and sometimes determined by the local interest rate. However, these loans always have an interest cap that gives the borrower some protection.

Consumer tip: If you can get a fixed-rate loan, you're probably better off. True, the economy could go into a period of deflation whereby the variable-rate borrowers would make out better,

but that's very unlikely. Also, if you have a fixed-rate loan and the rates drop, you can always renegotiate the rate.

See also Section II, "Borrowing."

variable-rate mortgage (VRM)
also *adjustable-rate mortgage;* a mortgage loan that provides for interest rate adjustments. This type of mortgage was designed to help lenders avoid the trap they were in during the late 1970s, when they were paying interest rates as high as 18 percent on new money while their mortgage portfolios were heavily invested in 6 and 7 percent loans. The adjustments allow lenders to benefit from rising rates, and, conversely, they allow borrowers to benefit from falling rates.

There are many plans, but typically the loan is originally written below the current conventional loan rate and is fixed for from six months to a year. Thereafter, every six months the lender adjusts the rate to some current inflation index, often the "cost of funds" index issued by the Federal Home Loan Bank Board. Usually, there is a cap on each rate adjustment and a total cap on the entire loan, so that a mortgage originally written at 13 percent will not go over about 17 percent over the life of the loan. Conversely, there is no downward floor, so the borrower can benefit if rates drop sharply.

Consumer tip: Here's a rule of thumb: If you have a good chance of moving in five years or less, don't let a variable-rate loan bother you. On the other hand, if you plan to stay in your house permanently, shop for a conventional loan. Even if rates drop, you can always renegotiate downward; and if they go up, you will benefit greatly. If you must get a variable-rate loan, shop for one with the lowest cap.

See also *conventional mortgage; graduated-payment adjustable mortgage; rollover mortgage;* Section II, "Home Financing."

vault cash in a financial institution, cash on hand that is not necessary for routine business. Such cash is usually under a separate time lock in the vault, which means that a teller must set the combination, then wait for a period of time before the lock will open. This delay is designed to discourage robbers, who are almost always in a hurry.

Consumer tip: If you have a small business, take a tip from bankers and keep a minimum of cash where it is at risk from robbers. Lock the rest in a secure place, preferably off the premises. You will always have time to get cash, but robbers can't wait.

vendor seller.

venture capital money invested in a new undertaking that may be raised by a new issue of stock or, because many new businesses do not have access to conventional lending sources, directly from investors.

Consumer tip: The most common venture capital investment vehicle for most people is that available through penny stocks or new issues. You can make—or lose—a fortune through such investments, so be very careful. Seek the advice of a competent broker.

See also *penny stock;* Section II, "Investments."

vested interest a legal and permanent right of ownership in property.

vesting the legal and permanent right of an employee to share in a pension plan under the terms of his or her employment agreement. Vesting implies the right of an employee to carry pension benefits from job to job within an organization. The Employee Retirement Income Security Act (ERISA) defines employee rights.

See also *Employee Retirement Income Security Act (ERISA).*

Veterans Administration (VA)

a federal government agency established to administer the rights of veterans as defined by law. For most people, these rights break down into:

- Mortgage-loan guarantees, which enable qualifying veterans to borrow up to 100 percent of the appraised value of a home. That means the possibility of a low- or even no-down-payment loan, and at reduced rates.
- Education benefits, which vary depending on when the veteran saw service. A college veteran's advisor can provide details.
- Life insurance benefits. Because some veterans qualify for excellent life insurance benefits, people at a VA office should be consulted for details.
- Funeral benefits. Veterans are entitled to free burial in a national cemetery, or their dependents may receive up to $450 to help defray funeral expenses. This amount in-

creases if the death is service-related.

Consumer tip: If you or a close relative are a veteran, check out any benefits that are due you. Be sure to leave a copy of your military discharge papers where the executor of your estate can find them.
See also Section II, "Home Financing."

VISA a popular bank credit-card system that issues credit cards, traveler's checks, and point-of-sale (POS) services as well. VISA was originally called Bank Americard, and was founded under the aegis of the huge west-coast Bank of America.
See also *MasterCard*.

voidable contract a contract that may be cancelled by either party in the event of fraud, incompetence, or some other justifiable reason.

volatile stock a stock that tends to increase or decrease in price at a rate much higher than the market as a whole. Obviously, highly volatile stocks are much more speculative than those with low volatility.

volume usually, the total number of shares traded on a stock exchange in a single day. Volume may also be used to measure trading during other specified time periods.

voluntary bankruptcy See *bankruptcy, personal.*

voting rights, shareholder the right to vote at shareholders' meetings at the rate of one vote per share of common stock owned. Few stockholders actually attend meetings, so voting rights are usually given by proxy to a person or group who represents the shareholder's interests.

voucher check a check with a voucher attached that shows the purpose of the check and is extremely handy for bookkeeping and tax purposes.

voucher system a bookkeeping technique for the orderly payment of bills. With this system, vouchers for payment are prepared that authorize payment. The actual checks are prepared from these vouchers.

VRM See *variable-rate mortgage.*

wage compensation for employment paid on a per-unit basis. Such units may be time, as in dollars per hour; or they may be production, as in payment for each piece produced (piece work). Typically, wages are paid for blue-collar work and salaries are paid for white-collar work.

See also *salary*.

wage assignment a legal agreement signed by a borrower at the time a loan is made that permits the lender to receive a portion of the borrower's pay, directly from his or her employer, if loan repayments are not made in full and on time.

wage earner plan the popular name for the debt reorganization plan authorized under Chapter 13 of the Bankruptcy Act.

See also *bankruptcy, personal*.

wage freeze a government edict locking in wages at current levels, except for merit increases.

waiver of premium an added clause, or rider, available at an extra charge under most life insurance policies, by which the policyholder need pay no further premiums if he or she becomes permanently and totally disabled.

Consumer tip: The waiver-of-premium rider is usually a good choice and worth the few extra dollars it costs each year.

See also Section II, "Life Insurance."

Wall Street 1) a street in New York City; 2) commonly, the name for all of that city's financial district.

ward a person who, because he or she is a minor or incompetent, is placed under legal guardianship by a court.

warehouse 1) to store or stockpile; 2) a place for storage.

warrant a certificate issued by a corporation that gives a shareholder the right to purchase a specified amount of additional stock at a specified price by a certain date. Warrants are transferable and thus have the same value that fractional shares of stock would have. For this reason, they are traded on the market.
See also *rights*.

warranty a guarantee, either written or implied. An *implied warranty* exists on most products and services and simply means that the buyer has the right to believe that the product or service will reasonably fulfill normal expectations. Thus, an item sold as a toaster is assumed to toast bread and not to burn it.
A *limited warranty* is in writing and attempts to limit the liability of the producer as much as possible. Thus, if a roll of film fails to work, the manufacturer may be responsible for replacing the film, but not for paying extra for customer annoyance.

warranty deed title to real estate that states that the seller is giving the buyer good title, free of debt, and that guarantees the seller will defend the title against all claims.
See also *perfect title*.

watered stock stock that is worth less than its market price because of false representations of assets made by the issuing corporation.

weak market a stock market period during which there is more interest in selling than in buying.

wealth in popular usage, the sum total of the value of the possessions of a person. Probably more conflicting definitions of wealth have been written by economists than of any other term. In general, however, economists define wealth as material objects that are useful, relatively scarce, and that can be owned. Money, stocks, bonds, and mortgages are regarded by some as evidence of wealth, but are not wealth itself.

white elephant an unwanted possession that is difficult to dispose of; property that costs so much to maintain that it produces a loss. In ancient India, when a prince wished to destroy another prince, he would give him, as a gift, a white elephant. These rare, sacred beasts, which were never used in work, cost so much to maintain that, while to own one was an honor, it could also bankrupt the owner.

whole life insurance See *ordinary life*.

wholesale price index a measure of inflation, issued by the U.S. Bureau of Labor Statistics, which shows the changes in the prices of over 2,000 commodities at the wholesale level.

widow's allowance an award of her husband's property made by a court of law to a widow immediately following her husband's death. The purpose is to provide for the widow pending the settlement of the estate.

widow's exemption the deduction allowed a widow under state inheritance taxes.

will also, *testament*; a legal document in which an individual details his or her bequests. Anyone may make a will who is of age, of sound mind, and free of undue influence. The different kinds of wills are:

- *Witnessed wills*, which are written or typed and signed in the presence of two witnesses. A properly witnessed will drawn up by an attorney is the best of all wills.
- *Holographic wills*, which are written, dated, and signed in the handwriting of the person whose will it is. They are recognized as valid in many, but not all states.
- *Nuncupative or oral wills*, which are wills made verbally before witnesses that may be recognized in some states if they are later transcribed. A determining factor in recognizing an oral will is the circumstance under which it was made. In other words, if death was imminent and the maker could not have it written down, it has a better chance for being accepted by a probate court.
- *Mutual wills*, which are made by married couples or others with close relationships. Each will is a separate document, but each relies on the terms of the other to some degree.

Consumer tip: If you have any property at all, have a will drawn by an attorney. The fee is modest, and the potential savings in court costs, attorney's fees, taxes, and hard feelings are huge. Keep a copy at home in an easy-to-find place, and have your lawyer keep a copy.

See also *Simultaneous Death Act;* Section II, "Estate Planning."

wiped out when all cash and liquid assets are gone and obligations still remain.

wire transfer an exchange of funds between one bank and another for credit to a customer's account. For example, suppose that Joe, in Houston, owes Mike, in Seattle, $1,000. Mike needs the money immediately, so rather than risk a delay in the mail, Joe instructs his bank to wire transfer the money to Mike's bank for credit to Mike's account. In most cases, wire transfer orders given before noon can be executed that same day, and the fee is modest. What actually happens is that Mike's bank has its balance on deposit with the Federal Reserve Bank increased by $1,000 and Joe's bank has its balance decreased—which means an immediate transfer of cash.

Consumer tip: Wire transfer is an ideal way to send a large amount of money quickly during an emergency. Ask your bank about charges and time schedules.

withdrawal the act of taking money out of an account.

withholding tax federal, state, or city income taxes set aside by employers from the paychecks of employees and remitted to the taxing authorities.

without recourse   a limiting of the rights of a holder in due course in a transaction involving a negotiable instrument. A note endorsed "without recourse," for example, limits anyone to whom the note is assigned from collecting from the endorser should the maker fail to pay.

See also *endorsement; holder in due course.*

witnessed will   See *will.*

working capital   cash or other current assets available for the day-to-day operation of a business. Lack of adequate working capital is a prime reason for the failure of many small, new businesses.

workmen's compensation   state supervised insurance plans designed to give relief to workers injured while doing their jobs. Most people are covered, except for farm workers, domestics, casual laborers, the self-employed, and those who work for religious or charitable institutions. Benefits are typically between 60 and 80 percent of the employee's wages, and are paid to make up for income lost, to compensate for medical bills, and as death benefits for those who are killed on the job. Employers pay premiums either to private insurers under state regulation or to the state itself, depending on the state laws.

A worker may collect Social Security disability payments as well as workmen's compensation so long as the benefits combined do not exceed 80 percent of his or her last wage. Private health insurance usually does not pay for any conditions covered by workmen's compensation.

See also Section II, "Health Costs."

World Bank   See *International Bank for Reconstruction and Development.*

wraparound mortgage   a mortgage under which the seller of a property agrees to continue to make the payments due on the original loan, extending a second mortgage to the buyer for the difference between the outstanding balance on that loan and the sale price, less the down payment. The result is that the buyer gets part of his or her financing at the interest rate on the original mortgage loan.

See also *creative financing;* Section II, "Home Financing."

write-off   charging off a loan that is uncollectible to a reserve for bad debts.

X-C See *ex-coupon*.

X-D See *ex-dividend*.

Xmas Club See *Christmas Club*.

yield the rate of return on an investment, expressed either as a flat amount or, more commonly, as an annual percentage.

yield to maturity the annual rate of return on a certificate of deposit or bond if it is held to maturity. This figure gives investors a basis for comparison between various investment choices.

Z

zero-balance account an automatic transfer checking account in which a customer, by agreement with a bank, keeps no funds. As checks come in for payment, funds are transferred from another account to cover them. This arrangement is more common with business accounts, because individuals can take advantage of NOW accounts.

zero bracket the basic amount allowed for deductions from federal income taxes. This amount is built into all tax-computation formulas so that, if a taxpayer itemizes his or her deductions, only the amount in excess of the zero-bracket amount may be subtracted from adjusted gross income. A taxpayer who must itemize deductions by law may end up with an unused zero-bracket amount that can add to his or her adjusted gross income.

Consumer tip: You may have an unused zero-bracket amount if you are married and file a separate return and your spouse itemizes deductions; if you are a U.S. citizen who elects to exclude income from a U.S. possession; if you are filing a short-year return because of a change in accounting period; or if you have earned and unearned income above a certain level (this changes, so check the current figures) and are a dependent on someone else's return.

zero-coupon bond See *bond*.

206

SECTION II
FINANCIAL PLANNING

FINANCIAL PLANNING

An Introduction

Financial planning is a popular subject, but few people, even some of those who call themselves "financial planners," really understand what it covers. Financial planning involves nothing more or less than resource allocation and conservation, and risk management. What exactly does this mean to you?

Most of us receive a relatively fixed income. When things are tight, you can't simply say, "Well, next year I'll just earn more." Therefore, you must devise a way of allocating your financial resources to your best advantage and you must know how to conserve them:

- The first part of that allocation goes to *federal income and Social Security taxes*. The government insures this by deducting money for the taxes directly from your paycheck or by requiring you to pay estimated taxes quarterly under threat of severe penalties. So the first step in resource conservation is to reduce your taxes as much as legally possible.
- The second part of your resource allocation goes to *fixed expenses*—mortgage or rent payments, utility bills, insurance premiums—those recurring month-after-month bills that take precedence in your after-taxes budget. The second step in resource conservation is to reduce those fixed expenses by as much as you can and then to budget to pay them.
- The third part of resource allocation goes for *variable expenses*—clothing, food, and other necessities, and those luxuries that make life enjoyable, such as dining out and spending for entertainment or hobbies. In many cases, variable expenses, even those for food, can be drastically reduced if it is absolutely essential. Overreduction can make life miserable, however, so for most people careful resource conservation means keeping variable expenses within the framework of a reasonable standard of living.

- The fourth part of resource allocation is to provide for *special expenses*; keeping a child in college or the purchase of a new car are the most common such expenses. The goal of resource conservation here is to choose realistic options you can live with that will allow you to achieve your objective.
- The fifth part involves risk management—*protection of the assets you have acquired*. This means buying health and disability insurance to protect your earning capacity, buying life insurance to extend such protection beyond your possible death, buying property insurance to provide for replacement of any lost or destroyed assets, and buying liability insurance to cover you against loss from legal action.
- Finally, resource allocation must be concerned with the *accumulation of assets*. Naturally, building income is important; but the best goal of financial planning is to build net worth—the excess of total assets over total liabilities. This accumulation of assets has three phases: the building of readily available savings; investing in various vehicles such as stocks, mutual funds, or real estate; and setting aside sufficient funds for retirement security.

The problem that many people have is that their money runs out before they reach the savings, investment, retirement fund allocation stage. When that happens, their only recourse is to go back over each of the prior five steps and make reductions.

Money A to Z

Here's how this book can help with your financial planning. In Section I, the words and phrases that bankers, brokers, and other financial people use are defined in plain English. Where appropriate, a consumer tip is included that spells out how the information concerning that definition can be used to your advantage.

In this second section, an overview of each of the more important aspects of financial planning is summarized, along with a list of references to specific entries in Section I that will further cover any aspect about which you are concerned. If you're going to buy life insurance, for example, a good way to begin is to read the unit about life insurance in Section II, then cross-check any needed references in Section I. In addition, if you're confused about any technical terms your agent has used, look those up in Section I as well.

Remember that the goals of financial planning are resource allocation and conservation. You have only so many resources to allocate, so be sure you do it wisely. And be sure that you put risk-management dollars where they are most needed.

BANK ACCOUNTS

Until a few decades ago, services offered by banks and savings institutions were fairly simple to understand. They offered deposit accounts, made business and mortgage loans, and provided safekeeping services. Offering consumer loans was the first major change in their services; then automatic overdraft checking accounts, then issuing credit cards were added. Now, with federal deregulation increasing, banks and thrifts are expanding their services to include insurance and brokerage services as well as all types of traditional banking services.

The average person needs a relationship with a bank before establishing one with any other type of financial institution, because, in our society, one cannot function effectively without money, and banks are the primary clearinghouses of money transactions.

Choosing Your Bank

To choose a bank or savings institution, consider the following factors:
- *Convenience* is the first requirement in a successful banking relationship. What banks are near your home or where you shop or work? The best choice is a bank that is reasonably close to all three, even if this involves using two or more branches.
- *Friendliness* is the second requirement. Where will you be treated like someone important?
- *Availability of loans* is also important. Where can you get a loan, for any purpose, with a minimum of red tape and waiting?
- *Cost advantage* is also a determining factor. Most banks are quite similar when it comes to fees, rates charged, and interest paid, but there are exceptions. Decide on which services you'll need, then make cost/earnings comparisons.

Services

Here are the minimum services every working adult should have:
1. *A checking account.* For most people, the best deal is the interest-paying or NOW account. A checking account is your basic bookkeeping tool, and one that gives you great safety for your funds as well.
2. *A regular savings account.* While such an account pays the lowest of interest rates, it offers safety of funds and a convenient place in which to accumulate

211

money for such purposes as vacations, Christmas shopping, and, most important of all, investment in high-yield certificates of deposit, money market funds, common stocks, or other vehicles.

3. *A bank credit card.* Bank cards now offer the same universal acceptance as the major travel and entertainment credit cards, at much lower cost. Note that husbands and wives should each have cards in their own names for future credit rating protection.

4. *Loans, as needed.* These include personal loans of all kinds and loans for home financing, automobiles, and education costs.

5. *A safe deposit box*, in which important papers—except life insurance policies, cemetery deeds, and wills—should be kept. In some states, executors may have access to a box to remove these documents, but in other states they may not.

Although there are many other services offered by banks and savings institutions, the following are also very useful for most people:

1. *A money market deposit account.* These accounts pay rates that are competitive with money market mutual funds, but they are covered by deposit insurance. Depositors may make as many as six transfers per month from these accounts, three of which may be checks; or they may make an unlimited number of in-person transfers.

2. *Certificates of deposit.* CDs are savings deposits with varying maturity dates, ranging from as little as a week to 10 years or even more. The rule of thumb is that the larger the amount and the longer the term, the higher the interest rate that the bank will pay. When interest is dropping, try to invest for long periods, so as to lock in a high rate, and when interest is rising, for short periods, so as to be able to take advantage of higher rates when they come.

3. *An Individual Retirement Account or Keogh Plan.* While these accounts are offered by all brokerage and most insurance firms, banks and savings institutions are far and away the favorite depositories for most people. IRAs or Keogh Plans may be funded with certificates of deposit.

4. *Trust services*, which include trust administration and estate planning. Anyone with assets in excess of $100,000 should talk to a bank trust officer to see if these services can conserve an estate from excess taxes and other costs.

Using Your Bank

Here are some important ways to use your bank effectively:

1. If possible, use one bank or savings institution for all of your accounts. This gives you preferred-customer status when it comes to getting loan approval.

2. Get to know the manager of each office you use in order to get personal service.

3. Keep your banker informed about your financial status and goals. In this way, he or she can make recommendations to benefit you as financial conditions change.

Section I References of Special Interest:

bank
bank services
certificate of deposit (CD)
check
deposit insurance
direct deposit
endorsement
escheat
home improvement loan
inactive account
individual account
insufficient funds
MasterCard
money market deposit account
(MMDA)

night depository
NOW account
overdraft checking account
pay-by-phone
returned check
safe deposit box
safekeeping
teller
time deposit
Totten trust
traveler's check
trust
uncollected funds
wire transfer

BORROWING

Borrow only when you must; but when you have to borrow, get enough money to do the job required and then pay the lowest rates possible.

Under what circumstances should you borrow? Here are two reasons:

1. If there is a necessity you must have and you simply don't have the cash available.
2. If the cost of the loan will be more than offset by a savings or profit that can be earned by borrowing.

Where should you borrow? Wherever you can get the best terms, of course. A few years ago, for those who were eligible, this frequently was at a credit union. Nowadays, however, credit unions are competing more and more directly with banks; as a result, their loan rates have risen. Thus, for most people, the best place to borrow is at a bank. But you should shop around, even from bank to bank. During these days of deregulation and stimulated competition, it is not impossible to find competing banks with loan-rate differentials of as much as 5 percent per year. This isn't true for common consumer loans, such as credit-card rates or auto loans, but it is possible for negotiated loans.

Real estate or chattel mortgage loans are fully collateralized and thus have competitive rates. But when it comes to other personal loans, it is to your advantage to avoid the traditional installment-repayment variety and opt for the single-payment loan if it is possible to get one. The following example shows why.

Suppose you borrow $1,200 for one year with an annual percentage rate of 12 percent. Your monthly payments will be $106.61, and your total finance charge will be $79.32. In effect, you will have the use of $1,200 for only one month. After your first payment, you will have the use of about $1,100, and so on. Now consider this: If you borrow that $1,200 with a single-payment loan at the same rate, you will repay the same $1,279.32—your finance charge will be the same. But you will have the use of the $1,200 for the entire year if you need it. And if you put that $106.61 into a regular savings account each month, even at a modest 5.5 percent interest, compounded daily, you will accumulate $1,318.68 and thus reduce your interest cost by $39.36, making your effective loan rate not an annual percentage rate of 12 percent, but closer to an APR of 6 percent (about 3.25 percent under the old add-on rate system).

The problem with a single-payment loan is that, despite a person's good intentions to save the payments on his or her own, they don't always succeed.

But if you have the discipline to save, it's the best way to borrow; and if you have the credit rating, many banks will make the loan that way.

Thirteen Dos and Don'ts on Borrowing

Keep the following money-saving rules in mind the next time you borrow money:

1. Avoid finance companies, if possible. Try to qualify for bank credit.
2. Avoid credit-card installment repayments—it's an expensive way to borrow.
3. Borrow enough to do the job.
4. Shop around for the lowest annual percentage rate.
5. Don't just concentrate on how much the monthly payments are; the most important factor is the finance charge, or the total cost of credit.
6. If you make an installment loan, choose the shortest term for repayment that your budget will allow; you'll save a lot of money that way.
7. Try for a demand loan if your credit rating is good enough. This means, in effect, that you may repay when you wish.
8. Don't sign a loan contract with a confession of judgment, acceleration, or other discriminatory clause.
9. Don't borrow under a conditional sales contract.
10. Know your rights under the Fair Credit Billing Act, the Fair Credit Reporting Act, and the Equal Credit Opportunity Act.
11. Consider using the equity in your home through a second mortgage when you need a long-term loan.
12. If you have an old life insurance policy, consider a policy loan as a low-cost source of money.
13. Don't ever borrow from a loan shark.

Section I References of Special Interest:

acceleration clause	interest
add-on rate method	judgment note
annual percentage rate (APR)	level-payment loan
balloon payment	line of credit
conditional sales contract	loan
Consumer Credit Protection Act	loan fee
credit card	loan shark
credit rating	note
demand loan	passbook loan
discount	policy loan
discount rate method	prime rate
down payment	promissory note
Equal Credit Opportunity Act (ECOA)	Rule of 78
Fair Credit Billing Act	second mortgage
Fair Credit Reporting Act	Title I FHA loan
finance charge	total of payments
finance company	unearned interest
home improvement loan	usury
installment loan	variable-rate loan

CASH MANAGEMENT

The principle of cash management is simplicity itself. It consists of using all funds received with minimum costs and maximum earnings. Like most simple principles, stating it is much easier than acting upon it. Keeping in mind these two concepts will help:

- *The time value of money.* A dollar today is $1; but earning at a rate of 6 percent, compounded daily, for one year, it's $1.0627; at 10 percent, it's $1.1067.
- *The cost of money.* If you pay $100 in cash for an item, the out-of-pocket cost if $100; if you pay by credit card with installment repayments, the cost rises to $110.16 over a one-year period.

Then there are some basic steps you should take to achieve effective cash management. Like dieting, cash management largely means sticking to good habits, including these:

1. Deposit all checks as soon as they are received. This sounds basic, but an amazing number of people sit on checks received for weeks and even months. Get your money earning for you as soon as possible.

2. Keep all deposits that you can in interest-paying accounts. For many people, this means a NOW checking account. Here's a tip: If you use a NOW account, keep a minimal balance in it, even if this means incurring service charges, and keep the excess thus created in short-term CDs or in a money market deposit account or money market mutual fund. You'll earn more that way.

3. Pay bills as late as possible without hurting your credit rating or incurring a late charge. For example, life insurance payments have a 30- or 31-day grace period; use it, as well as any grace periods on your other bills. In addition, take advantage of the "float," that is, the period it takes your checks to clear. This can result in real savings over the long run.

4. Avoid finance charges whenever possible. Buying on time adds substantially to the cost of any good or service.

5. Unless you are very affluent, don't consider using the cash management accounts offered by brokerage houses or banks. By using them, you will be paying rather stiff fees to do something you can easily do on your own.

Section I References of Special Interest:

cash flow

cash-management account

float

grace period

NOW account

repurchase agreement

service charge

COLLEGE COSTS

The largest investment most middle-class families will ever make is the purchase of a home. Sending a child or children through college is the second largest. And it's a good investment. A college education means additional lifetime earnings of about $340,000 above those of the average high school graduate.

But college costs are extremely high. The most prestigious institutions now cost about $15,000 a year—and that doesn't include travel and all of the other peripheral expenses. You can save money by sending your children to a state college, but even then, the costs can be staggering. At a typical state college, tuition, room and board, books, an allowance, travel expenses, health insurance, and all of the other plusses can easily total $7,500 a year. For a family in the 30 percent tax bracket, that means $10,715 in pre-tax income must be earned to have $7,500 left to pay for college.

Ideally, parents should save well in advance for college costs. This can be done by making annual deposits to a custodial account set up in the child's name under the Uniform Gifts to Minors Act, which allows the interest earned to accumulate tax-free, unless the child earns enough to pay income taxes. Or, if the parents have income-producing assets and their children are near college age, they might consider setting up a Clifford Trust.

Seven Sources of Help

Despite their good intentions, many parents and children face college costs with insufficient savings. In this case, the following tips can help:

1. Write to Octameron Associates, Box 3437, Alexandria, Va. 22302, for a list of their excellent booklets on college financing, which are updated at least annually and cost about $3 each. You will gain valuable information by reading them.
2. Choose a college that offers grants and scholarships that need not be repaid.
3. In order to reduce expenses, consider attendance at a local community college for the first two years, while the student lives at home.
4. Consider military help. An ROTC scholarship pays all expenses plus an allowance. Even nonscholarship ROTC membership pays $100 a month during the last two years of college. In addition, in most states, there is a National Guard program that helps with costs at state colleges. Another alternative is

for the prospective student to join the service and save for college through the Veterans Educational Assistance Program, under which the government contributes $2 for every $1 saved by the future student, up to a maximum of about $20,000.

5. Look into grants, especially the Pell grants if your family income is low enough. And that's the key—if the parents' discretionary income (arrived at by a complex formula) is $15,000, they must contribute $2,100 plus 5 percent of their available assets to their child's education each year. They must contribute an additional 25 percent of all income over $15,000. Thus, if the parents earn $30,000 a year and have $50,000 in savings, they must contribute $8,350 a year to the child's education before he or she becomes eligible for a Pell. Obviously, these grants do not help many who are in the middle class.

6. Try to plan to meet expenses in such a way that neither you nor your child will be saddled with long-term debts. If that isn't possible, as a last resort, consider student loans. There are two basic types—those repaid by the student after graduation (Guaranteed Student Loans) and those repaid by the parents beginning at once (PLUS loans). Of course, such loans can mean years of debt. Consider the student who takes out a GSL and repays it over 20 years; as he makes his last payment, he may be taking out a loan for his own child's education. He could be in debt until he is 65!

7. As another last resort, if you have substantial equity in your home, consider taking a second mortgage loan to finance college. This is a very feasible plan, despite the general bad press that second mortgates have had. In some cases, a second mortgage is actually better than a student loan, so it is a good idea to shop around and compare monthly repayments as well as total finance charges.

Section I References of Special Interest:

Clifford Trust	gift tax
education loan	guaranteed student loans
equity	Uniform Gifts to Minors Act (UGMA)

CONSUMER FRAUDS

Some years ago, when the police asked Slick Willie Sutton why he robbed banks, he is supposed to have replied, "Because that's where the money is." Many con men and women see consumers as potential sources of "where the money is." In general, these con artists' schemes break down into three categories: the out-and-out criminal fraud; the sometimes legal but always shady deal; and the legal, nonfraudulent scheme that takes advantage of the consumer's trust.

Criminal Fraud

Much criminal fraud is built around a simple premise: The con person offers a deal that appeals to the victim's greed—his or her chance to get something for nothing. Thus, the best way to avoid this kind of fraud is never to try to get something for nothing. If a deal sounds too good to be true, it very probably is.

Criminals also sometimes pose as bank officials or law enforcement authorities in an attempt to get their victims to hand over money for a variety of "official" purposes. Real officials, however, *never* ask anyone to make a withdrawal from a bank.

New swindles are being planned almost daily. Here are a few of the classic types to avoid:

1. *Tricks to get the victim to withdraw funds from his or her bank account.* These include the well-known "pigeon drop," in which a con artist shows the victim an envelope full of cash and offers to share it if the person will put up some "good-faith" money until a distribution can be made. Or a con artist may pose as a policeman or even as a Social Security official and ask the victim to make a withdrawal in order to test the honesty of a bank teller. Of course, the victim never sees the money again.

2. *The cheap merchandise scheme.* In this case, the con artist offers to sell, from the back of a truck or other unlikely place, expensive items for next to nothing. When the victim gets the merchandise home, he or she finds that the TV set or other item is just an empty chassis.

3. *The home repair scam.* Here, a contractor comes to the door of a private resi-

dence and offers to make an inspection, in the course of which he finds a bad roof, defective furnace, or the like, and immediately calls in a crew to make shabby but expensive "repairs" for which he gets paid a hefty fee at once. There is one notorious "family" that literally tours the U.S. with this scheme.

Sometimes Legal But Shady Schemes

Caveat emptor ("let the buyer beware") was once the rule, but more and more consumer protection laws are now on the books. The following schemes are not legal, but they are often hard to prove:

1. *"Bait-and-switch"* describes a situation in which a merchant advertises an obvious bargain, then, when a person responds to the ad, the merchant switches him or her to more expensive merchandise.
2. *The so-called Ponzi scheme* exists when a company uses dollars received as investments to pay earnings to earlier investors. Obviously, this just can't work, yet every few years there is a new such scam and people always fall for it.
3. *The chain letter or pyramid club* are simple variations of the Ponzi scheme, in that dollars collected from new members go to pay off old members. In any case, there simply aren't enough people in the country to sustain these swindles for very long, as a quick bit of arithmetic can easily prove.

Legal Schemes That Take Advantage

There are also schemes that, although perfectly legal, victimize consumers. They include:

1. *"Charities"* that mail out unordered merchandise along with a request for a "donation." When this happens, the recipient should simply reseal the package and write on it, "Merchandise not ordered—return to sender" and drop it in the mailbox. The sender will have to pay the return postage, which may discourage him or her from continuing.
2. *Insurance plans*, often sold by mail order or through magazine ads, for hospitalization coverage for which benefit payoffs are usually not authorized until after a one-week waiting period. Since the average hospital stay is under four days, those who sell these plans are safe in offering them. Such companies usually charge very high premiums and pay very low benefits. And if a person ever does collect from one, he or she may quickly find the coverage canceled under an obscure clause. "The large print giveth, but the fine print taketh away."
3. *Direct-selling plans*, which mathematically resemble the Ponzi scheme in that salespeople can earn more by signing up new salespeople than by selling the goods. These schemes are legal, but they are based on excessively expensive merchandise to support the pyramid of payments. Sadly, these companies often sign up the elderly to sell; and the friends of these people, often also elderly, feel pressured to buy even though they have limited funds.

CONSUMER FRAUDS

Section I References of Special Interest:

bait-and-switch
blank check
blue sky laws
boiler room
caveat emptor
chain letter
fleece

forgery
fraud, consumer
lamb
Ponzi scheme
pyramid scheme
raised check
right of recision

DEBT MANAGEMENT

Borrowing is a fact of economic life. The trick is to contain it within reasonable limits. Ideally, installment payments—not counting payments for a home mortgage or credit-card payments that are for the balance in full made during the grace period—should not exceed 15 percent of your income after taxes. Thus, if your take-home pay is $300 a week, your monthly payments should not exceed $195.

The Do-It-Yourself Approach

Everyone occasionally gets behind the financial eight ball. When this happens to you, here's what to do about it:

Try the do-it-yourself approach. This means:

- Plan a realistic budget and stick to it.
- Stop using credit cards and charge accounts at once. Give yourself a chance to catch up.
- Call your creditors and try to arrange for more reasonable repayments. They may balk; if they do, you might casually mention the possibility of personal bankruptcy. That may make them more agreeable, because they'd rather have a total repayment made slowly than a partial repayment.
- Stop writing checks for cash, except for amounts needed for within-budget shopping.

Debt Counselors

If the do-it-yourself plan doesn't work, contact a member agency of the National Foundation for Consumer Credit and go to its people for help. Look for your local agency in the Yellow Pages under debt counselors. If you can't locate an agency, write to the National Foundation for Consumer Credit, 8710 Georgia Avenue, Silver Spring, Md. 20910, and ask for the name of the agency nearest you.

These agencies charge no fee except for postage and mailing costs; they are supported by banks and merchants who are glad to get their help and who pay them 10 to 15 percent of monies collected as a fee. The agency will do the following:

1. Contact your creditors and stop all dunning efforts on their part.

2. Help you contact any governmental or charitable agencies that may be of help, as might be the case when medical expenses are the problem.
3. Help you plan a budget.
4. Arrange for realistic monthly payments to wipe out your debts.

The Next Step

If that approach fails or isn't acceptable, the next recourse is Chapter 13 of the Bankruptcy Reform Act of 1978. To qualify, you must have a regular income and have no more than $100,000 in unsecured debts and less than $350,000 in secured debts. You must propose a repayment plan that will give your creditors at least as much as they would receive under a regular bankruptcy, and you must pay off the debts within a three-year period.

To undergo Chapter 13, you should contact an attorney who specializes in such matters, and he or she will:
1. Contact your creditors and immediately stop all collection actions against you and all accruing finance charges and late penalties.
2. Have a realistic repayment plan approved by a federal judge.
3. Make the resulting monthly payments to the creditors as monies are received from you.

The Last Resort

Chapter 7, or personal bankruptcy, is the last resort. A person may file for bankruptcy if he or she has liabilities that exceed assets; has obligations not secured by purchases, such as auto or boat loans; has not either received a discharge in bankruptcy or had a Chapter 13 that paid less than 70 percent of unsecured debts within six years; has not lied on a credit application; and has no co-signers on his or her debts.

The attorney will file for bankruptcy, and, under the current law (bankruptcy laws are constantly revised), the debtor will be able to keep a substantial number of his or her possessions. A record of a bankruptcy may be kept in a credit file for up to 14 years.

Section I References of Special Interest:

bankruptcy, personal	garnish
charge account	late-repayment penalty
charge-off	lien
consolidation loan	loan shark
co-signer	net balance
credit card	post-dated check
debt counselor	repossession
delinquency	right of recision
Fair Debt Collection Practices Act	second mortgage
foreclosure	slow pay

ESTATE PLANNING

Your personal estate plan should be designed to attain these three goals:

1. *To leave an adequate amount to your heirs.* A good first step toward achieving this goal is to purchase life insurance, at least to establish after-death assets while other assets are accruing. It is usually a good idea to buy the cheapest life insurance available—term coverage—and then begin a savings/investment plan that will eventually reduce the need for all life insurance except a basic ordinary life policy to cover final expenses. The young person with family responsibilities needs a more substantial amount of coverage, while an older person with other resources needs much less.

2. *To distribute your estate properly.* This requires writing a will that is drawn by an attorney. Handwritten (holographic) wills are not allowed in many states, and in those states where they are allowed, they may be difficult to probate. Begin by making up a list of your assets and your wishes for their eventual distribution, then take this list to your lawyer. This will avoid accidentally omitting a beneficiary as well as the attendant expense of changing your will later.

3. *To protect your estate from excessive taxes and administrative fees.* The conservation of the estate breaks down into three areas:

- *Federal estate taxes*, which, for all intents and purposes, no longer exist for most people since everything may be left to a spouse tax free, while, for other heirs, the lifetime exemption on an estate will effectively total $325,000 in 1984, $400,000 in 1985, $500,000 in 1986, and $600,000 in 1987 and thereafter. That means that only estates in excess of those amounts will be federally taxed.

- *State taxes*, which are not as easy to escape. In this case, big problems can arise over the matter of legal domicile. Here's an example: Joe and Mary lived in New York for 40 years, then they retired to Florida. But they keep an apartment in New York, which they use frequently. Joe's car has Florida plates, Mary's has New York plates. Mary voted in Florida in last year's election, Joe voted in New York in this one. Where is their legal domicile? If Joe should die, which state can claim taxes? Unfortunately, the answer may be that both states can. To establish domicile, vote in one state only, register cars in that state, have your will(s) drawn in that state, leave a letter of intent stating your choice of domicile, and take all other steps that might prove your residence in that state should a question arise.

- *Administrative expenses*, which can be avoided through a properly drawn will. If your estate is based on simple assets—savings, investments, house, car, and personal property—and if your heirs are all close family members, designate your next-of-kin as executor to serve without bond or fee. This will save an administrative fee of about 5 percent of the value of the estate. For a $100,000 estate, this would amount to a substantial $5,000. If your lawyer insists that he or she or a bank be named as executor, find another lawyer.

Five Dos and Don'ts

1. Don't use joint property agreements as a "poor man's will." This does not exclude property from estate taxes. Sometimes it is simply wiser to put major property in one name. For example, if a husband is 65 years old and has a bad heart and his wife is 50 and healthy, why not list the house in her name alone?
2. Ask your lawyer about the Simultaneous Death Act. If you are married, both you and your spouse should have a clause in your wills that establishes which of you is to be deemed the last to die in the event of a simultaneous disaster. This can prevent having your estate go to someone you'd rather it didn't. For example, suppose that a husband and wife, Fred and Alice, leave everything to each other, but Fred designates his poor, sickly sister as his secondary heir whereas Alice makes no such provision. If Fred and Alice are killed in an auto crash and the court rules that Alice took her last breath one second after Fred, the estate may go to her wealthy father, even though Alice and Fred have been estranged from him for years.
3. Talk to an estate planning officer at your bank if your assets exceed $100,000 in value. It won't cost you anything and it may be unnecessary, but on the other hand it might pay off in tax savings.
4. Don't get estate planning advice from anyone who can sell you something and earn a commission.
5. Preplan your funeral. Best of all, join a memorial society that is affiliated with the Continental Association of Funeral and Memorial Societies, Inc., 1828 L Street NW, Washington, D.C. 20036. The lifetime membership is only a few dollars, and it allows you to protect your heirs from being overcharged for funeral services.

Section I References of Special Interest:

beneficiary
codicil
decedent
domicile
Economic Recovery Tax Act of 1981
escheat
estate
estate planning
estate tax
heirs
inheritance
inheritance tax
in terrorem
inter vivos trust
intestate
irrevocable trust

joint property
last will
legacy
letter of administration
letters testamentary
life estate
life insurance trust
living trust
marital deduction
nuncupative will
short certificate
Simultaneous Death Act
trust
trust agreement
will

FAMILY ACCOUNTING

A simplified family accounting system has three goals—to determine how the family finances stand, where they are going, and how to save the maximum on income taxes.

Where Your Finances Stand

Knowing where you stand is important because it shows how well your planning has worked to date and gives you a clear picture of the financial base on which you can build. This knowledge is also vital should you need to borrow.

To determine your financial status, it is necessary to compute your net worth, or where you stand as of a particular time. Use the following form.

FINANCIAL STATEMENT

Name_____ Date _____

Assets
Cash, including checking account $
Savings accounts
Savings bonds
Home, market value
Life insurance, cash value
Money due from others
Other real estate
Certificates of deposit
Money market funds
Stocks and mutual funds
Bonds and savings bonds
Personal property
Other
Total assets $
Liabilities
Mortgage outstanding $
Auto loan
Personal loans
Credit-card balances

Other loans due
Money due to others
Outstanding bills
Total liabilities $
Net Worth (total assets less total liabilities) $

As an additional step, you can compile a statement reflecting income and expense on an accrual basis. Simply use the above form, but add in portions of money earned but not yet due, and portions of expenses incurred but not yet due. If this is done carefully, it will give an accurate current picture of your finances.

Where Your Finances Are Going

The next step is to develop a workable spending/savings plan. The expense figures below are adapted from averages developed by the U.S. Department of Agriculture. They have been modified to include substantial savings:

MONTHLY FAMILY INCOME, AFTER TAXES

	$1,700	$2,000	$2,250	$2,500	$3,000	$3,500
Housing	$612	$720	$810	$900	$1,080	$1,260
Food and alcohol	306	360	405	450	540	630
Transportation	289	340	382	425	510	595
Savings	170	200	225	250	300	350
Apparel	102	120	135	150	180	210
Medical care	68	80	90	100	120	140
Entertainment	68	80	90	100	120	140
Other goods and services	51	60	68	75	90	105
Personal care	34	40	45	50	60	70

Use the above figures as a guideline to monitor your own spending/savings on an ongoing basis. It takes only a few minutes to do this when you balance your checkbook and make your credit-card payments. In other words, let your checking account and credit/charge cards take the place of the old-fashioned budget envelopes.

Reconciling Your Checking Account Statement

It is important to reconcile your checking account statement as soon as possible after you receive it. It will only take a few minutes, and it will assure that you know exactly how much you have in your account, and will also verify the bank's accuracy. Here's what to do:

1. Get an up-to-the-minute checkbook balance by subtracting any charges made

by the bank and adding in any interest that it paid. Write down these amounts in your register or on your check stubs and correct your balance.

2. On the back of your bank statement or on a separate piece of paper, write down the balance for your account as shown on the bank statement. Add to that the amounts of any deposits that have not yet been credited to your account.

3. Now arrange in numerical order the checks that were returned with your statement. Mark off each one in your register or on your check stubs. Then make a list of any checks that you wrote that have not yet been returned, including those from previous statements. Add up their amounts and subtract the total from the amount arrived at in step 2.

4. Compare the final result with your corrected checkbook balance. If the two agree, your account is balanced.

Here's a brief summary of the steps outlined above:

checkbook balance − bank charges + interest = (a) $_____

bank balance + deposits not credited − outstanding
checks = (b) $_____

The amounts for (a) and (b) should agree.

Tax Preparation

Finally, set up a simple system to keep track of tax-deductible expenses so that you don't pay Uncle Sam a dime more than he is entitled to. Here's a simple system:

1. Get a supply of plain business-size envelopes.
2. Label them to correspond with the items on Schedule A, Form 1040:
   a. Medical and dental expenses
   b. Taxes
   c. Interest expense
   d. Contributions
   e. Casualty or theft losses
   f. Miscellaneous deductions
   g. Interest income
   h. Dividend income
3. Now make up envelopes for your Form 1040:
   a. Income
   b. Payment to IRA or Keogh plans
   c. Political contributions
   d. Other envelopes (Look at a Form 1040 and see if any of the less common categories apply to you.)
4. As you incur each tax-deductible expense, put the receipt into the proper envelope. At tax time, sort your canceled checks, credit-card slips, and other proofs of tax-deductible expenses into the proper envelopes along with your receipts. Using an adding machine with a tape, add up the slips, checks, and receipts that are in each envelope and staple the tape to the face of the envelope. If you remember to get receipts and to file them faithfully, you will

have a really complete and provable set of records so that you or a tax preparer can fill in your tax forms in short order.

Section I References of Special Interest:

accounting	income and expense statement
accrual basis budgeting	liability
allowances, children's	net worth
balance sheet	reconciliation
budget	statement
financial statement	statement of condition

HEALTH COSTS

Types of Health Insurance

By 1984, the average family's annual health costs reached $4,064, and they are rising. For many people, a large portion of this expense goes to pay for insurance. Basically, health insurance breaks down into these types:

1. *Blue Cross/Blue Shield (the "Blues")*, which are nonprofit organizations that provide varying degrees of coverage. In general, the best all-around deal in terms of cost and benefits is Blue Cross/Blue Shield major medical insurance under a group plan.

2. *Commercial hospitalization insurance*, which provides coverages similar to those offered by the Blues. This insurance ranges from good to poor in terms of cost and coverage, but a good group plan is an acceptable alternative to the Blues. In general, however, realize that there is a sales commission on commercial insurance that tends either to make the costs higher or the benefits lower than the nonprofit Blues.

3. *Hospital indemnity insurance*, which is frequently sold through the mail and pays benefits after a period of hospitalization. In general, these policies are best avoided because they are costly and often provide little in the way of benefits. Some begin to pay benefits only after a week in the hospital; since the average stay is three to four days, the chances of collecting are slim. (See "Consumer Frauds," page 221).

4. *"Catastrophic illness" or "dread disease" policies*, which cover only a specifically named condition, usually cancer. In some cases, coverage is provided for several diseases, ranging from cancer to encephalitis. The cost, though low, is seldom justified considering the odds in favor of the insurance company.

5. *Disability insurance*, which provides coverage against the loss of income due to accident or illness. Social Security offers some protection in this area, although the Reagan administration did its best to reduce the benefits paid by stiffening the eligibility requirements. Also, workmen's compensation covers most employees. In general, there is no need for commercial disability insurance for most people who are not self-employed.

6. *Medicare and Medicaid*, which provide coverage for the elderly, the very young, or those on welfare or other social-assistance programs. Medicare and Medicaid can be financial lifesavers for those who need them, and detailed infor-

232

mation on current coverages can be obtained through your doctor or hospital.

7. *Health maintenance organizations*, or HMOs, which are a relatively new alternative to standard insurance coverages. With HMOs, the insured pays a fixed monthly fee for which he or she receives comprehensive health care, including physicians' and hospital services and sometimes even dental care. The biggest advantage of an HMO is that it is in the interest of the doctor or hospital to keep the insured healthy, thus they tend to stress preventive medicine. For people who are not eligible for group coverage in the Blues, HMOs are a viable alternative. They are low-cost; the savings average 10 to 40 percent on the cost of health insurance if you include fees not covered by insurance, but which are covered under an HMO. For information about your nearest HMO, watch your local paper for ads or check with your local hospital.

Reduce Your Health Care Costs

Here is a list of suggestions to reduce your health care costs:

- Try to stay healthy. Don't smoke; do exercise.
- Join a group plan for Blue Cross/Blue Shield, if possible.
- The next best choice is a group plan with a commercial company—if the coverage is adequate and if the company pays its claims. (Some fight almost every claim.)
- If you must get coverage as an individual rather than as part of a group, the best choice is to join an HMO; the second best choice is to join the Blues.
- Check any policy to be sure that your individual premiums cannot be raised unless all policyholders' premiums are raised.
- Realize that you may have other coverage. An auto policy, for example, may have some medical benefits in case of an accident; a life insurance policy may have a disability rider; you may be covered by Social Security or workmen's compensation; or you may be eligible for Medicare or Medicaid.

Section I References of Special Interest:

corridor deductible
elimination period
group insurance
health insurance

Medicaid
risk management
workmen's compensation

HOME FINANCING

The Down Payment

Obtaining the down payment is a major problem for many first-time home buyers. Typically, a down payment is set at 20 percent of the purchase price. People who have a home to sell can use their equity as the down payment on their next house. But if you don't have the equity from a present home and must face the prospect of raising a down payment in cash, you have two alternatives. Realize that you very likely may have to use a combination of the two:

1. *Savings.* If you are thrifty, you may amass a substantial sum. For example, if you begin at the age of 22 to save $1,000 a year, with interest compounded daily at 10 percent, by the time you reach 27, you will have about $6,000 after taxes to put into a home.

2. *Borrowing.* You may be able to borrow from relatives; if so, keep the loan businesslike by signing a note. Or, if you've had a cash-value life insurance policy for a while, you may be able to borrow on that. In any case, avoid making a loan for your down payment with a commercial lender because chances are good that you'll become overextended.

Types of Mortgages

Getting a mortgage isn't too difficult if you have the down payment and a steady income. Try your local bank, thrift institution, or mortgage company. But buying a home in a market in which mortgage rates fluctuate, even by a point or two, is tricky. If you were to make a 20 percent down payment and then pay $500 a month in mortgage repayments, you could buy a home valued at $77,600 with a 9 percent loan—but you could buy a home valued at only $60,800 if the rate were 12 percent. Naturally, you will want to buy at the lowest possible rate.

Here are the types of mortgages you may have to choose from:

- *Conventional fixed-rate mortgages.* These loans are the most sought after, but are not always the best. With this type, the interest rate is fixed for the life of the loan, usually from 20 to 30 years. These loans are ideal for people who are not likely to move in a few years. Realize that the lender can't renegotiate the rate upward, but that you may be able to refinance at a lower rate if mortgage rates drop enough to make the cost of reclosing worthwhile.

- *Variable-rate mortgages*, or VRMs, are also known as adjustable-rate mortgages. Typically, they begin with a rate one or two percentage points lower than that for fixed-rate loans. Also, they usually have a built-in rate cap that limits increases over the life of the loan—for example, to 5 percent. Thus, if you begin with a 10 percent rate and if fixed rates are at 12 percent, you may, over 25 or 30 years, have rate increases that take you up to 15 percent. If you are in a job that requires a move every three to five years, or if you upgrade your lifestyle every few years, you'll do well with a VRM.
- *Graduated-payment adjustable mortgages* are variable-rate mortgages for which payments are lower in the early years, then they rise. The idea is to meet the needs of those whose incomes will rise as time goes by. The lowered payments are achieved in the early years by deferring principal reduction—which means a higher overall net cost. It is usually best to avoid this type of mortgage. If you should have to sell the house in the first few years, you might even owe the lender additional interest under the terms of the contract.

In general, the fixed-rate mortgage is best for the older borrower or for the family that will tend to stay put in a house; the variable-rate mortgage is better for young homeowners who are likely to move within five or six years.

Home Financing

Here are some general tips on home financing:

- Avoid so-called "creative financing," which is usually a euphemism for "we can't raise the down payment so we'll borrow it." This includes buyer take-backs and second mortgages of all kinds. The risk is in overcommitting yourself to huge monthly repayments. When you want a house, it's easy to think, "Well, we'll sacrifice"; but as the months and years go by, sacrifices become onerous. And don't forget the cost of a growing family, which can shatter the best laid plans. The only reason that the people who indulged in creative financing didn't lose money when mortgage rates peaked in 1980 was that rates thereafter dropped. If they had stayed high, many people would have lost their homes. The only person sure to benefit from creative financing is the real estate agent.
- Avoid tricky mortgage plans, such as "shared-appreciation mortgages," in which the buyer shares equity growth with the lender, and "balloon mortgages," for which the loan comes due in full in a short period—usually five years—at which time the loan must be renegotiated.
- Apply for an FHA- or VA-insured loan if you can. You'll get a lower rate and, often, a break on the down payment.
- Realize that during the first five years of a mortgage loan, over 90 to 98 percent of each payment is for interest, which is tax deductible. In effect, this reduces your actual cost of borrowing considerably. If you are in the 30 percent tax bracket, for example, and have a 10 percent loan, your effective loan rate during the first five years will average out to about 7 percent after figuring in the tax advantages.

HOME FINANCING

Here's a *really* creative financing scheme for those with great willpower: Buy a home on which the payments will be about half of what you can afford. Ask the lender for an amortization schedule, which will list the monthly payments due for the entire life of the loan. (There may be a few dollars charge for this.) Then, as you make each month's payment, also pay the principal due on the loan, working from the other end of the schedule. In other words, make the first payment and the principal portion of the last payment at one time; the next month, make the second payment and the principal portion of the next-to-the-last payment, and so forth. Your 30-year loan will become a 15-year loan, you'll retain your greatest tax advantages, and your finance charges will be greatly reduced.

Section I References of Special Interest:

amortization
annual percentage rate (APR)
assumption of mortgage
balloon payment
closing costs
conventional mortgage
creative financing
deed
Federal Housing Administration (FHA)
first mortgage
flexible-payment mortgage
graduated-payment adjustable mortgage
mortgage

mortgage loan
mortgagor
origination fee
owner financing
point
prepayment penalty clause
purchase-money mortgage
real estate mortgage
rollover mortgage
shared-appreciation mortgage
variable-rate mortgage (VRM)
Veterans Administration (VA)
wraparound mortgage

INVESTMENTS

In the minds of most people, the difference between savings and investments is that all savings are highly liquid—that is, readily convertible to cash—and that investments range from liquid to downright illiquid. Another basic difference is that savings dollars are extremely safe, whereas investment dollars range from safe to speculative.

Before you get into any kind of investment program, there are two financial essentials you must meet:

1. You should have the equivalent of at least two and preferably six months' income in safe and liquid savings, such as bank certificates of deposit or money market mutual fund shares.
2. You should have enough life insurance to cover final expenses for illness and burial plus enough to create any necessary estate, and enough health and disability insurance to carry you through a crisis without having to liquidate your investments at a loss.

After meeting these requirements, it is a matter of which investments to make. Consider the following:

- *Real estate* is a viable investment, but should only be considered by those who are experts in the field. Besides a personal residence, the only really attractive real estate option for the average person is a rental property with less than five units, which is exempt from many onerous regulations.
- *Mutual funds* are the ideal investment vehicle for many people. They offer the safety of diversity plus almost unlimited goal choices in that funds exist for growth stocks, income stocks, growth/income stock mixes, municipal bonds, treasury securities, and so forth. You can even find funds that invest only in nondefense industries or environmentally-safe industries if that is important to you. Basically, funds are of three types—load, no-load, and low-load. Load funds are sold by commission representatives and charge a sales fee, usually when the purchase is made. No-load funds charge no sales fee; and low-load funds charge a fee of about half that of the load funds. Buy a no-load fund, all other things being equal. You'll have to make the purchase yourself since no salesperson will call on you. Many people who buy load funds don't realize that no-load and low-load funds exist.
- *Common stocks* are what most people mean by investments, and they can be

237

extremely useful as a long-term hedge against inflation as well as a source of future growth. But common stocks should never be counted on for short-term profit—that's speculating, not investing. Here are some guidelines on how to buy stocks:

1. Select those with low price-earnings ratios; some experts suggest seven or lower, although 10 or lower is more common.
2. From that group, select those with a book value (liquidation value) that is at least that of the market price of the stock.
3. From the remaining group, select those with a reasonably consistent pattern of growth and that also seem to offer future prospects for growth. In other words, if automobiles are coming in, don't invest in a buggy-whip company, no matter what the P/E ratio, book value, or growth history.
4. From the few stocks that are left—if you can find 25 at any given time that meet the above requirements, you're doing well—select a few whose products or services appeal to you. Then invest at least several hundred dollars in four or five stocks, each in a different industry, to gain the safety of diversification.

Things to Avoid

- Don't bet the rent money on any investment or speculation; remember, if you must liquidate to meet expenses, you may take a loss, even if the stock is just temporarily depressed in price.
- Don't speculate unless you can afford a loss, and then not unless you develop real expertise. This means avoiding the commodities market, options of all types, precious metals, and other highly volatile "investments."
- Don't count on big winnings. Those who consistently profit from investments are satisfied with small but regular gains.
- Don't just jump in. Read, investigate, and ask questions of real experts.

Section I References of Special Interest:

apartment house	dollar cost averaging
bear	Dow Jones Averages
beta	earnings yield
bid and asked price	equity fund
bond	equity investment
book value	gold
broker	growth fund
bull	growth stock
calls	high flyers
churning	income fund
closed-end fund	investor
commodities	leverage
customer's representative	load
devaluation	lot
diversification	low-load
dividends	make a market

margin
money market mutual fund
monthly investment plan
Moody's ratings
mutual fund
National Association of Securities Dealers Automated Quotations (NASDAQ)
no-load
no-par-value stock
option
over-the-counter stock
penny stock
price-earnings ratio (P/E)
puts
random walk
real estate investment trust (REIT)
sell short

settlement day
smart money
speculator
spread
Standard and Poor's bond ratings
Standard and Poor's Composite Stock Index (S&P 500)
stock, common
stock exchange
stock market index futures
stock market index options
stock, preferred
Treasury securities
trust
U.S. Savings Bonds
venture capital
warrant

LIFE INSURANCE

Life insurance is an absolute essential in the financial planning of everyone except the very wealthy or those with no dependents or obligations. It does what no other financial vehicle can—it creates an instant estate for the insured person and guarantees that his or her dependents will not sufer undue financial strain if he or she should die.

There is a basic problem in buying life insurance, however, and it is this: Agents are paid a commission, not on the face amount of insurance they sell, but on the premiums; in addition, the policies that are more profitable to the companies pay a higher commission rate. Therefore, many people are sold too little insurance at much too great a cost.

Most unbiased financial experts agree that, in almost every situation, it is far wiser to buy a basic amount of ordinary life insurance that will remain in effect for the lifetime of the insured to cover final expenses. Additional coverage should be bought as needed in the form of convertible renewable term insurance; the savings represented by the difference between premium costs for this form of insurance and ordinary life insurance can be invested meanwhile in a tax-deferred Individual Retirement Account or other program. To use life insurance as a savings/investment vehicle is simply not sufficiently profitable to be attractive.

The insurance industry is offering many new plans, such as universal life and variable life, but again, the high commissions and low earnings usually do not make for an attractive investment program.

How to Save Money on Life Insurance

1. Know your needs. If you have a growing family and a mortgage, you need more insurance than if you are single and have no debts. As a rule of thumb, have the equivalent of one year's gross income in permanent, cash-value insurance (sold as ordinary life, whole life, or straight life). This is for final expenses—last illness costs plus burial—and should stay with you for life. Then calculate how much more would be needed and buy that amount in renewable term insurance to cover your dependents should you die. As your obligations decrease and your assets grow, phase out the term coverage until, when you retire, you have only the ordinary life left.
2. Buy your insurance from the least expensive source possible. Check rates for

the best buys. Consult the latest *Consumers Union Report on Life Insurance*, which should be available at your local library.

3. Pay your premiums annually to get the discount. In order to avoid having a huge bill come due all at once, stagger your policy dates so that an equal portion is payable each quarter. Of course, if you're affluent enough to buy all of your insurance at once, pay your premium annually by putting money aside in savings to cover the payment when it comes due.

4. Avoid such high-cost policies as endowments and limited-payment life.

5. If you're a nonsmoker, take advantage of special discounts for such people.

6. Never buy life insurance from a mail-order solicitation, from a television or newspaper advertisement, or from a door-to-door salesperson.

Section I References of Special Interest:

accelerated option
accidental death benefit
agent's commission
American Society of Chartered Life
  Underwriters
cash-surrender value
cash value
convertible policy
dividend options
endowment insurance policy
equity fund
extended term insurance
industrial insurance
insurable interest
insurance
lapse
life insurance

limited-payment life
mortgage life insurance
nonforfeiture provisions
nonparticipating life insurance
ordinary life
paid-up additions
paid-up insurance
participating life insurance
risk management
Savings Bank Life Insurance (SBLI)
settlement option
standard mortality table
term life insurance
twisting
universal life insurance
variable life insurance
waiver of premium

MONEY MATH

You can do most of the money math that you will ever need to do by using a simple pocket calculator. The formulas given below assume that you have only an inexpensive calculator without an exponent function. Most such calculators operate as described below. If yours doesn't, check the instructions that came with it. Also, for those who have the equipment, a simple program is included at the end of this summary that will run on most home computers.

Computing a Percentage

To calculate a percentage of an item is simple: If you have a percentage key on your calculator, just enter the amount of the item, press the multiply key, enter the percentage you wish to calculate, and then press the percent key. If you don't have a percent key, then just multiply the amount of the item times the percentage to be calculated, then divide by 100.

Thus, to calculate 23 percent of 124 with a percent key:

124 × 23 (percent key) = 28.52
Without a percent key:
$$\frac{124 \times 23}{100} = 28.52$$

Computing a Discount

Is an item a good buy? Suppose you see an item marked down from $55.95 to $49.50—that's a reduction of $6.45. And at a competing store, the ad reads "20 percent off on all items." Which should you take? There are two ways to solve this problem. The simplest is to multiply $55.95 times .20, which would yield $11.19—a much better cash discount than $6.45. The other route is to multiply the cash discount of $6.45 times 100, then divide it by $55.95 to determine that the actual percentage discount is 11.528 percent. Here are the formulas:
1. price X percentage discount = cash discount
2. cash discount X 100 ÷ original price = percentage discount

Computing Tax-Free Earnings Equivalents

This computation is useful when investing in municipal bonds or other tax-free investments. It allows you to determine just what the tax-free yield is equivalent to in taxable dollars. Here's how to do it:

TR= taxable return
TFR= tax-free return
TB= (marginal) tax bracket
The formula is $TR = \dfrac{TFR}{1\text{-}TB}$

Applying this, assume that you are in the 33 percent marginal tax bracket. Also assume that you are thinking of buying some county school bonds, which pay 9.4 percent annual interest. What would that equal in taxable earnings?

First, convert the stated percentages to decimal equivalents; thus 9.4 percent becomes .094, etc.

$$TR = \frac{.094}{1\text{-}.33}$$

$$TR = \frac{.094}{.67}$$
$$TR = .1403$$

The tax-free return, in this case, would equal a taxable return of 14.03 percent. To do a reverse calculation, that is, to compute what tax-free interest would be necessary to equal a known taxable interest, simply modify the formula. Thus, if you know that you can earn 12 percent in CDs, what tax-free interest would you need to equal or better that rate if you were in the 33 percent marginal tax bracket?

The formula is:
$TFR = TR \times (1\text{-}TB)$; thus,
$TFR = .12 \times .67$
$TFR = .0804$

You would need a tax-free interest in excess of 8.04 percent to top the taxable interest in this case.

Computing Future Value

How much will $100 saved today be worth 10 years from now? And, more complex, how much will $20 a week saved for the next 10 years be worth after that amount of time? Computing future value is essential in making a personal financial plan.

MONEY MATH

In computing the future value of a one-time investment:

FV= future value
P= principal amount
i= the interest rate expressed as a decimal
n= is the number of compounding periods, used as an exponent.
Here is the formula:
$FV = P(1+i)^n$

It's easier to use than it sounds. Suppose you have $1,000 to invest now and can anticipate earnings of 10.25 percent, compounded annually, for 8 years. How much will that $1,000 grow to? The formula is:

$FV = 1000(1+.1025)^8$

To calculate this, enter 1 in your calculator, add .1025, and press the multiply key; your amount is now factored in once. It must now be multipled by itself seven more times to equal the exponent of 8. To enter it the additional seven times, press the equals key seven times. Your display will now read 2.182874. Now press the multiply key and enter 1,000, then press the equals key. The final answer is 2,182.874. Your $1,000 will grow to $2,182.87 in 8 years at 10.25 percent, compounded annually.

Now here's the way to calculate the future value of regular deposits. In this case:

FV= future value
PMT= periodic deposit amount
i= the interest rate expressed as a decimal
n= the number of compounding periods
This formula is more complex:

$$FV = \frac{PMT}{i}[(1+i)^{n+1} - (1+i)]$$

Here's the way to use it: Assume that you can save $1,000 a year in an IRA and that you project your earnings (the rate will be only an assumption) at 12 percent per year. You are now 45 and expect to retire at 65. How much will you have?

$$FV = \frac{PMT}{i}[(1+i)^{n+1} - (1+i)]$$

$$FV = \frac{1,000}{.12}[(1+.12)^{20+1} - (1+.12)]$$

$FV = 8,333.3333 \times (1.12^{21} - 1.12)$

$FV = 8,333.3333 \times (10.803845 - 1.12)$

$FV = 8,333.3333 \times 9.683845$

$FV = \$80,698.71$

The only tricky calculation is the exponent. Here, enter the value 1, add the .12, press the multiply key (now it's in once), then press the equals key an additional 20 times to multiply the number by itself the required number of times. And remember always to do all of the calculations inside the brackets before doing those that are outside.

Computing Present Value

To compute present value, keep in mind that it is the corollary of future value. How much is needed today to equal a certain amount tomorrow? Here, the formulas are:

1. For one-time deposits: $P = \dfrac{FV}{(1+i)^n}$

2. For regular deposits: $PMT = FV \dfrac{i}{(1+i)^{n+1} - (1+i)}$

Consider an example: How much must be invested today at 11 percent annual interest to yield a total of $20,000 in 7 years?

$$P = \frac{FV}{(1+i)^n}$$

$$P = \frac{20,000}{(1+.11)^7}$$

$$P = \frac{20,000}{1.11^7}$$

$$P = \frac{20,000}{2.0761599}$$

$P = \$9,633.17$ invested today at 11 percent, compounded annually, will yield a total of $20,000 in 7 years.

Second example: How much must be saved each year for 12 years at 9 percent, compounded annually, to yield a total of $50,000?

$$PMT = FV \frac{i}{(1+i)^{n+1} - (1+i)}$$

$$PMT = 50,000 \times \frac{.09}{(1+.09)^{12+1} - (1+.09)}$$

$$PMT = 50,000 \times \frac{.09}{1.09^{13} - 1.09}$$

$$PMT = 50,000 \times \frac{.09}{3.0658041 - 1.09}$$

$$PMT = 50,000 \times \frac{.09}{1.9758041}$$

$$PMT = 50,000 \times .045551$$

PMT = $2,277.55 invested each year at 9 percent, compounded annually, will yield a total of $50,000 in 12 years.

Computing Earning Power

To compute lifetime earning power (used in the settlement of insurance claims) calls for value judgments. How much will your income rise each year? What will be the rate of inflation? To illustrate the example given in Section I (see *earning power*), assume that a person is now earning $20,000 and is 55 years old. If experienced people in his or her field earn $40,000 at retirement, that means he or she will earn an average of $30,000 during those years. If you assume an inflation rate of 6 percent, you can easily calculate the person's earning power using the future value of regular deposits formula:

$$FV = \frac{PMT}{i} [(1+i)^{n+1} - (1+i)]$$

$$FV = \frac{30,000}{.06} [(1+.06)^{10+1} - (1+.06)]$$

$$FV = 500,000 \times (1.06^{11} - 1.06)$$
$$FV = 500,000 \times (1.8982982 - 1.06)$$
$$FV = 500,000 \times .8382982 = 419,149.10$$

A Program for Your Personal Computer

The following computer program will be very handy if you often use the formulas in this summary. Programmed on a TRS-80, Model III, it may require minor modifications for your brand of computer. Also, note that in the future value and present value calculations, the deposit/compounding periods must be entered on an annual basis.

```
10 REM ** MONEY A TO Z —MONEY MATH ASSISTANT **
20 REM
30 PRINT "WELCOME TO MONEY MATH ASSISTANT!"
40 PRINT
50 PRINT "THIS PROGRAM CAN ASSIST YOU IN CALCULATING..."
60 PRINT
```

```
70  PRINT "1—CASH DISCOUNT"
80  PRINT "2—PERCENTAGE DISCOUNT"
90  PRINT "3—TAX-FREE EARNINGS"
100 PRINT "4—TAX-FREE RETURN"
110 PRINT "5—FUTURE VALUE (ONE-TIME DEPOSIT)"
120 PRINT "6—FUTURE VALUE (REGULAR DEPOSITS)"
130 PRINT "7—PRESENT VALUE (ONE-TIME DEPOSIT)"
140 PRINT "8—PRESENT VALUE (REGULAR DEPOSITS)"
150 PRINT
160 PRINT "WHICH TYPE OF CALCULATION DO YOU WISH TO MAKE?
    (ENTER 0 TO STOP):";
170 INPUT Q
180 IF Q=1 THEN 1000
190 IF Q=2 THEN 2000
200 IF Q=3 THEN 3000
210 IF Q=4 THEN 4000
220 IF Q=5 THEN 5000
230 IF Q=6 THEN 6000
240 IF Q=7 THEN 7000
250 IF Q=8 THEN 8000
260 IF Q=0 THEN 9999
270 PRINT "PLEASE ENTER A NUMBER BETWEEN 0 AND 8 . . ."
280 GOTO 150
500 REM ** FUTURE VALUE PROGRAM **
1000 REM ** CASH DISCOUNT PROGRAM **
1010 REM
1020 PRINT "ENTER THE ORIGINAL PRICE:";
1030 INPUT P
1040 PRINT "ENTER THE DISCOUNT AS A PERCENTAGE:";
1050 INPUT D
1060 LET C=P*D/100
1070 PRINT "PURCHASE OF A $";P;" ITEM AT A ";D;"% DISCOUNT
     WOULD SAVE $";C
1080 GOTO 40
2000 REM ** PERCENTAGE DISCOUNT PROGRAM **
2010 REM
2020 PRINT "ENTER THE ORIGINAL PRICE:";
2030 INPUT P
2040 PRINT "ENTER THE CASH DISCOUNT:";
2050 INPUT C
2060 LET D=C* (100/P)
2070 PRINT "A CASH DISCOUNT OF $";C;" ON A $";P;" PURCHASE
     REPRESENTS A"
2080 PRINT D;"% DISCOUNT"
```

```
2090 GOTO 40
3000 REM ** TAX-FREE EARNINGS PROGRAM **
3010 REM
3020 PRINT "ENTER THE TAX-FREE RETURN AS A PERCENTAGE:";
3030 INPUT F
3040 PRINT "ENTER THE (MARGINAL) TAX BRACKET AS A PERCENT-
     AGE:";
3050 INPUT B
3060 LET R=F/(100−B)
3070 PRINT "THE TAXABLE RETURN EQUIVALENT IS ";R*100;"%"
3080 GOTO 40
4000 REM **TAX-FREE RETURN PROGRAM **
4010 REM
4020 PRINT "ENTER THE TAXABLE RETURN AS A PERCENTAGE:";
4030 INPUT R
4040 PRINT "ENTER THE (MARGINAL) TAX BRACKET AS A PERCENT-
     AGE:";
4050 INPUT B
4060 LET F=R*(100−B)/100
4070 PRINT "THE TAX-FREE INTEREST EQUIVALENT IS ";F;"%"
4080 GOTO 40
5000 REM ** FUTURE VALUE PROGRAM **
5010 REM
5020 PRINT "ENTER THE PRINCIPAL:";
5030 INPUT P
5040 PRINT "ENTER THE INTEREST RATE AS A PERCENTAGE:";
5050 INPUT I
5060 PRINT "ENTER THE NUMBER OF COMPOUNDING PERIODS:";
5070 INPUT N
5080 LET F=P*(1+I/100) [N
5090 PRINT "THE FUTURE VALUE WILL BE $";F
5100 GOTO 40
6000 REM ** FUTURE VALUE W/REGULAR DEPOSITS PROGRAM **
6010 REM
6020 PRINT "ENTER THE PERIODIC DEPOSIT AMOUNT: ";
6030 INPUT M
6040 PRINT "ENTER THE INTEREST RATE AS A PERCENTAGE:";
6050 INPUT I
6060 PRINT "ENTER THE NUMBER OF DEPOSIT/COMPOUNDING PE-
     RIODS";
6070 INPUT N
6080 LET I=I/100
6090 LET F=M/I*((1+I)[(N+1)−(1+I))
6100 PRINT "THE FUTURE VALUE WILL BE $";F
6110 GOTO 40
```

```
7000 REM **PRESENT VALUE PROGRAM FOR ONE-TIME DEPOSITS
     **
7010 REM
7020 PRINT "ENTER THE FUTURE VALUE:";
7030 INPUT F
7040 PRINT "ENTER THE INTEREST RATE AS A PERCENTAGE:";
7050 INPUT I
7060 PRINT "ENTER THE NUMBER OF COMPOUNDING PERIODS:";
7070 INPUT N
7080 LET P=F/(1+I/100)[N
7090 PRINT "THE PRESENT DEPOSIT MUST BE $";P
7100 GOTO 40
8000 REM ** PRESENT VALUE PROGRAM FOR REGULAR DEPOSITS
     **
8010 REM
8020 PRINT "ENTER THE FUTURE VALUE:";
8030 INPUT F
8040 PRINT "ENTER THE INTEREST RATE AS A PERCENTAGE:";
8050 INPUT I
8060 PRINT "ENTER THE NUMBER OF DEPOSIT/COMPOUNDING PE-
     RIODS:";
8070 INPUT N
8080 LET I=I/100
8090 LET M=F*(I/((1+I)[(N+1)-(1+I)))
8100 PRINT "EACH DEPOSIT MUST BE $";M
8110 GOTO 40
9999 END
```

Section I References of Special Interest:

compound interest
earning power
future value
nontaxable income

percent
present value
Rule of 72

MONEY MISTAKES

Why do some people earn a substantial income each year and have impressive assets while others with the same earnings just manage to stay one step ahead of the bill collector? In many cases, it has to do with their financial attitudes and habits. The following 13 basic mistakes cost many people a great deal of money. Learning to avoid them can add to your financial stability.

Mistake 1: *Assuming that money management is only for the rich.* Suppose a rich man earns $1 million a year, while you earn $30,000. He needs cash management and you don't—or so you may think. But you really need it just as much as, if not more than he does. For example, if you can save $1,000 on your income taxes, that amount is worth the same to you as a taxing savings of $33,300 would be worth to him. However, because you have less to start with, the $1,000 is actually going to mean more to you. The difference between you is that you should be prepared to be your own money manager; he can afford expensive professional help that you can't.

Mistake 2: *Failing to be businesslike.* Budgeting is boring, so many people never budget. The very same people who knock themselves out working on their employers' finances often don't take even a few minutes a week to put their own on a businesslike basis. As a result, they really aren't sure what's coming in or going out, and they often wind up with no savings and even with crippling debts. Make a once-a-year budget at tax time and live within it the rest of the year.

Mistake 3: *Signing legal papers without understanding them.* Never believe the interpretation a salesperson gives to a contract. If you can't understand it, don't sign it. Ask someone you trust and who does understand it to read and approve it before you sign.

Mistake 4: *Counting on two incomes.* Today, with over 50 percent of women aged 16 through 60 in the work force, it's easy for working couples to count on two incomes. In fact, the Equal Credit Opportunity Act requires that lenders rely on both incomes when they consider extending credit. The fact is, though, illness can strike anyone, anytime; or, because birth control doesn't always work, an unexpected bundle of joy can mean financial sorrow. Avoid hardship by realizing that there is a possibility of illness or an unplanned pregnancy and budget accordingly.

Mistake 5: *Failing to expect unexpected expenses.* Murphy's Law of Spending says that everything always costs more than you think it will. Planning to send a youngster to college? Allow hundreds of dollars per semester for unexpected costs. Getting married? Budget hundreds of dollars for dishes, glassware, tools and utensils, household gadgets—the list is endless. The principle applies no matter what your plans may be; always allow extra for the unexpected.

Mistake 6: *Failing to face financial realities.* Sadly, many people suffer from the ostrich syndrome. They hide their heads in the sand when dunning letters start coming in and they quit reading the mail or answering the phone. Or the bills mount up and they count on winning a lottery. This is the prelude to disaster. Know your financial status, even if it hurts. Then, if necessary, take steps to improve it.

Mistake 7: *Failing to keep basic savings.* Almost every money expert agrees that people should have the equivalent of two to six months' income in highly liquid savings before they invest in anything. Yet the average new investor in common stocks has less than $2,000 in total financial assets. What happens if money is needed for an emergency and such a person must sell immediately?

Mistake 8: *Failing to understand the time value of money.* A penny saved is more than a penny earned if it's invested at compound interest. For example, suppose your boss gave you a choice between a bonus of $10,000 in cash or one cent to be invested for one month with interest compounded at the rate of 100 percent per day. Should you take the ten grand? No way! In five days, that one cent would grow to 32 cents; in 10 days, it would grow to $10.24; in 15 days, it would amount to $327.68; in 20 days, it would grow to $10,485 (you'd now be ahead on the original offer); in 25 days, it would grow to $335,544.32; and in 30 days, it would amount to $10,737,418! With compound interest, the rate and the period of time for which the money is invested both count. They figure mightily in the time value of money.

Mistake 9: *Failing to factor in opportunity cost.* If you buy a stereo for $1,000 in cash, that's $1,000 you don't have the opportunity to invest. If you assume the life of the stereo to be 10 years and assume 10 percent as the possible annual interest that that $1,000 could have earned, the *opportunity* cost of the stereo is not $1,000 but $2,593.74—that's $1,000 plus 10 percent annual interest, compounded annually, over a period of 10 years.

Mistake 10: *Ignoring the cost of credit.* Credit-card purchases paid in installments add from 18 to 23 percent per year to the cost of goods financed in this way. Thus, unless you pay cash, buying a car for $7,000 doesn't mean the cost is $7,000. With an annual percentage rate of 10 percent, a $7,000 car financed for five years actually costs $8,923.76, less the value of the interest paid as a tax deduction. If the person in this example were in the 30 percent marginal tax bracket, the net finance charge, after tax savings, would be $1,346.63, and the net cost of the car would be $8,346.63. When you buy on time, add in the cost of credit.

Mistake 11: *Having a garage-sale mentality.* Many people buy the latest fad item at a premium price, use it two or three times, then sell it a year later at a garage sale for 10 percent of the original cost. The loss? Ninety percent per item. For example, if your children nag you to buy a computer game system, just wait—they'll become common at garage sales.

Mistake 12: *Trying to keep up with the Joneses.* When a person buys things he or she can't afford just to impress friends and neighbors, it can waste a great deal of money. Younger people are especially vulnerable to snob appeal. Some years ago, a cigarette company suggested that smokers buy its more expensive brand just to impress people. Ogden Nash, the humorist-poet, suggested in verse that he would smoke cheaper cigarettes and, when he offered one to someone, he would also give them a nickel to show he wasn't a piker.

Mistake 13: *Failing to cut losses.* Whatever the investment or item involved, don't count unrealistically on future growth in value to recoup loss. Sell while you can for what you can get. For example, if an investor buys a stock and it's plummeting with no apparent hope of regaining ground, he or she should sell it and take a minimal loss before losing everything.

Section I References of Special Interest:

acceleration clause
cancellation of insurance
conditional sales contract
confession of judgment
contract
cutting your loss
excess coverage clause
finance charge

future value
gentlemen's agreement
line of credit
opportunity cost
power of attorney
present value
right of recision

PROPERTY AND LIABILITY INSURANCE

It is estimated that Americans spend about one month's gross pay per year on insurance premiums of all types, including life, health, property, and liability coverages. The sad fact is, as a people, we pay far too much in premiums.

To understand the concept of and needs for property and liability coverage, it is a good idea to put aside the word "insurance" altogether, since "insurance" implies a guarantee—and as Benjamin Franklin said, ". . . in this world nothing is certain but death and taxes." Therefore, a better term is the more modern "risk management." To most people, "insurance" implies a guarantee of total coverage against loss. "Risk management" implies the sharing of risk, assuming a reasonable portion of risk for oneself. By applying this concept, the insured person can save hundreds and possibly thousands of dollars in insurance premiums each year.

Automobile Insurance

Automobile insurance covers certain specific risks. Coverage includes the following:

1. *Bodily injury liability coverage* insures you against claims arising from the injury or death of persons injured in accidents involving your car. These people may be in your car, in someone else's car, or not in any vehicle. Bodily injury coverage is listed as a fraction, such as 100/300, which expresses your liability coverage in thousands of dollars. In this case, 100/300 means that you are covered for up to $100,000 per person to a maximum of $300,000 per accident. This is where you face the greatest risk in your automobile liability; a huge judgment awarded by a jury could financially ruin you for life if you are inadequately covered.

   Here's a tip: have at least 100/300 in coverage. On top of that, add a $1 million umbrella rider under your homeowner's policy that will cover you for all amounts above those limits. Any good agent can write this for you, and it will cost very little—often less than $75 a year.

2. *Property damage liability coverage* insures you against losses arising from damages to the property of another. The amount of the coverage should be adequate to protect you if you cause a catastrophic loss—say a 15-car pileup on

the expressway. Always assume, if you should have an accident, that it will involve a rich person who has a Lincoln, a weak neck, and a good attorney.

3. *Medical payment coverage* insures you against claims arising from medical fees associated with an accident. Again, carry the maximum you can afford.

4. *Protection against uninsured motorists* covers you if you are hit by a person who has no insurance, too little insurance, or who hits you and runs.

5. *Collision insurance* covers you for damages to your car, no matter who is at fault.

6. *Comprehensive coverage* protects you against loss from fire, theft, glass breakage, vandalism, and other hazards.

To save money on auto insurance:

- Take the maximum deductible you can afford on your collision and comprehensive coverages. If you take a $500 deductible, this can save you as much as 30 percent of your premiums for this coverage per year.
- Drop unnecessary coverage—this means collision and comprehensive coverage on a car that is four years old or older.
- Shop agents and companies. This can effect huge savings.
- Drive carefully. In most states, you can earn a merit discount for safe driving amounting to a substantial percentage.
- Have all minor drivers complete an approved driver ed program.
- If you have a child, particularly a boy, put the car he drives in his name, with his own insurance. This may cost a bit more, but it greatly limits your personal liability. If such a child should have a costly accident that exceeds the coverage of your auto insurance and if the car is in your name, you could lose your home or other assets.

Homeowner's and Tenant's Insurance

Homeowner's insurance covers a variety of possible property and liability losses under one blanket policy. Tenant's insurance is simply a modified version of the basic homeowner's plan. With a typical policy, the perils for which you are covered include fire, windstorm, hail, explosion, riot, damage from aircraft or vehicles, smoke, vandalism, theft, glass breakage, falling objects, weight of ice or snow, collapse of the building, pipes bursting, pipes freezing, and electrical damage. You are not covered for damage caused by flood or earthquake (unless you carry specific coverages for them), or for war or nuclear accidents.

You are covered for:

- Your house.
- Other buildings on the property.
- Personal property, with restrictions on furs, jewelry, and art, but including losses to property when it is away from home.
- Additional living expenses, such as the cost of hotel accommodations while repairs are being made.
- Personal liability should anyone sue you (if, for example, he or she should be bitten by your dog or slip on your walk).

- Medical payments to anyone injured on your property.
- Damage to the property of others.
- Damage to landscaping on your property.

Here are some tips on buying homeowner's insurance:

1. Shop around because rates vary widely.
2. Compare policies. There are several types available and the coverage varies widely.
3. Keep your coverage up to date. Insure your home for its replacement cost, not its market value, and have at least 80 percent coverage of that replacement cost or you will become a "coinsurer," which means that you won't collect in full on a loss.
4. Save money by taking the maximum deductible available. Again, your savings can really lower your premiums.
5. Ask for credit for smoke detectors, burglar alarms, and devices that automatically notify the police or fire department should you have a break-in or fire.
6. Ask for nonsmokers credit if no one in your family smokes.
7. Limit your personal liability coverage to $100,000 and ask your agent to write an umbrella liability rider for $1 million to tie in with your auto coverage (see above).

Section I References of Special Interest:

actual cash value
all-risk insurance
American Society of Chartered Property and Casualty Underwriters
assigned risk
automobile insurance
coinsurance
Federal Crime Insurance
homeowner's insurance
indemnify

insurable interest
insurance
lapse
replacement value
return premium
risk management
self-insurance
tenant's insurance
tort

Retirement Planning

There are three sources of money for retirees: Social Security, company pension plans, and personal savings.

Social Security

Here is a very safe prediction: If you are under 55, you can't count on Social Security for adequate retirement income. If you're over 55, the odds are more in your favor, but they're still not good. Here's why. Social Security benefits are paid out of current revenue—there is no backlog of "trust funds." And the ratio of workers to retirees is dropping every year. In 1937, when Social Security began, there were 50 workers for every retiree; by the end of the 1980s, there will be less than three. Can three people pay enough in current Social Security taxes to support your retirement? The answer, of course, is no. So eventually Congress will have to cut benefits or restructure the entire system.

Another problem for retirees was created in 1984 when Social Security benefits became subject to federal income taxes. Calculated according to a formula so complicated that only a bureaucrat could have designed it, the tax, at the regular federal income tax rates, will be levied on:

- Fifty percent of the excess over the base amount of the sum of the adjusted gross income plus most of the tax-exempt income plus 50 percent of Social Security benefits; or
- Fifty percent of the Social Security benefits—whichever is less.

For calculations, the base amount is $25,000 for an individual or $32,000 for a married couple filing jointly.

If you receive Social Security, the important thing to realize is that the source of your additional income is now important. The following chart, reprinted from *The Week in Review*, the excellent accounting newsletter published by Deloitte Haskins & Sells, illustrates this clearly. In this chart, the assumption is made that a retired couple, both 62 years old, are in three different earnings situations. In case A, all of their income is earned; in case B, 50 percent is earned and 50 percent is in taxable interest; in case C, none is earned—50 percent is in taxable interest and 50 percent is in nontaxable interest.

IMPACT OF TAXATION OF SOCIAL SECURITY BENEFITS GIVEN VARIOUS SOURCES OF INCOME

	A	B	C
		Income Assumptions	
	All Earned	50% Earned 50% Taxable Interest	50% Taxable Interest 50% Nontaxable Interest
Soc. Sec.			
Benefits	$12,000	$12,000	$12,000
Reduction	−12,000	−6,040	—
Net	–0–	$ 5,960	$12,000
Taxable			
Benefits	–0–	$ 2,490	$ 4,000
Total			
Income	$34,000	$39,960	$46,000
Tax	$ 5,664	$ 6,411	$ 2,416
After-tax			
Income	$28,336	$33,549	$43,584

There are two important points here: Retirees under age 70 (when the limit on earned income ceases) should watch the impact of their earnings; and, at any age, retirees should consider investing in tax-free securities.

Company Pension Plans

Here's another sad fact: Some experts say that only one person in seven gets the company pension plan he or she counted on; other experts say it is one in nine. Either way, the odds are against your getting very much in the way of company pension funds.

The actual breakdown of sources of retirement income for the typical retiree looks like this:

Source	% of income
After-retirement employment	30%
Social Security	26
Savings/investment	25
Company pension	5
Other, including VA, welfare, and miscellaneous	14

The message is clear—if you want a decent lifestyle after retirement, you're going to have to provide for it yourself by saving for it. Yes, you may continue to work, but what if you can't?

Personal Savings

Here are five do-it-yourself retirement options that merit special attention, all of which require you to plan ahead. The younger you are when you start, the better.

1. *The Individual Retirement Account.* Any employed person may have an IRA. The annual deposit limits as of 1984 were $2,000 for an individual account; $2,250 for a spousal account in which one party is not employed; or $4,000 for a married couple with both partners employed and filing a joint tax return. However, raised limits are under consideration, so check with your bank for the latest figures.

   With an IRA, you get an immediate tax break because all deposits made during the tax period are deductible from income. The deposits also accumulate interest or gains on a tax-deferred basis. An IRA in which you deposit as little as $25 a week for as little as 10 years can mean the difference between a modestly comfortable old age and misery.

2. *The Simplified Employee Pension.* This type of retirement plan is similar to an IRA, except that both the employer and employee make contributions. SEPs, unlike most pensions, are fully vested immediately; and employee contributions, like those made to an IRA, are fully tax deductible for the tax year in which they are made. In addition to an SEP, the employee may also have an IRA.

3. *The tax-deferred annuity* is an option available only to employees of nonprofit organizations, such as teachers and most hospital employees. All premiums are deductible from taxable income, and there is no maximum annual allowable contribution limit. Here, too, the employee may have an IRA in addition to a tax-deferred annuity.

4. *The Keogh Plan* allows retirement accounts for self-employed persons. Annual contribution limits are frequently increased by law, but as of 1984, the self-employed person could contribute up to $30,000 or 20 percent of annual self-employment income, whichever is less, each year. The Keogh Plan is especially attractive for the one-person or husband-and-wife business; and a self-employed person may have an IRA in addition to a Keogh Plan.

5. *The mini-Keogh Plan* is a nickname for accounts opened under a clause in the legislation that authorized the original Keogh account. Under this clause, a person with $15,000 or less income from all sources may contribute 100 percent or $750, whichever is less, of self-employment income to a Keogh Plan each year. This choice is especially attractive for persons with part-time self-employment.

Realize that your investments in an IRA or Keogh Plan will keep right on earning while you are waiting to cash them in. The way to make retirement funds last a lifetime is to withdraw enough to live on each year from maturing investments and deposit the money in a high-yield money market mutual fund, while the balance keeps on earning. In this way, you can create your own annuity with no commissions.

A Last Resort

But what if you're already at retirement age and have no savings and no company pension—just Social Security? Consider a *reverse annuity mortgage*. They come in several varieties, but all have the same premise—you can augment your retirement income with a loan against the equity in your home. Typically, the borrower gets a monthly income for life, and the loan plus interest plus (usually) a percentage of the profit on the sale of the home gets paid back on the death of the borrower. It's a good last resort. Because they're not available everywhere, ask a mortgage lender in your state if they are.

Section I References of Special Interest:

Age Discrimination Act
annuity
Employee Retirement Income Security
  Act (ERISA)
Individual Retirement Account (IRA)
Keogh Plan
life annuity
old age and survivors insurance (OASI)
pension

Pension Benefit Guarantee Corporation
  (PBGC)
profit sharing
qualified retirement plan
reverse annuity mortgage (RAM)
Simplified Employee Pension (SEP)
Simultaneous Death Act
Social Security
Supplemental Security Income (SSI)

SAVINGS

The Effect of Inflation

Your savings should be put aside with as close to absolute safety as you can get. Since few banks fail and almost all are insured, the primary danger to savings is erosion by inflation. Consider inflation's comparative effects on the following three people:

Assume that Sue, Sally, and Sandy each have $1,000 to save. Sue puts her money into a cookie jar. Sally puts hers into a regular savings account that pays 5.5 percent annual interest, compounded daily. And Sandy puts hers into a bank certificate of deposit that pays 10 percent annual interest, compounded daily. Further assume that the annual inflation rate is 6 percent. At the end of five years, if the money in Sue's cookie jar hasn't been stolen, her $1,000 will have been eroded by inflation to $747.26 in purchasing power. Sally's $1,000, saved at 5.5 percent annual interest, will have grown in dollars to $1,316.50, with purchasing power of $983.77. But Sandy's $1,000, saved in an insured bank CD, will have grown to $1,648.61, with purchasing power of $1,231.94.

Things That Affect Earnings

Three things affect the earnings on your savings: the rate of interest, the method of compounding, and the length of time the money is left on deposit. Here are some examples of their relative effects:

- *The rate of interest*: One hundred dollars at *5.5 percent* annual interest, compounded daily, will grow in one year to $105.73. At *7.5 percent* daily interest, it will grow to $107.90; at *10 percent* daily interest, it will grow to $110.67.
- *The method of compounding*: One hundred dollars at 5.5 percent annual interest, compounded *annually*, will earn $5.50 in interest in one year. Compounded *monthly*, it will earn $6.40 in a year; compounded *daily*, it will earn $7.30 in one year.
- *The factor of time*: One hundred dollars at 5.5 percent annual interest, compounded annually, will grow *in 30 years* to $498.40. Then add in the effect of compounding methods: With monthly compounding, it will grow to $518.74; with daily compounding, it will grow to $532.70.

Thus, you can readily see that the secret of getting top earnings from your savings is to find the highest annual rate and the most frequent compounding; then, let the money grow for as long as possible.

Points to Remember

1. Put aside the equivalent of two and preferably six months' income in savings before you put money into any other investment.
2. Be sure to put your savings into an *insured* bank or savings institution.
3. Use a passbook, or regular savings account as a place to accumulate funds for special short-term purposes, such as vacations, Christmas shopping, or, best of all, until you get enough to transfer into a better savings plan.
4. As soon as possible, move regular savings dollars into higher-paying savings, such as bank CDs.
5. Always try to have your savings earn at a higher rate than the current rate of inflation. High-yield bank CDs traditionally pay 4 to 5 percent above the inflation rate.
6. Don't be afraid to take penalties in order to move into more lucrative savings plans. The "substantial penalty for early withdrawal" that banks, by law, must impose is usually offset whenever you can move up two percentage points for at least six months.
7. Above all, save regularly. Ten dollars a week will rarely be missed from the amount that you spend, but saved faithfully in a regular account, it buys a $500 CD every year. Start doing that when you're 35, put the $500 CD (assume a 10 percent annual interest rate, compounded daily) into an Individual Retirement Account, and at age 65, you'll have an extra $103,372. If you start when you're 25, you'll have $172,539!

Available Savings Plans

The following savings plans are currently available to you:

- *Regular, or passbook savings accounts.* These pay interest set at a maximum of 5.5 percent annually, although the bank may compound as frequently as it wishes. By 1986, government controls on the rate will be completely eliminated.
- *Money market deposit accounts*, with banks, or *money market mutual funds*, through brokers, offer moderate rates of interest with some check-writing privileges.
- *Certificates of deposit.* CDs have maturities ranging from as little as a week to as long as 10 years. There is no government regulation on rates; but generally the rule on interest followed by banks is, the higher the amount deposited and the longer the term, the higher the rate paid. When buying CDs, consider the future. If rates are high but seem likely to drop, buy a long-term CD; if rates are low and seem likely to rise, buy a short-term CD.

SAVINGS

Section I References of Special Interest:

certificate of deposit (CD)
Christmas Club
compound interest
interest
money market deposit account
  (MMDA)
money market mutual fund

nest egg
passbook savings account
payroll savings plan
penalty clause
savings account
Small Saver Certificate

TAX SAVINGS

When people speak of saving money on taxes, they usually mean federal income taxes. However, there are other taxes that can be substantially reduced as well. Here are some tips that relate to federal, state, and property taxes.

Federal Income Taxes

There are four ways to reduce federal income taxes without actually reducing income:

1. *Increase nontaxable income.* For most people, this means investing in federally tax-exempt municipal bonds. The average investor can get expert management and the safety afforded by diversifying risk by investing in a good municipal bond fund. Such funds are frequently advertised in *The Wall Street Journal.* The portion of Section II titled "Money Math" details the formula for computing the net effect of nontaxable income (see p. 243).

   In summary, realize that the higher your tax bracket, the better off you are with municipal bonds. If you are in the 30 percent bracket, a nontaxable investment that pays 9 percent is equal to a taxable investment that pays 12.85 percent; in the 40 percent bracket, this jumps to 15 percent; and in the 50 percent bracket, it jumps to 18 percent.

2. *Increase deductions.* The largest single deduction most people can make is the amount paid for mortgage interest on a home. During the first five years of a mortgage loan, over 90 to 98 percent of each payment is for tax-deductible interest. So if you recently bought a home and have mortgage payments of $800 a month, that means an annual deduction of over $9,000.

   The second largest deduction is an optional one—your contributions to an Individual Retirement Account; or, if you are self-employed, to a Keogh Plan; or, with the cooperation of your employer, to a Simplified Employee Pension plan.

   A third common large deduction is the amount paid for alimony. In this case, it is important that the alimony be paid under a separation agreement between the former spouses or the deduction may be disallowed.

   And a fourth common large deduction is the amount paid for real estate property taxes.

   In addition to the above four, don't overlook the "little" deductions. If you are in the 30 percent marginal tax bracket and find just $100 in deductions, you save $30 in taxes. A typical family should be able to find $1,000 or more in perfectly legal "little" deductions. These might include payment for a safe deposit box, cost of special work clothes, finance charges, union or professional dues, sales and gasoline taxes, charitable contributions, early-withdrawal-of-savings penalties, and so on.

When it comes to considering all your possible deductions, there are two important steps to take. First, find out what expenses are deductible. To do this, it pays to buy a good book such as Robert Holzman's *Take It Off*, which lists allowable items. And then write down every allowable deduction, no matter how small it may be.

3. *Defer taxes whenever possible.* For most people, this means contributing to an IRS-approved retirement plan, such as an Individual Retirement Account, a Simplified Employee Pension plan, a Keogh Plan, or a tax-deferred annuity. The deposits for all of these plans are deductible from income in the tax year for which the contributions to the accounts are made. Taxes must be paid when the funds are withdrawn, but by that time, you will probably be retired and in a lower tax bracket and will certainly have additional personal exemptions.

4. *Invest in a tax shelter.* In an attempt to stimulate certain essential industries, Congress has made investment in those industries advantageous from a tax standpoint. In general, if you are in the 50 percent marginal tax bracket, a shelter makes sense. For most people, the most accessible and sensible shelter is real estate. Interest income may also be sheltered by passing it on to a child who pays no taxes, by establishing a custodial account under the Uniform Gifts to Minors Act or under a Clifford Trust.

State Income Taxes

Many states follow the federal tax rules, so reducing your federal taxes proportionately reduces your state taxes.

In addition, there are several other factors to consider: A state will exempt municipal bond earnings that come from governmental bodies in that state. Thus, if your tax bracket suggests buying municipal bonds, you should first consider those bonds issued in your own state. There are also money market funds that are tax-exempt within the borders of certain states, such as Fidelity's Massachusetts tax-free funds. What's more, states cannot tax savings income generated outside their borders, so you may want to keep some CDs in out-of-state banks.

Property Taxes

The key here is fairness. Be sure that your property is assessed at a fair value relative to that of your neighbors. It is illegal to assess property inequitably, so if you feel you are being discriminated against, see an attorney. Inequities often result from the fact that property may be reassessed when it changes hands, which means that "old-timers" in an area may enjoy relatively lower assessments than newcomers.

Section I References of Special Interest:

adjusted gross income
assessed valuation
bracket creep
capital gains
Clifford Trust
deduction, tax
depreciation
disposable income
Economic Recovery Tax Act of 1981
gift tax
Individual Retirement Account (IRA)
Keogh Plan
marginal tax bracket
marriage penalty

nontaxable income
policyholder
property tax
sales tax
Social Security
sweat equity
tax deferral
tax exemption
tax penalty
tax roll
tax shelter
Uniform Gifts to Minors Act (UGMA)
U.S. Savings bonds
zero bracket

ABOUT THE AUTHORS

Don and Joan German are a husband-and-wife writing team. Full-time professional writers since 1964, they specialize in retail banking and consumer finance.

Money A to Z is the Germans' 21st book. They have also written hundreds of articles and are the editors of two widely read and respected newsletters for bankers, the *Bank Teller's Report* and the *Branch Banker's Report*. In addition, they are the executive editors for a consumer newsletter, *Financial Directions*.

The Germans are members of the American Society of Journalists and Authors, Inc., for which Joan serves as the chairperson of the Berkshire Hills Chapter in western Massachusetts.